About The Author

John Searancke is restaurant reviewer for the Canary Islands newspaper *Island Connections*. He also provides independent book reviews for a well-known English publishing house. Born in 1943 at Derby Royal Infirmary, and thus a war baby, he lived his early life in Ashby-de-la-Zouch and was sent away to be educated at Kings Mead Preparatory School, Seaford and afterwards at Rugby School. Later commissioned into the Territorial Army, he has been variously an hotel and restaurant owner, director and chairman of a marketing consortium, and latterly a partner with his wife in a commercial legal services company. He has enjoyed his working life in England and Switzerland and now lives with his wife Sally in northern Tenerife. His first book, *Dog Days in The Fortunate Islands* received much acclaim. *Prunes for Breakfast* is his second book.

Please visit the website for more information about both books.

www.johnsearancke.com

PRUNES FOR BREAKFAST

One Man's War:
Based on a True Story

John Searancke

Copyright © 2015 John Searancke

The moral right of the author has been asserted.

Cover design by John Harding
www.johnharding.net

Apart from any fair dealing for the purposes of research or private study, or criticism or review, as permitted under the Copyright, Designs and Patents Act 1988, this publication may only be reproduced, stored or transmitted, in any form or by any means, with the prior permission in writing of the publishers, or in the case of reprographic reproduction in accordance with the terms of licences issued by the Copyright Licensing Agency. Enquiries concerning reproduction outside those terms should be sent to the publishers.

Matador
9 Priory Business Park,
Wistow Road, Kibworth Beauchamp,
Leicestershire. LE8 0RX
Tel: 0116 279 2299
Email: books@troubador.co.uk
Web: www.troubador.co.uk/matador
Twitter: @matadorbooks

ISBN 978 1784625 054

BRIDGEND LIB & INFO SERVICE	
3 8030 60143 652 3	
Askews & Holts	4924305
B SEA	£9.99
	ML1

For
My Son Marcus
And My Grandchildren Josh & Sam
In Remembrance
Of Their Grandfather & Great Grandfather
With Love

&

In Memory Of All Those That Served In
'The Good Old 59th'

Contents

Prologue   IX
Notes on Military References   XIV

1.	All Change	1
2.	A Call to Arms	7
3.	No Going Back	16
4.	Stepping Up	25
5.	Barrage Balloons	31
6.	Pip!	38
7.	East Coast Shuttle	47
8.	The Four Airfields	54
9.	Target Practice	68
10.	Pip Pip!	83
11.	Ireland Beckons	91
12.	Over the Water	99
13.	Building Bridges	108
14.	Salisbury Plain	122
15.	Church Parade	130
16.	Harlequin & Canute	138
17.	We'll Meet Again	151
18.	D-Day +	161
19.	Beachhead Salvoes	173
20.	Hell Alley	189
21.	Battle Lines	201

22.	Cattle Trucks	221
23.	Border Crossing	227
24.	Halfway House	236
25.	POW Camp	241
26.	White Cliffs	259

Epilogue	*268*
Itinerary after landing in France	*270*
Glossary	*272*
Acknowledgements	*276*
Thank you!	*278*

Prologue

Did I really know my father? It's a question that I have pondered often, and I always come up with the same answer: no, not really. I was born in 1943, and therefore too young to remember him before D-Day came around in 1944. Then there was the inevitable gap until his release from a POW camp and return to the family in England in 1945. Sadly, I have no early memory of him. I remember little of my early years until, in short order, I was sent away to board at a prep school at the other end of the country (so precluding most term-time visits) and then onward to Rugby School, a boarding school *par excellence*.

I never seemed able to see eye to eye with my father as I grew up. He and I just did not seem to get on. There appeared to be no common ground between us, and conversation was difficult and stilted. Inevitably we drew further and further away from each other, and it is pointless now to speculate who might have been to blame, even if there was blame to apportion.

But I do remember a number of people saying that the war had changed him. Was that true? Sadly, I shall never know, because my mother, my father and all my close relatives are gone now. I, so stupidly, never asked any of them the questions that I should have.

Years after the deaths of my parents, my Aunt handed me a box filled with letters that my father had written to my mother over the period from 1940 to 1945. I did not read them for a number of years, preferring wounds to heal with the passage of time, and wondering, indeed, if it was right for me to read them. Just before my Aunt died,

PRUNES FOR BREAKFAST

she told me that there was another batch of letters (from my mother to my father, I presume, but maybe I am far wide of the mark on this) that she had destroyed on the instructions of my mother after her death. What to make of that?

And so, to my writing of this book. I chose to write in a diary format, reconstructing the story of my father's war through research and reproducing sections from his letters verbatim in between the telling of the tale. I have not found (although I am sure that it must exist) another book which details the humdrum and mundane, as well as the exciting and dramatic, experienced and recorded in writing by one man over the full period of World War Two, as he was turned from a civilian into a fighting soldier and leader of men.

Whilst making full use of letters handed down to me, I have tried to capture the times and places mentioned therein to the best of my ability. Only you, the reader, will know whether the combination of letters and imagined diary works for you. I hope that it does, but, in any event, I shall be content with at last being able to tell his war story and with it, lay some of my bugbears finally to rest.

My father had what might well be known as 'a very good war'. He even managed to be away from his base in England when it was bombed, returning to find devastation all around him.

This is the story of my mother and father, told mostly from the side of my father, from the time of his calling up in early 1940 until his release from a prisoner of war camp in Germany in 1945, thence to return to England to try to pick up the pieces of his old life. Nothing could ever be quite the same afterwards.

We travel through those five years, learning of the ups and downs, the plots and counterplots, as my father rose through the ranks to end his war as a captain, elevated to that rank in the field as his troops faced the formidable might of the SS Panzers – where his battle came to an abrupt end, surrounded in an orchard by the enemy, captured after a series of bloody skirmishes as the British army spearheaded its way from the beaches, through the *bocage* of

Prologue

Normandy, aiming for the liberation of Paris and then the final conquest of Germany. Such was the fighting that a VC was won that day, the action taking place in plain sight.

His journey across France and Germany in a truck, with comrades dying each day, is as hard to tell as it may be to read, particularly when a new life and new harsh rules had to be learned and rigidly enforced in a prison camp in northern Germany, his final destination. Not all was doom and gloom however; who else, for example, would order a new car whilst in that German prison camp, so certain that he would be home in time to take delivery?

Because letters were subject to censorship, very often the date was missing, and equally the identifying Unit. The recipient, of course, would usually be privy to the real or approximate date. Particularly when letters were written after D-Day, the actual day of the week mentioned may be inaccurate. After living in a foxhole and being shelled for a number of days, very few knew, or even cared, as to the actual day of the week. Some of the letters were not relevant enough to include, and some paragraphs of a more personal nature have been omitted. Any grammatical errors have been left in, for authenticity.

Certain things puzzled me. For example, when my father wrote to my mother from Salisbury Plain, he mentioned the major operation he was involved with, Operation Fortescue, and I could not understand why he would have mentioned this or how it could have got past the censor. References to certain events are obscure, and now I can only guess at their meaning, but I have left them in, again for authenticity.

The letters themselves helped explain some other pieces of my parents' story that have come to me over the years. In 2004, a friend of a friend still living near Ashby-de-la-Zouch, who had an interest in pre-war MGs, was told that there was a 'barn find' MG languishing on a farm in Norfolk. He went over there and took some details of the remains. The car still had its original number plates. A call back to my friend, Derek Box, who had worked for my father after the war, established that it was indeed my father's old car. Derek had it trailered back to Woodville (near Ashby), where he lived, and immediately telephoned me. Derek is acknowledged as one of the major national players in the restoration of pre-war MGs and over a number of years has rebuilt the car to new 'concours' standard. It now looks better than the day that it left the factory.

On the other hand, my grandfather's house also is no more. It has long made way for the entrance road to a housing estate. That would have made him chuckle at the irony – he, a builder, having his own house knocked down to make way for the entrance to a new housing estate.

Once, whilst a child on the way back from a family holiday in Brittany, I visited, with my parents, the sites of the Orne battles. I was shown the exact orchard in which my father and his men were captured (including bullet holes in the walls) and also the local war memorial to the fallen of his Regiment. Although it was so many years ago, it remains vividly in my memory to this day.

Whilst the imagined 'memoir' that links the letters together is fictional, as my father did not write it, it is true in essence. At times I may have compressed events to better assist the flow of the story. I have occasionally embroidered the storyline, but not often, for similar reasons. The majority of characters are real. The attributes, actions, resemblance and/or words of any character should not be ascribed to any real person, however, living or dead. With a view to protecting privacy or anonymity, names of people, locations and businesses and other identifying details may, where appropriate, have been changed. If there are mistakes in the narrative, or in dates attributed to particular actions, then they are mine, and I hope that

Prologue

I may be forgiven, and that they do not affect the enjoyment of what is meant to be an enjoyable and informative story. This is in no way meant to be a definitive historical treatise.

This book is a kind of catharsis for myself, and a method of recording the extraordinary period through which my family lived, namely the Second World War, and also a semi-historical work for my son Marcus and his children, Joshua and Samuel, so that they may learn, and most importantly, never forget, what so many of my countrymen suffered so that they may remain free.

Notes on Military References

It may be helpful for me to record the following notes, the better for the reader to understand some of the context of the book.

British armed forces were generally made up thus, although there were many variations, particularly with the addition of headquarters staff, support units or amalgamation through battlefield losses:

Section – 10 men
Platoon – 3 Sections (usually commanded by a Lieutenant)
Company – 3 Platoons (a Captain or Major)
Battalion – 6 Companies or thereabouts (a Lt. Colonel)
Brigade – 3 Battalions (a Brigadier or Maj. General)
Division – 3 Brigades (a Maj. General or Brigadier)
Corps – 2 or more Divisions (a Maj. General or Lt. General)
Army – 2 or more Corps (General or Lt. General)
Army Group – 2 or more Armies (Field Marshal or General)

The original name of the 59th Division was the 59th (Motor) Division. It was soon updated to become the 59th (Staffordshire) Motor Division and then the 59th (Staffordshire) Infantry Division before eventually becoming the 59th Division (59 Div.).

59 Div. was part of the 176th Infantry Brigade (176 Bde.) with original HQ at Burton on Trent, and which later became part of X11 Corps. X11 Corps was to become part of the British Second Army, itself finally part of the 21st Army Group under General Montgomery.

Notes on Military References

My father (Army number 2198674 on enlistment, and later 193377 post commission) initially joined the Royal Engineers and was subsequently moved about from one Unit to another, ending up with the 7th Battalion of The Royal Norfolk Regiment (7 RN) which joined 59 Div. in October 1942 as part of 176 Bde. This all came about because of the requirement for duplication to double the size of the existing armed forces as quickly as possible, and then further amalgamation of geographically placed Units once fighting commenced and Units became scattered, or even wiped out in conflict.

59 Div. was the only Duplicate Division to see active service overseas in World War Two. Until arrival in France, it was tasked for the first three years of the war with strengthening and guarding the East Coast defences and VP (Vulnerable Point) establishments from enemy air or land attack. Examples of VPs would be the bomber and fighter aerodromes, docks and ports; the Division was also responsible for the training of personnel already located there in those particular skills, the defence of the East Coast from air or sea assault, anti-parachutist attack, ongoing security of all the aforesaid, and general aid to the civil powers. Then they went to France, still with the title of Reserve Division, but almost immediately were drawn into the fray, and acquitted themselves with distinction on the battlefields of Normandy.

A further explanatory note may be appropriate concerning the four aerodromes that my father was stationed at during the early part of the war. There is often little to distinguish one venue from another, particularly in that he does not generally discuss operational or geographical topics because of censorship, but mainly concentrates on his own woes or small triumphs. The four are Collyweston, Wittering, Kings Cliffe (that he called Kingscliffe) and Easton-on-the-Hill. All four were, at that time, grass runway aerodromes with hard standing for dispersal areas and camouflaged hangars. All except Wittering (which has a distinguished ongoing record) have been returned to agriculture, like so many others, and little remains of them other than derelict control towers and some camouflaged hangars now doing duty for agricultural purposes.

Arthur Eddie Fisher Searancke

Date of birth: 22nd March 1912
Date of marriage: 2nd July 1938
Enlisted: 13th June 1940
Commissioned as 2nd Lieutenant: 21st June 1941
Promoted to 1st Lieutenant: 1st October 1942
Departure for Normandy: 27th June 1944
Promoted to Captain: 10th July 1944
Captured in Normandy: 8th August 1944
Liberated from POW Camp: 13th April 1945
Release Leave: 30th January 1946
Final Discharge: 6th April 1946
Date of death: 19th December 1975

1
All Change

A buff envelope landed on my doormat one morning. The contents stated that I was urgently required to go to Leicester to attend the main army recruiting office hard by the old Territorial Army barracks. It seemed that things were beginning to move.

What was then being spoken of as the Second World War was tightening its grip on the country. It had been a very strange feeling for me, that of my country being engaged at war, but myself not actually being part of it. The world was about to change for ever. And within it, now, my own small world.

I should explain. It was then early 1940. Although war had been declared on Germany almost six months earlier when Poland was invaded, nothing much had altered around me, save that, keen to serve my country, I had immediately visited my local recruiting depot that had been set up in Burton on Trent to enquire about signing up. The posters for that were stuck up everywhere in my home town of Ashby-de-la-Zouch, an old market town complete with ruined castle on the borders of Leicestershire and south Derbyshire. My name and other details were taken, and I was told to go away and await further contact. Wartime administration seemed to grind exceedingly slowly, and so I must wait my turn to take up arms and serve. The tentacles of bureaucracy would delay my enlistment for a month or two. It had been almost a phoney war so far, everyone was saying; and in the boundless confidence of youth, I and my friends were sure that when it got properly started, it would be short.

PRUNES FOR BREAKFAST

And so I set off for Leicester, 19 miles away, a number of my chums with me, filling two cars as we made our way out of Ashby-de-la-Zouch towards the city. We chattered excitedly on the way, as young men were wont to do, displaying a bravado that was only surface deep, like a sticking plaster covering the concern of being about to step into the unknown.

At last it seemed that I was to be enlisted, to take my part in whatever my country might demand of me. Full of pride and trepidation in equal measure, our little group lined up. It was Thursday the 13th June 1940, which, although not a Friday, I hoped would not be unlucky. After various investigatory questions, laboriously hand written down onto a lengthy form, I was sent off to appear before an Army Medical Board, where I was passed fit for service and then, before I could change my mind, rather painfully vaccinated. From the papers handed to me, it seemed that I had been enlisted (without any option!) into C Company of the 2nd Training Battalion of the Royal Engineers. I was given the army number of 2198674 and rewarded with the grand title of Sapper, Clerk, Class 3 (Temporary) – whatever that meant.

Why the Royal Engineers, I wondered? Who knew? It appeared that the maxim of the army was to put you where you had absolutely no knowledge or experience, rather than to integrate you into a Unit where your experience in your present job might be helpful to the war effort.

Because of the shortage of trained manpower within the existing armed forces when war had been declared, I was told that there was to be a brand new Duplicate Division created, and that, as a local person living in the catchment area, I had been earmarked for a place in it. A Duplicate Division was, I was informed, a sort of mirror image of one that already existed, in order to more quickly train and assimilate extra troops into the army. At that stage, nobody was prepared to inform me of the name or title of the new Duplicate Division, on the basis that *'walls have ears'*. I was not even exactly clear what a Division was. And what my role in all of that would be, I had no clue at all.

And so, back home, at least for a few days. But very soon now, I pondered, it would be time to say goodbye.

I had emerged into this world on the 22nd March 1912, the son of a middle-class family living in Church Gresley, and was educated at the local grammar school in Ashby-de-la-Zouch, before inevitably joining my father Fred Rosslyn Searancke, a master builder, in his contracting company. By the time that war was declared in 1939, I was 27 years old and a director with responsibility for land acquisition for housing, new houses being the mainstay of our business. Father still worked hard in the firm that bore his name; he was no figurehead, despite playing an increasing part in local area politics, moving upwards from councillor to his present position as mayor of his small town.

Yes, it had been a good life so far, for a young man on the cusp of his maturity. Girls and sport were the two things that occupied most of my waking thoughts before work came a-calling. But I had fallen into my work with much enthusiasm, enjoying being in the family business and quickly realising that I had something to contribute, not just as my father's son.

Looking back on it, so many years later – those five long years or so of my war service – I reckon that the young matured a lot earlier and quicker than they do nowadays. By 1940 I had bought my own quite large detached house, a rather racy two-seater MG motor car, and enjoyed a hectic social life which encompassed golf, hockey, tennis and squash, and of course, girls. But I had been blessed with having found a beautiful young lady (of impeccable family, her father a solicitor in Derbyshire with his own practice) who had deigned to

PRUNES FOR BREAKFAST

become my steady girlfriend, and Violet Elizabeth Ellis-Fermor and I had become engaged to be married with the imminence of the war bringing forward the date of our formal union to the 2nd July 1938. It had been a very grand affair, but I was soon to learn that Elizabeth, who had been sent away to school at Roedean and was used to several servants in her family home in Ripley in Derbyshire, would not take kindly to the running of my house, Grantchester, on the Moira Road in Ashby-de-la-Zouch, where there was nobody to look after her every whim other than myself, of course, and a weekly cleaning lady and part-time gardener. Despite her protestations, I would have to work hard, I knew, to overcome the shortfall and make her feel at home in her new surroundings.

Now, quite suddenly, my charmed life seemed to be heading for a major fall, courtesy of that chap we had all been hearing so much about, Herr Hitler.

Within a couple of weeks, my time had come around. Those new papers were all in order, detailing my enlistment into the Royal Engineers, and I had been poked, prodded, and received stern warnings about the future care of my feet; the worst example of fallen arches, I was gloomily informed, that they had seen for a long time. Nevertheless, still good enough (just) to fight for King and Country.

And so it was now time for me to leave my new wife and my family. Time to go to war. It seemed strange: in all my twenty-eight years I had never been apart from my immediate family for any length of time until now, and this was an enforced parting, with no end in sight. But a stiff upper lip was required at that moment, and the call to serve could not be denied. All too soon, the final moment was upon us.

Both sides of our families had come together and were drawn up at the front door of my father and stepmother Lou's home in

All Change

Church Gresley. My father had remarried after the sad death of my mother. Their eyes all focused on me, ready to wave their goodbyes, apprehension and sadness visible in all of their faces. What must they all have been thinking?

We kissed, my new bride Elizabeth and I, so briefly, so chastely, and clung on to each other for a moment. I buried my nose in her hair and sniffed deeply – savouring every bit of her to the last moment. I wanted to remember the smell of her. I wished that I could have bottled it and taken it off to war with me. We were not long married, and I ached with longing for her.

Everyone called out their good wishes for a safe journey and, unspoken, an even safer homecoming, whenever that might be. My two younger sisters started to move, to run towards me, but a stern glance from my father, standing by the driver's door of his car, was all that it took to stop them in their tracks. It was not to be a time for the showing of emotion. But I was sure that, from the corner of my eye, I saw him momentarily turn his head away. He was standing ramrod straight, but could no longer bear to look directly at me. I sensed that tears were not that far away.

I knew instinctively that he was wondering whether he would ever see his only son again after that day.

And I was wondering what my future held in the great unknown.

I didn't want anyone to see the tears in my eyes either, so I quickly turned and got into the front passenger seat of his car. I remember clearly, almost as though it was yesterday, that it was a lovely day, crisp and sunny. With a cheery backwards wave, which I did not feel, and my head facing firmly forwards, and my father gripping the wheel, he and I set off towards Burton on Trent, towards whatever this war was going to throw at me.

On the way I tried to put out of my mind all the normal day to day issues that had until then concerned me. My mind had to quickly become a blank canvas, onto which I would paint my future as a soldier. From that moment, I must have no more thoughts of business; my father must do all that. Nor must I think of my house and home. Nothing should be on my mind from that moment save the conflict to come, and the part that I might be called upon to play in it. It was a rather liberating feeling, putting my whole life behind me, and trying to start again with that blank canvas.

2
A Call to Arms

It was an early summer afternoon, the sun was shining, the trees were still a vivid summer green and my mind had indeed, I suddenly realised, gone completely blank. Was this the calm before the storm? It was an almost surreal moment, not knowing how long I would be away, months or possibly years – even for ever, should I fall abroad – wherever the army would have sent me.

Driving down the long hill to Burton on Trent, past the old square brick-built water tower on our left, we stopped to pick up a couple of friends, Alastair Winfield and Bill Sinclair, who were sitting with others on their kitbags at the side of the road by the bus stop, just opposite the Waterloo Inn. There was no room for more than two, so the others would have to wait for their own transport to come along. They gave us a cheery wave, and I expected that I should see them later in the day at our destination; I was pleased that there would be at least a few others there that I knew.

My small suitcase was strapped on the back of the car. I had brought it with me despite the orders that I had received stating that I should bring just the bare minimum by way of personal belongings, because henceforth the likes of me would be wearing army uniform, and using army kit, for the duration.

We were still hopeful that, as the wireless kept telling us, this war was going to be shorter than the last one, The Great War.

Burton seemed quiet as we crossed over the long bridge into the town centre and then motored the length of the High Street. My mood darkened perceptibly the further we went. There were few people out and about on the streets, and those that there were, walked with a single-minded purpose as if to get done what they needed to do and then to be off into the safety of their homes. Already, there was black sheeting taped across the windows of offices and private houses alike. The breweries had their huge windows boarded up, so that they could continue to produce their fine ales for the likes of us new squaddies. It was impossible, in wartime as it is today, to go through Burton without that all-pervading smell of roasted hops getting into your nostrils. I sniffed appreciatively as we drove past Ind Coope's brewery. Not a chink of light must be visible through those blackout blinds to give aid or identification to an airborne enemy. Could enemy bombers really reach inland as far as Burton? It seemed strange to believe that it could be so.

I think that my father interpreted that sniff for one of anguish. 'Are you alright, Eddie?'

'Yes, father, fine, but I shall be glad when this bit is behind me. I just think that I need to get on with it now.'

'Well, not long now. You are doing the right thing, and we are all very proud of you. You will keep in touch, won't you?' I think that I detected a slight choke in his voice.

'Yes, don't worry, father. I will be OK, you know.'

We had been told to assemble in the lorry park of an old factory at Branston, just out of town, which had been converted to the manufacturing of munitions materiel for the war effort. We turned in at the great wrought-iron gates, on which was emblazoned the legend of the pickle manufacturer, and received a smart salute from the soldier standing in front of the temporary guardhouse. They must be so pleased to see everyone, I thought. Pulling up in the main yard, we were saluted once again and I was courteously asked for my identification papers.

'Good afternoon, sir. Welcome to the battalion. There is a temporary Officers' Mess in that large building off to the right, where you will receive all your information. Please park over to the right hand side, by those other cars.'

'Thank you kindly,' said I, 'but I think you should know that I am not actually an officer. I have just enlisted and have been told to turn up here.'

The change was instantaneous and dramatic. The man looked as though he was about to have an apoplectic fit. He spluttered and turned puce in the face. It appeared that we three were the only enlisted men to have shown up by car. He was clearly embarrassed, but whether for himself or for us was not clear.

Leaning over towards my father in the driver's seat, he shouted: 'Park that ruddy car over there immediately whilst you unload, and then get it out of here. These lads are in the army now.' And pointing at me: 'I don't like you at all, turning up like this and pretending to be an officer! What's your name anyway?'

I was less than amused, and told him my name rather stiffly, reminding him that I was not pretending to be an officer but that was a conclusion he had drawn himself. He was clearly the sort of man that left his sense of humour at home the moment that he donned a uniform.

'Quiet! So that's Private Searancke, then, is it? And what's your number?'

'My number?' I enquired.

'Yes, your army number; you must have been given one when you enlisted. Even you.'

I pulled out my paperwork, and sure enough, there it was. I had quite forgotten all about it in the pressure of the moment. It was, after all, very new and unnerving.

I told him, stumbling a bit over the numbers, in my own unease and anger.

He ticked off my name on his clipboard and muttered: 'Oh, I'm going to remember you, Private Searancke.'

I didn't think that it would be worth my while to tell him that he had mispronounced my name. And so I received my first taste of army life. It was quite a blow to my already low morale.

PRUNES FOR BREAKFAST

'And what about you two other lads? Sure you aren't officers as well?' he growled, poking his nose through the open car window.

'No, no, we aren't.' Bill and Alistair nodded as though transfixed like a rabbit caught in the headlights of an oncoming motor car. They were quick to scuttle out of the car.

After formally shaking my father's hand for the last time, we moved away and joined a long line of men queuing outside one of the factory buildings, jostling others out of the way so that we could all stay together. I looked back towards the car, and saw my father standing by it, one hand leaning on the roof. When he saw me looking over to him, he briefly raised his hand, got in, and drove away without looking back. I didn't know who was the sadder. Very soon we reached the front of the line, and there was yet more paperwork to be completed all over again. It seemed that the army really did do everything in triplicate, and we must be officially signed in yet again.

Later, standing in yet another long queue at the quartermaster's stores, I was told to hold out my arms to receive my sets of kit, my clothing, a tin hat, a new pair of boots (brand new, hard as nails and unpolished) and all of the other paraphernalia that appeared to be required in order to turn me into a soldier. No rifle was offered, and nor did any of us think to ask for one.

After standing around for what seemed like hours, we were allocated to a bizarre collection of civilian lorries which had thundered into the parking area, throwing up clouds of choking dust and exhaust fumes; those with canvas backs rolled open in the evening sunshine, ready for everyone to scramble on board. There were open-backed lorries, large and small vans, in fact anything, it seemed, with wheels and a functioning engine that could be pressed into service on an irregular basis to help out the sorely pressed armed forces, who as yet had a dearth of proper vehicles. It really did look as though the butcher, the baker and the candlestick maker had all turned up to throw their weight behind the war effort. I chucked my newly acquired kit bag up in front of me, and helping hands dragged me up into the back of a furniture removals company van emblazoned on both sides with a well-known local company's name. For some reason, I found it quite hilarious to think that my first approach to this war was to be from the back of a removals van.

Eventually everyone was on board the motley collection of vehicles, a roll call was taken once again, and the convoy trundled out, looking for all the world like the advance guard for the local Statutes (the Ashby annual fair, enshrined by the written authorisation of the then king to the townspeople long ago). As we pulled out of town, perched uncomfortably on the temporary wooden slats masquerading as seating, I looked back longingly at Burton, wondering how long it would be before I might be back again.

So, were we on the road to war at last?

No: we were on our way to our assigned induction and training barracks. The war would still be a long way off for the likes of us. Within a few minutes of leaving Burton, the convoy split into two halves. We found out on the way, through shouted gossip with the driver and his mate, that we were going to the Leicester area, and that the other half of the convoy was going to a staging area at Cannock Chase, up in Staffordshire. It seemed that Leicester was where we should be meeting up with the rest of the members of this newly to-be-formed battalion, and perhaps others as well.

It was already getting quite dark when we pulled into the old Territorial Army centre at South Wigston, just outside the old city limits. Workmen were still hard at work, frenziedly grafting away, erecting sleeping blocks, larger toilet facilities and a communal Mess hall. Further away in the gloom were blocks that looked vaguely like classrooms, forming three sides of a large parade ground. Arc lights, set high on tripods, had been almost taped over to comply with the new blackout regulations. Aimed downwards, the small area of their lenses left uncovered hardly emitted enough light for the workmen to continue with their labour. There was much cursing and swearing, hammering, drilling and banging in the encroaching darkness.

My feet were aching as we were told to get down from the trucks, and not to forget to take our kitbags with us. Inevitably, another long line formed whilst we waited for someone in authority to arrive and tell us what we were to do. I was not at all impressed that they did not appear to know that we were coming.

So far, none of that had been a good beginning to army life for me. Nobody seemed to be properly in charge, although lots of chaps were strutting about like peacocks in their fancy uniforms. I took them to be officers. And there was nobody to inform us of what was expected of us. We were herded like the proverbial sheep to the old Mess hall, where a simple meal of stew and potatoes was awaiting us. I dug around looking for the meat, but found very little. There was super-strong stewed tea in big urns, nothing else. Builder's tea, it was called. I should know, because my trade was that of building, but never had I had to endure a mug of stuff like that, stewed quite beyond redemption.

Afterwards, we were allocated to our billets, dormitory-like with row upon row of simple iron bedsteads with a locker and shelf to one side, no privacy in between. After a kit briefing shouted at us by a lanky Corporal, and which nobody could by then be bothered to try to understand, we got our heads down. We were all too tired to talk, and I dare say too nervous too. It had been a long day, although we had travelled all of 30 miles. We might as well be on a different planet. As I pulled the rough blanket over my head, I could only think of my wife, safely tucked up at home in our marital bed, cossetted by cotton sheets and Witney blankets, facing her newly married life without me, and I eventually fell asleep worrying about what the morrow might bring.

Reveille sounded from outside, and I jerked awake, disorientated for a moment. It was still pitch dark. Morning came so very early when one was in the army, even if there was nobody out there yet for us to fight, nor light to do it by.

Some of the lads with me had never heard the call before, and wondered what was going on when the rest of us jumped out of our beds. But they soon learned when the peace was shattered by the door to our hut being thrown open and the stentorian tones of that same Corporal bellowing at us, demanding our immediate readiness.

Was it really necessary for him to be banging on a dustbin lid with a swagger stick?

There was no time for the niceties of life. In the new lavatory block, we shivered and shaved, doing what we needed to do, and then pulled on our coarse and itchy new uniforms and went to breakfast. Afterwards, we returned to stand by our beds, with our kit laid out and ready for inspection. We had been told all about this the night before, but nobody had taken it in. Every single person in our room failed the inspection, and we had to do it time and time again until we had it off perfect. Were all Corporals sadists once they got their first bit of promotion, I mused to myself?

I had joined up to fight the Hun, not to have to lay out my kit in some petty regulation order. There had to be a better way, and I was determined to find it.

With more paperwork to be processed that morning, it was then confided to us a few of the details of this new Royal Engineers training battalion that we were to form part of. Realistic information was in short supply though, other than the fact that we were to be turned into soldiers as rapidly as training schedules would allow. My papers showed that I had been formally graded as a temporary clerk, which I considered an affront considering that the day before yesterday I was a company director of a well-known local building firm. Come to think of it, I suppose that I still was.

The first few weeks passed by in a blur of activity. Most of it was taken up by 'square bashing', that army ritual where one learned to march in quick time and slow time, and do it all unceasingly round the parade ground until all the men maintained rigid straight lines and every foot hit the ground at the same instant with perfect synchronicity. Some got it quickly, but there were always a few that did not seem to be able to kick off on the same foot, or about turn at the same time, forming endless collisions in the early days. We used to laugh at those poor clowns and ribbed them unmercifully when we got back into barracks.

At some stage I stopped to draw breath and think anew of Elizabeth. We had made a pact between us to stay regularly in touch, however difficult that might become. I promised myself that as soon as there was time I should write my first letter to her, although I knew in advance that it would not come naturally to me. I have never been one of nature's born letter writers.

17th July 1940.
My dear Elizabeth,
I am feeling excessively miserable at the moment, up at 2 a.m. this morning for Inlying Picket for the next 27 hours. I have just discovered that it is Wednesday. I am feeling very fed up, on Monday we had to parade at 10 a.m. and marched up to Beacon Hill and were kept there until 3 p.m. Coming home, Renwick and myself had to walk back on our own, our feet being so bad.

To make things worse, we have a new CO, Captain Charteris, a martinet, and have to parade for every meal which means that time is more restricted than ever. I am not sure of getting a pass out yet

because of on my first spot of duty with a party of men, I omitted to give the salute.
    All my love,
    E.

The days wore on and we were drilled and drilled until we were bone tired. In between those endless drills, we sat in classrooms, being instructed in the finer arts of basic infantry warfare for our new role in the Royal Engineers. I found it a bit of a joke to be instructed about weapons that not only had I never heard of, but were not yet available to our new Division to even have a sight of. We were that short of everything. Even the officers had been told to bring their own private cars with them to drive whilst on army duty.

Just how much basic training did there need to be before we could go to the front line? Anyway, where was the front line nowadays? If anyone actually knew, they were not telling us. The most we heard was from sitting round the wireless in the evening, after our meal, and before lights out; due to censorship, it was not a lot. We seemed to be living in a vacuum, with little or no hard information coming in our direction.

My depression set in even further when, almost on a daily basis, we were woken with the dreaded word 'PT' and we had to do half an hour's physical training before breakfast. Rather uncivilized, I reckoned.

I had only one question that I wanted answering: 'When can I go on leave, please?'

3
No Going Back

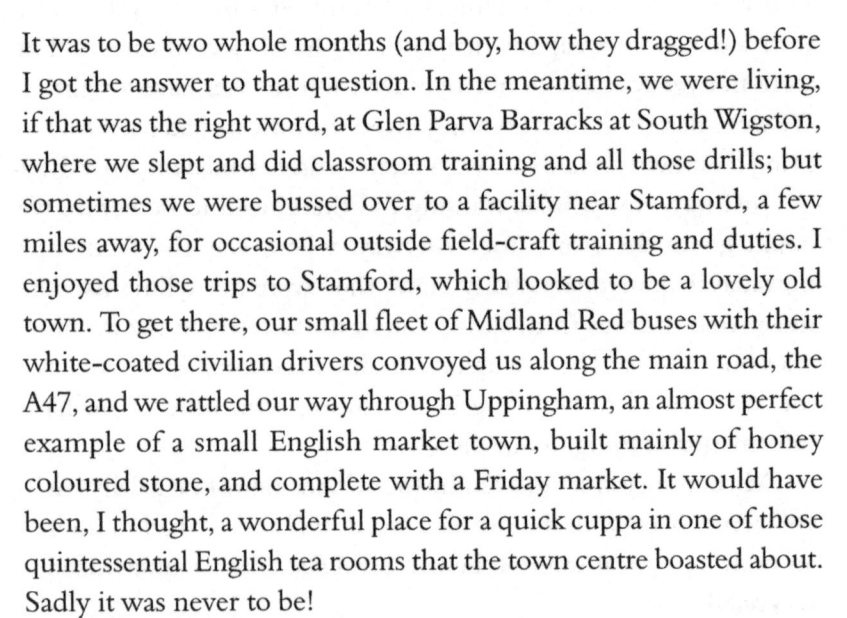

It was to be two whole months (and boy, how they dragged!) before I got the answer to that question. In the meantime, we were living, if that was the right word, at Glen Parva Barracks at South Wigston, where we slept and did classroom training and all those drills; but sometimes we were bussed over to a facility near Stamford, a few miles away, for occasional outside field-craft training and duties. I enjoyed those trips to Stamford, which looked to be a lovely old town. To get there, our small fleet of Midland Red buses with their white-coated civilian drivers convoyed us along the main road, the A47, and we rattled our way through Uppingham, an almost perfect example of a small English market town, built mainly of honey coloured stone, and complete with a Friday market. It would have been, I thought, a wonderful place for a quick cuppa in one of those quintessential English tea rooms that the town centre boasted about. Sadly it was never to be!

One evening, back at Glen Parva, I spotted a notice informing us that we were now eligible to apply for a weekend pass to go and see wives, friends or family. There was an instant queue formed and soon a truck was laid on for a group of us, one of its destinations Burton. I hitched a lift on it.

My father was at Burton station, all ready to collect me and take me home to my parents' house. Elizabeth would also be there. There was my old bedroom where we could sleep.

The weekend was not a complete success.

Elizabeth and I met again seemingly almost as strangers. Neither of us found it easy to be in any way demonstrative. Our old intimacy was a million miles away and I think that both of us felt uncomfortable even holding hands in private, let alone in front of the others.

The family wanted to know what had been happening to me, and I was able to tell them so very little. In truth, there was nothing much to tell, because we had done nothing of particular interest or importance. Just learning drills and field-craft and getting ourselves assimilated into what was eventually to become, we were told *ad nauseam*, a fighting Unit: this new Duplicate Division.

Dinner that evening, all of us together for the first time in what seemed like ages, was a bit of a stilted affair. By now, rationing was in full swing, and everyone was pleased that I had been able to bring a few oranges away with me to grace the table.

I had forgotten what a comfy bed felt like, and when it was time to retire, we said our goodnights to everyone, and I fell asleep almost instantly. It was not a good way to improve relationships with a new wife! In retrospect, perhaps we should have made the effort to get back to Ashby, but Elizabeth had not thought to open up the house to be ready for us, thinking that I would have made all the arrangements.

The next day we tiptoed around each other, went to church just down the road for the Sunday service, and afterwards enjoyed a splendid roast lunch with all the trimmings. I didn't like to ask where everything had come from, but I was sure that my father must have pulled a few strings or called in some favours. Later, Elizabeth and I went for a walk, wanting to be alone together. We went down into the dell, traipsing along woodland paths by the brook that we had known for years. Weak sunlight dappled the leaves, and any that had fallen on the path I scuffed out of the way, moody at all the changes that had so abruptly altered my life.

Much later, we returned to the house, coyly holding hands and smiling to the family. Very discreetly, without anyone else noticing, my mother liberated a leaf from Elizabeth's hair.

PRUNES FOR BREAKFAST

All too soon my weekend pass was over, and my father took me back down to Burton. Before long I was again sitting uncomfortably in the rear of yet another un-camouflaged civilian lorry – this time the proud property of a vegetable wholesaler, keen to do his bit for the war effort – swapping notes on the weekend with my chums, and discussing how we could get in some sports practice.

It had all been a bit like the curate's egg – good in parts.

'Eddie, when do you think that you will be promoted to become an officer?' This was the big question posed by my father over that last weekend that we had spent all together. It seemed to ring in my ears for days afterwards.

Well, hang on a moment! I had only been in the army for a few weeks. As I had explained to him, one did not, as far as I was aware, become an officer just like that. First, as I understood the system, you had to progress through the lower pay grades of non-commissioned officers, lance corporal, corporal and then sergeant, onwards and upwards. After that process, if you were lucky and efficient at what was asked of you, you might be singled out as potential 'officer material' and go on to become commissioned.

I was as determined as he that this should happen as soon as possible, though. After all, I was already running a business with my father, employing a large number of men, so I really ought to be officer material, oughtn't I? I was keen to get back to the barracks to find out what I could do about it.

Never volunteer for anything. That was THE Golden Rule in the army. It was one of the first things that you learned after you had joined up, often the hard way; never volunteer for anything. You could get into all sorts of scrapes, most of which you would prefer to avoid.

But I had set my sights on becoming an officer, and to achieve my goal I realised that I must go out of my way to impress my seniors and encourage them to feel that I should be joining their ranks. So I had to volunteer for something, just to stand out from the crowd.

My social upbringing helped me enormously to feel comfortable being around the officers that I had met so far, and I liked to believe they saw in me something of a kindred spirit. I had always been confident; though a few others might perhaps say big-headed. Most of our existing officers had been transferred from other Units in order to get this new Duplicate Division started. They had either been career soldiers in the case of senior commanders, or had seen action in other theatres. We younger enlisted men would have to go through the mill in order to stand out and be identified as possible future officer material.

I believed that the key to stepping up my game, so to speak, would be my love of sport. The downside was that I had these awful flat feet with their fallen arches. They gave me no end of pain and trouble when I was on them for any length of time, the bones seemed to scrunch and grate together. By the end of a hockey match, for example, I would have been in a bit of agony. It was touch and go at that initial medical examination as to whether I would be allowed to join up or not. Just think, I might have had to end up in the RAF instead…They seemed to take virtually anyone!

9th August 1940.
My darling Elizabeth,
A quick note here, as I thought that you might like to know my news today.
You remember that I was enlisted as a temporary clerk, although I have done no clerking whatsoever? Well, I took the

Grade Test yesterday and they have confirmed to me that I have passed it. So I am no longer Class 3 (temporary), but now Class 3! I nearly told them what to do, but I thought that I might have my next leave chitty suspended, so I smiled politely and left them to it.

But I am still graded as a clerk! It's a disgrace, I didn't join up to be a clerk!

All my love,
E. xx.

And so the drudgery of my day-to-day life went on. At Glen Parva we were being chased from pillar to post by our instructors and, in between the drills, we were on rotation for outside picket duty: supposedly practice for temporarily 'guarding' a facility, the location of which I was forbidden to divulge, for fear of a lot of blue pencil from the censor.

13th August 1940.
My dear Sweetie,

We have just had a terrible few days. For example, we started yesterday morning at 7 and did not finish until 5. I then bathed and massaged my feet and went to the Baths. Then we had another parade at 9.15 to get our rifles, and this took until 10.30. This morning we had Bathing Parade at 6.20 and have been drilling and working all day until 5. I have just put my feet in water for half an hour and am now trying to write a letter or two. We have another parade at 9.15 tonight and Breakfast Parade is at 6.45 tomorrow.

The food is much better when we are over here at Stamford. You will be pleased to learn that I was spoken to by my CO yesterday for about 15 minutes (the only person so honoured in the Company). He informed me that I should get my stripe as L/Corporal at the end of this month. Of course it will mean working very hard and I shall not have to slack up a minute. As you will realise, my feet are at somewhat of a disadvantage with most of the others, but I shall stick with it.

We are being worked at twice the speed than any other batch has been worked, and I was told that we are now doing drills today that the last lot did not do for nearly 3 weeks more.

Well, I must hurry away now my Sweet. I will 'phone you on Friday about 7.30.

All my love, darling.

Edward. x.

Before all this war business started, I played golf adequately, perhaps a little better than just adequately. I played squash on a regular basis, tennis too in summer, and I was almost county standard at hockey, having had a trial. I also played bridge, solo and dominoes, all well. I was determined that some or all of these were going to stand me in good stead.

Now, we played our army games all week and we were all starting to come together as a team, although if we had been put into a fight, it was anyone's guess how we would have fared. But now that we were about to move on to proper outside training, it meant that the usual round of weekend passes would be suspended for a while because we would likely be away on operational duties and courses elsewhere.

I was determined to excel on those courses, and in our spare time at the weekends, I was going to organise some proper sport for the men. None of us had any equipment, but I had seen some of the officers had sets of golf clubs propped up in corners of their offices.

In one of my letters to Elizabeth, I asked her to arrange for somebody to get my hockey stick and my golf clubs over to me at the barracks in South Wigston. I had no idea how she would do this, but a week later I got a call in the evening telling me that a large package would be arriving at Leicester station, and would I collect it within the next two days.

I thought that I might be in business!

In readiness for the next free Saturday afternoon, I got together a rudimentary hockey team from various ranks, and then went in search of some opposition from another Unit.

Saturday came around and due in part to luck, and in part to rather canny play, our team scraped home victorious, watched from the side-lines by some of the officers, including the CO. I was determined that he would notice me. It helped because I scored twice for my side and afterwards I quite forgot to mention to anyone that I had had that county hockey trial and that one of the people that I had chosen to be on my team was a chap that also played hockey very well. We had played at home in the past, his name was Norman Tarry, and he was a very good friend. Little did I or anyone else know at that time that Norman would go on to have a distinguished war service and that he would be promoted to join regimental HQ staff. Last but not least, he would become godfather to my son. Anyway, my first sporting event had turned out well.

The young lieutenant in charge of my platoon, a chap by the name of Giles Benson, was a keen golfer, and I offered him a challenge, which he accepted. He brought along another lieutenant and, with great good fortune for me, also my Company Commander, whose car was allowed on the base and who had an army petrol allowance. Where to play? I suggested a four-ball at Willesley Park, just outside Ashby-de-la-Zouch, provided that they could between them scrounge enough petrol coupons to get us over there.

I quite forgot to mention to them that Willesley Park was my home club, where I supposed that I was still technically a member, although subscriptions had been suspended during the war. When we arrived there, it was nice to be greeted by people that I knew, and my colleagues were clearly impressed.

They were also much more impressed when I and Giles Benson trounced the other pairing, mostly, I have to say, due to my knowledge of the course. A good drive from the seventh tee, for example, could cut the dog-leg corner, but it had to be a good one. The opposition drove off and both balls landed squarely in the back garden of the Joyces' property. I had forgotten just how many balls I had lost in that garden before; too many to count. My partner and I both chose to lay up short, and that was another hole to us. When we left, they all agreed to a return match. But when? Nobody could say. It would not be for a while, as I wasn't entitled to as many leave passes as the officers. And I was seriously in the dog house for using up one of those passes to play that round of golf instead of going home over the weekend to spend the time with my beloved. The inevitable letter arrived in the post a couple of days later.

Undated.
Darling Edward,
You told me that you had got a leave pass for last weekend. I came to Burton station in the MG to meet the afternoon train from Leicester, but you were not on it. What happened? Are you able to telephone me? I am so worried…
Elizabeth. xx

I queued for the telephone that evening. It was a long queue, and therefore quite late by the time that I eventually got through to her parents' house in Ripley, where she was staying.

'Ripley 489.'

'Hello… is that you, my sweet?' I enquired.

'Oh, thank heavens you have called. I've been waiting by this phone all evening,' came the reply from Elizabeth.

'It is so lovely to hear your voice, although the line is pretty bad isn't it? I am so sorry about the weekend. I was going to come back home, but something came up. I was invited to make up a four-ball at golf, and since the other three were officers from my Unit, I felt that it would have been improper of me to ignore them and turn down the opportunity. I hope that you are not too angry with me?'

'You were playing golf when we were supposed to be meeting? I can't believe it!' She was fuming. 'How is that you are allowed time off to play games of golf?'

I was beginning to think that I was digging myself into a bit of a hole.

'Well,' I went on, 'apart from all that, the golf clubs that you sent on to me were put to good use, and our side won pretty handsomely. I believe that it can only stand me in good stead for the future. You remember that I want to get myself commissioned as soon as possible, don't you?'

'Yes, but…'

'And how are all the rest of the family? Oh, my money is running out now and there is still a big queue behind me. Must go now. I will write to you tomorrow. All my love, my sweet. Bye.'

Phew! I think I got away with that quite well in the end. I did miss her, I really did. I sometimes felt quite sick at the thought of being away from her, and what might befall me in the god-forsaken war. What was also concerning me rather a lot was the fact that she had never taken a driving test, and there she was, swanning about in my new MG!

4

Stepping Up

It was the middle of August when we had a leaflet raid over at Stamford. The Germans had decided to overfly us and dropped a huge confetti of leaflets telling us to give up because we were losing the war. What a load of rubbish – though it might unnerve a few of the civilian population, I supposed. I applied for leave for the weekend and hoped it would materialise.

Leave having been granted, it was a whirlwind of a weekend. I caught the train from Leicester back to Derby (thank heavens that they were still running – and almost on time, too) and was collected by Elizabeth who had motored down from Ripley. We spent one night at my home, Grantchester, in Ashby, and the rest of the time over in Church Gresley with my parents. There was so much to catch up on because the firm's building works, contrary to expectation, had not slowed down that much. We needed to devise some sort of strategy to keep it going forward albeit with fewer men being available. One of our best joiners, Norman Bond, had now been called up. So too had Reg Poole, who was one of our lorry drivers. All in all, we were now about six of the younger men short, and a couple of the older ones, too. I had an idea which had slowly been circulating round my mind for some weeks, but I had not fully developed it yet, so I kept it to myself for the time being, with a promise to my father that I had got my thinking cap on.

The weeks rolled on by, and the warmth of summer turned to the chill of autumn. Doing night-time picket duty was not as pleasurable as it had been, because I now needed to wear a greatcoat and the night-time dew made it heavy and damp. I was unable to get it fully dry during the day, and so I had to heave it on the following evening and it was becoming so heavy and beginning to smell fusty. I was beginning to think that this must be the wettest autumn ever.

But training pushed on ahead, day after day, week after week. We marched, then we marched some more. I was not the only person in our hut that had sore and swollen feet. Although at the most basic of levels we had learned how to stick a bayonet into the Hun (you had to do it very hard, and shout very loudly at the same time, in order to terrify the sacks filled with straw that were deputising for the aforesaid Hun), we had little idea of how a fighting battalion would go about its proper business.

But things could be about to change on one front. I had finally been put up for a stripe. I had been very lucky that I had been able to talk on level terms with my Unit officers, and they had been very welcoming to me, whilst maintaining their officer status and not being seen to get too friendly in front of other enlisted men. Those irregular games of golf, hockey and tennis (and dominoes and bridge in the evenings, where I was handsomely in profit) had obviously helped no end.

After being marched in to stand before the CO one day, I was very soon marched out again, ready to sew on the chevron badges of a Lance Corporal. This was the first rung up the ladder, and I was therefore now everyone's dogsbody. But it was progress of a sort, and I must make of it what I could. My primary task was to show leadership to the small band of men now nominally under my command for low level tasks, and to interact between them and the officers. It was my first move to becoming commissioned as an officer.

When I got back to our sleeping block, I had been expecting a number of caustic comments, but in fact, quite the opposite was the case. The men had taken the news of my promotion in their stride, and seemed to look naturally to me for guidance in a lot of day-to-day areas.

I decided that the time was now ripe to sign up for some extra courses to raise my levels of army knowledge and awareness, and at the same time learn how to lead my men along in a kind way without resorting to any bullying tactics, which had been a bit prevalent elsewhere. The courses were a bit of a bind, because I had to do them in my spare time, and spare time was not something that there was a lot of when one was titularly at war. Nevertheless, burning the midnight oil had brought me some good results, and my next target was to make a quantum leap onto the short list for the Officer Cadet Training Unit (OCTU), though I expected the next intake still to be way beyond my reach. I would be jumping a few other pay grades if it came off. OCTU would establish whether or not I was good officer material, and I couldn't wait for the call, as and when it might come, the sooner the better.

Other things were beginning to move a lot faster now. Our basic training had been completed, we had been through our passing out parade, and the battalion was being posted to more active duty, albeit still in England.

One of the benefits of having been raised to the lofty heights of a Lance Corporal was that, although I had many extra duties to perform and must look after my charges, there was occasionally some extra spare time in which to think. It was a bit of a two edged sword because I kept thinking of Elizabeth without me, at her parents' home in Ripley, and when my next leave would be granted. On the plus side, I had been thinking about the family business. That idea was still rattling around in my head.

In the middle of all this, on the 15th December 1940 I was, almost without warning, transferred to Depot Company, 2nd

PRUNES FOR BREAKFAST

Training Battalion RE based at Newark, on temporary assignment. Not far from Nottingham, it was easy to get from there to Ripley on leave, as Elizabeth could bring my car. It was also not too bad for getting back to Ashby and Church Gresley. I could easily take a train to Derby via Nottingham instead of going in to Leicester via Stamford, and either my father or Elizabeth could pick me up at Derby station. More importantly, I was hoping that this date would signal a new chapter in my own personal wartime development.

Indeed it did, because within a couple of months I was advised that I would be on the move once again. I was only told that advanced training for my battalion would be accelerated and a destination would be announced nearer the time. Talk about playing things close to the chest, but, once again, as I was forever being reminded: *'those walls have ears'*.

On the 13th February (another 13!) 1941 we were all posted up to Lancaster to the Infantry Training Centre (ITC) at Bowerham Barracks, home to The King's Own Royal Regiment, on a special training assignment. A train had been laid on, and although I could have wangled a seat in one of the jeeps or private cars (yes, we were still using officers' own private cars, so short was the battalion of army issue vehicles), I opted to stay with my men. It was a good decision, because we got there before any of the officers arrived, and so could get our bearings and sort ourselves out more easily, much to their embarrassment.

Once we were settled in, the very next morning hard training started with a vengeance, and time passed in a blur. One day merged into another, and in between the days, we slept the nights away, sleeping the sleep of the just, completely exhausted by the punishing regime. We were really being pushed to our physical and mental limits.

I had no idea that the Lake District was so beautiful, or so wet. Wet it was indeed, and there cannot have been anybody who could have derived any pleasure from field-craft exercises taking place in driving rain against our set-piece opposition. Both sides were simply soaked each day, and the treacherous ground underfoot made walking, let alone the placing and camouflaging of heavy equipment, an absolute nightmare. A number of my friends and colleagues suffered from sprains or broken ankles, and it seemed to me that, apart from undertaking tasks in simulated battle conditions, it was all a bit of a waste of time.

Little did I realise how naïve that assumption was, and just how wrong I was in my assessment. Little did I know then how our early training there in The Lakes would be responsible for the saving of many of our lives in France.

In our month up there, we only saw a few glimmers of sunshine when the heavens ceased their relentless deluge and the lowering clouds lifted, parted, and revealed the landscape in any depth. Then, I had to admit, with a perfect rainbow shining overhead, the sodden Lake District took on an almost magical quality and became a place of infinite beauty.

Things must have been happening behind my back whilst I was away up in Lancaster. Only a few days after we all tumbled out of the returning train, our still-wet battledress uniforms steaming unhealthily from the closeness of everyone's bodies, I was called in to see the CO.

What had I been caught out at? Casting my mind back over that month, yes, I could admit to a few of the usual 'games' that we all played from time to time during our down time when we were not fast asleep, a few of which had become a bit roisterous, but nothing more than that, of which I was aware. We had left the city of Lancaster more or less as we had found it, and I had put in more than my fair share of effort during the war games.

Even the relentless rain could no longer dampen my spirits, which were at an all-time low because one of my men had deserted the previous night, and, of course, he being nominally in my charge, I had had to take the blame. There had been a few deserters since all this started. I guessed that I was going to get a rocket.

I was marched into the CO's office and brought swiftly to attention, before being told to stand at ease, and then to stand easy. The CO shuffled some of the papers on his desk and brought out one slim folder in particular. He had called me in to give me the news that he had heard my application for OCTU had reached the front of the queue.

5

Barrage Balloons

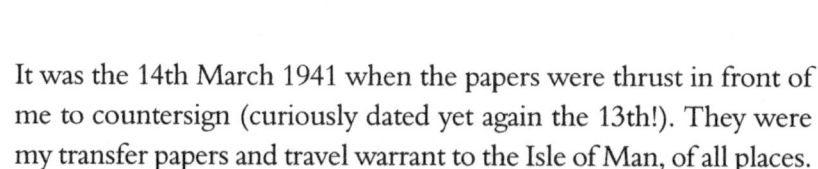

It was the 14th March 1941 when the papers were thrust in front of me to countersign (curiously dated yet again the 13th!). They were my transfer papers and travel warrant to the Isle of Man, of all places. It seemed that I had received a glowing report from the CO at Lancaster after the exercise was over, and as a result, together with my own CO, it had been decided to put me forward for 166 Officer Cadet Training Unit (OCTU) in Douglas, Isle of Man, for the next available course. My CO had some very generous words to say about the reports that he had, apparently, been receiving on a regular basis about me from his own senior officers, who were unanimous that the decision to put me forward for a commission was very well deserved.

I was not often at a complete loss for words, but all I could remember of the remainder of that interview was the inane smile plastered on my face, the formal shaking of my hand by the CO, some words of praise such as, 'I know you will not let me down… Well done so far, Corporal Searancke,' and with that I snapped to attention and saluted, and was marched back out into the corridor, where I was dismissed. All as quick as that.

Then it was all systems go as I had to get back to my billet, pack my kit, say a round of goodbyes and find someone who would give me a lift to the railway station early the following morning, all of which I was fortunate to accomplish in short order.

In the back of the truck rattling its way to the station, I wrote brief notes to Elizabeth and my father, telling them that I was going on a three-month course at OCTU, which I had been told was due to end on the 20th June. Naturally, I could not tell them where the course was being held, but I could hint a bit and hope that it got past the censor, and that they would be able to read between the lines. Once on the train, I had a couple of changes to make, the first at Derby and the second at Preston. Of course, I was familiar with Derby station, having passed through it a good few times when going on leave. I had been to Preston once before, on the way up to Bowerham Barracks in Lancaster, and frankly hoped that I never had to see it ever again. The long platforms, all side by side, half a dozen of them at least since it was a major terminus, were covered over by what must have been a lovely bit of Victorian architecture, all huge glass panels suspended in between the iron girder framework. But the glass was filthy from the myriad steam trains that had passed through down the years, blowing soot and steam from their funnels. Some of the glass was missing, and, with the war on, nobody had found the time or energy either to replace what had become broken, or to clean what remained. The huge canopy was roughly on a north-south axis, it seemed, and the prevailing cold March wind blew through as though it was a wind tunnel, chilling everyone and everything. Within a minute or two, I and a bunch of other lads heading the same way had given up on our swapping of stories about our Units and our heads had retreated downwards into the collars of our overcoats, our chins tucked inside the flaps, in an effort to preserve all our remaining available body heat.

'Bloody hell, but Jack Frost stays on late up here,' muttered some soft southerner.

Eventually our own train pulled in, venting soot and steam all around and over us. We climbed aboard, flashing our travel warrants at the guard, and collapsed onto the nearest free seats. Next stop for me, Liverpool. I tried to get some shut-eye, but there was incessant chatter from another batch of "new boys" who had joined us at

Barrage Balloons

Preston station, and in the end I gave up and looked gloomily out of the window at the passing countryside. A few miles short of Liverpool, way out in the country to the right hand side of the railway line, I could see a large aerodrome (the land was almost completely flat thereabouts) where a number of hangars were being camouflaged. Men were crawling about on the domed top. I couldn't tell whether it was being used for fighter or bomber aircraft, and it soon slipped by. To this day I have no idea what it was called, but it was about 10 miles short of Liverpool.

No sooner were we off the train at Liverpool main station than we were all pressed together like sardines in a can, in the back of a truck taking us through the city and down to the docks. There, life appeared to have taken on a sort of surreal madness. All around us there were workmen, teeming like colonies of ants, swarming around the ships tied up at the various quaysides. The noise of shouting, machinery clanking and grinding, revving engines and the hooting of klaxons as boats left their berths was quite overwhelming. There was continuous movement of larger ships as they came and went from the quays, many having to anchor further out mid-river to await their turn to dock. A haze of smog hovered over the city and the cranes on the dockside seemed to raise and dip in some sort of macabre mechanical dance as they proceeded about their business of loading and unloading the various cargoes. Above everything floated a bobbing carpet of immense grey barrage balloons, adding even further to the image of Dante's *Inferno* and offering, what seemed to me, scant defence against aerial attack.

There were so many ships tied up, or coming or going, because the Atlantic convoys were by then getting in full swing. One large ship had a gaping hole at the waterline, presumably as a result of a U-boat attack, and it was a miracle to me how she had made it back to the safety of port. Even firmly tied to her quay, she listed heavily to one side, and there was a continuous stream of water coming from her bilges as the pumps strove to keep her afloat. The docks were a hornet's nest of feverish activity, huge boxes and crates of cargo being loaded and unloaded, men running everywhere in their haste to keep the supply chain going.

Apart from the centre of the city, most of the barrage balloons appeared, from a distance, to be concentrated in one area and I asked where that was. *'Lairds,'* was the one word I got from an almost unintelligible and deeply Scouse stevedore. I came to understand that Lairds was the main shipyard of the port of Liverpool.

As eventually we cast off and left Liverpool behind, with the wind freshening as we moved out into the choppy grey open waters, we passed by a submarine about to go out on patrol into the Irish Sea; it was the first that I had ever seen other than in pictures. I could only thank the Lord that I was not to be cramped up inside one of those claustrophobic tin cans.

They said that the Isle of Man was a beautiful place... I wondered how much of it I would see during my three months in Douglas, the island capital. The down side was that I should not see my wife at all, because no leave was going to be allowed. I was not even sure that letters were going to be permitted. But, and it was a big but, I had brought along my tennis racket. I wanted to bring my golf clubs, but I had nowhere to stow or hide them.

As usual, we should just have to wait and see. We had to do so much of that.

Undated.
Darling Elizabeth,
　As you may see, I am now on the Isle of Man! I am not allowed to tell you exactly where though. It was a filthy journey and the crossing was rough, and I was sick as a dog. But there is a great group of chaps with me and we are determined to make our King and country proud of us. I am already taking bets with everyone that I shall pass out with flying colours.

Now, you must think of me every day, and I will write to you as often as I can. I do not know what the form is yet, but as soon as I do I will let you know.

I feel a lot further away from you over here, but you can be sure in the knowledge that the Isle of Man is a fairly safe place to be at the moment, certainly more so than the East Coast, so try not to worry too much.

I had to leave my golf clubs behind, but I did manage to pack a tennis racket.

Give my love to everyone. I love you very much.
Edward. xx.

I had not fully realised that there was so much involved in becoming an army officer. Our training was centred around instruction on how to lead men into battle, and how to look after them when they have been put in harm's way. Orders were to be clear and concise, and I had to be able to interpret information that was sent down the line from those above me. So, I had to be able to take orders, give orders, and think for myself, whilst looking out for my men.

I had to be able to read maps, interpret signals, be familiar with all sorts of different weapons both large and small, and how to be able to analyse the 'bigger picture' provided that it was passed down the chain of command whilst on active service. My map reading skills left a lot to be desired and I was determined to improve them. I was determined, too, to become a good leader of men. It was constantly drummed in to me that many lives would depend on my decisions once we were in the field.

All of that related very much to the sharp end of being an officer, but there was also the 'backroom' that must be attended to. I was learning all of the administration duties that must become second nature to an officer. I would be responsible for calculating different rates of pay and then paying money out in cash to my men. I would have to issue daily reports back to HQ from the field. I had to master

PRUNES FOR BREAKFAST

some basic medical skills for wounds on the battlefield, together with legal training, particularly regarding the Geneva Convention. In between learning all of this, I was to be found on exercises, crawling along wet stream beds in full camouflage with a heavy pack, learning how to plan attacks on the ground, or to organise my men to provide covering fire and support to others. I became on very intimate terms with Snaefell and the area around her. I was also determined to become a reasonably expert signaller, to be able to take over, as I was told quite frequently, should my attached signaller be shot.

I was exhausted. Totally, totally exhausted. And my feet...! As the possessor of those badly fallen arches, being laced into combat boots all day, particularly when they were soaking wet, was not a good recipe for my health and well-being. Any time off that we were allowed was spent feverishly reading through the mountain of paperwork that had descended on us. There were to be regular exams based on each core requirement. Some of the lads went into the capital, Douglas, at weekends, to have a good time and no doubt to meet up with the local ladies; but for me, any quiet period was spent either letter writing or boning up for the next exam to come. I was determined that I should not fail myself, my wife, or my father.

The moment that the final exams were completed, the course over, and farewells made, we were hastily bundled back onto the ferry, and found ourselves back where we started, after yet another rough crossing, on Liverpool docks. Poking out of my kitbag was my tennis racket, still unused.

The entire area had been severely bombed in May whilst we were away in the relative calm of the Isle of Man. Whole streets of the city that I had been driven along between the railway station and the dock area no longer existed. They had been reduced to piles of rubble, pushed aside by bulldozers as the roadways had been cleared for traffic again. So much for those barrage balloons. The bombers flew above them and just used them as aiming targets or markers.

My orders were to take an early train that same day if possible, and to report back to my Unit. But there was no train to be had, so I and a number of the others walked round to the Adelphi Hotel, Liverpool's oldest and finest, plonked our kitbags down in front of the reception desk, and asked if they had rooms. The manageress, a very smart dark haired lady – Carol, as I saw from the name on the card propped up on the desk in front of her – looked us up and down before breaking into a smile and pushing a form across for me to complete. They had rooms, but the cost meant that we should have to share. No, there would be no discount for us, despite my hopeful smile. Nevertheless, it was a forgotten taste of luxury that lasted for nearly ten hours. I wallowed in a shallow but hot bath and felt somewhat revived.

The next day, bright and early, well before any of us had the chance of sampling the unknown delights of the Adelphi breakfast, our train pulled out of the city in a cloud of steam and I was on my way back to the Midlands. On arrival in Leicester, I got off the train with what seemed to be a thousand others, and elbowed my way through the scrummage, out to the station yard, clutching my kitbag firmly in front of me, where I found that I was lucky enough to be able to hitch a lift on a truck that was going to Glen Parva Barracks.

Back on the base, I had no sooner thrown my kitbag onto my allocated bed, than I was required to report to my CO.

'Well, Corporal Searancke, how do you think that you got on? Do you reckon that you passed out of OCTU satisfactorily? We have quite missed you here, so it's good to have you back with us.' All this was said with a glimmer of a smile on his usually harassed features.

'I have no idea, sir. All I was told was that the results of the course would be put together over the next week or so, and then recommendations would follow, depending on the pass rate. I really do hope that I will have passed.'

'I am sure that you will.' He opined with a shrug and a further smile. 'Dismissed.'

6

Pip!

The next two weeks flew by after my return from the Isle of Man. Training was being accelerated once again, and I had catching up to do. One afternoon I was called in again to see the CO. I was sure that it could only be that he had received the results from my OCTU course, and my legs immediately turned to jelly. I marched rather poorly in to his office, and threw as smart a salute as I could manage.

'Come in. Oh, and you'd better sit down,' said the CO, shuffling yet more paper on his desk. He looked up and smiled.

'Well done, young man!' He beamed, waving a sheet of paper in my direction. 'You have passed the Selection Board at OCTU with flying colours, and you can now put up your pips as a Second Lieutenant. Congratulations!' Whereupon he came round his desk and shook my hand. 'I look forward to seeing you in the Mess tonight.'

Clearly the first round was going to be on me!

And with that he passed over a formal document with a seal on the bottom. It stated that I had received an immediate commission as a Second Lieutenant into The Leicestershire Regiment. Yet another stated that I would henceforth have allocated to me the army number 193377. And yes indeed, as he told me with a broad smile, it was the custom for drinks to be on me that evening in the Officers' Mess.

I thought that I could cope with that. Indeed, it would be a pleasure to stump up some cash for friends and colleagues in exchange for their welcoming me as an officer into their – and now my – Mess. I thought that I should get myself smartened up, dig out my best uniform, but first things first, I decided to make a beeline for the nearest hot bath to soak my poor feet, as ever the source of my main troubles.

It was then the 21st June 1941, and therefore almost exactly twelve months since I signed on as an enlisted man. I cast my mind back to that question posed by my father all those months ago. Now I had an answer for him, and I made for the phone – cheekily claiming priority over some of my seniors, and for once getting away with it – so that he could be the first to know. He was almost speechless with delight at the news. Later on in the evening I managed to make a call to Elizabeth, but I had to confess to her that by then I was more than slightly in my cups, and had spent what seemed to be more than a month's future pay in the Officers' Mess. I think that she was very pleased for me, but as she was roused from her bed to receive the call, I was not too sure. I found it very difficult to 'read' some women. I would have to put it right tomorrow with a letter.

The next day I was handed a day pass to spend in the town, to be measured up for the new uniforms that were required. I went to see Mr. Virgo, the military tailor and outfitter, and as soon as I had them, I strutted around like some puffed up pouter pigeon, until it dawned on me that I was still the lowest of the low and on the bottom rung of the officer ladder. Nevertheless, I had become an officer, and I knew that my father would be so proud to see me. I couldn't wait to see Elizabeth, and indeed all the family, wearing (at last!) my new uniform. But it would be a week or two yet before I could get a weekend pass.

In fact, that first evening in the Officers' Mess after slightly too much to drink, I was told that I was to be honoured by being given the opportunity to understudy the Orderly Officer on the following weekend. Only the next day did I find that this was a dastardly prank that was inflicted on all newly appointed junior officers, and was about the most boring way of passing time ever invented, whilst giving more senior officers a bit of a chuckle and extra leave-time in lieu of work.

PRUNES FOR BREAKFAST

My idea of leave was clearly out of the window now. I really had to try to ring Elizabeth, and perhaps she would be able to get over to me for a few hours so that we could celebrate together as soon as I could arrange it. Meanwhile, I supposed that a letter to her was well overdue...

22nd June 1941.
My darling,
I think that you may be interested to learn that the CO called me in late yesterday and told me that my commission has been confirmed. I shall be putting up my pips on my new kit at the earliest opportunity!
However, the trip back was a nightmare. We came on a very old merchant ship, long overdue for the scrapheap, but pressed back into service, and I was terrified that we would be torpedoed. But we got into Liverpool safely, and I then took the train to Derby, then to Leicester. All in all, it took over 24 hours from door to door. I am exhausted.
By the time that you get this we will have spoken on the phone, I trust.
All my love,
Edward. x.

Our training had taken us all around the Isle of Man, and I had discovered a wonderful place, that I would love to take Elizabeth to after this blessed war was over. The Golf Links Hotel was just outside the little town of Castletown, stuck right on the end of a promontory, surrounded on two sides by its own golf course, and with a little island at one end, and a lighthouse at the other. One evening I had stood quietly on the causeway to the island, called Fort Island, although no trace of a fort remained, and looked down over the parapet. There was utter silence except for the calling of the gulls, and the war could have been a million miles away. The sea below the causeway was crystal clear, and I could see the seaweed waving to and fro in the current, and I knew then that this was a place that we must come to together once this war was over. But I never quite knew how to tell Elizabeth such things.

And so I was formally transferred back to Leicester, and welcomed back to Glen Parva Barracks, the home of The Leicestershire Regiment, from where I had started out my army life. It was a strange feeling entering those portals again as a junior officer, compared to when I had first walked in as an enlisted man. Since then, I had learned so much, so much more than I had thought possible. I was now to be a leader rather than one of those that I could see lined up on the parade ground, about to undergo the start of their basic training. A sense of humility and nervousness set in, most unusually for me.

The newly appointed Adjutant turned out to be very nice, and, whilst I did not need to be shown around, he did point out some facilities that had been added on since I was last there, and I left him with my transfer papers. Later, I knocked on the door of the CO and re-introduced myself. I thought that he was rather pleased to see me again. I dined that evening in the Glen Parva Officers' Mess for the first time. Another boozy evening, but it signalled a bit of a milestone for me now to have my own small command, a platoon of local Leicestershire men. Hopefully, we should get on just fine and I soon settled in to the swing of things.

Undated. (Tuesday)
XVII Leicestershire Regiment, Glen Parva Barracks, South Wigston, Leicester.
My darling,
How do you like the notepaper?! Some bad news for you my sweet. Having understudied the Orderly Officer today, and the Duty Officer tomorrow, I find that I have managed to click for these 2 jobs, Saturday and Sunday, which means that I am confined to barracks the whole of Saturday and Sunday. I am very fed up, but of course it is an old fashioned custom that they work on new officers.

In the meantime, how are you getting on, my pet? Not missing me too much, I hope.

I am sitting in the dashed Orderly Room waiting to answer the telephone should it ring. We have just had supper, hors d'oeuvres, tongue, corned beef, salad and new potatoes, followed by cheese and coffee. Not bad is it?

I am very fed up. It has not taken me long to realise that this is a bit of a backwater with not much going on. They tell me that no-one ever gets promoted here and I am thinking of asking to be posted to Ireland for extensive training, what do you think? The other alternative is that some fellow officers have been shortlisted for overseas duty in Egypt. I am not too keen on that, far too hot for me.

I doubt whether I shall be able to post this tonight. Ah well.

All my love, sweetheart.

Edward. x

Such food as that - and there was meant to be a war on!

The CO took me to one side in the Mess a couple of evenings later and asked me if I had a car.

'Well, yes, sir, indeed I do. Why do you ask?'

'Now that you are an officer, you are entitled to ask whether you can bring your private vehicle onto the base. A number of my officers have their own here, as you will have seen. Actually, old boy, we need all the private vehicles that we can get hold of, because the dashed army is still not in a position to supply them for us. Want to bring yours along?'

Would I like to? You bet I would! I was absolutely delighted.

'Yes, sir! Thank you sir!' I resolved that my MG would be on the base by the next weekend. I wasn't too sure exactly how Elizabeth was going to take the news, though. The CO hadn't asked what sort of car I had, and I had not bothered to inform him that the MG was just a two-seater, and would therefore benefit the war effort not one whit. But I was going to be mobile. That was all that mattered to me.

Anyway, a few days later I received a notecard from Elizabeth. I sometimes wondered whether she thought that the army should be counted second to her, and that I should be available at her beck and call.

2nd July 1941.
My dearest Edward,
A most disappointing day. I have tried to phone you for the last half hour and can get no reply. I'm fed to the eyebrows as I did so want to speak to you if only for a minute as it happens to be our third anniversary.
I expect you have been very busy and have had no time to write so you are forgiven! Darling, I am thinking of you all the time and wondering what you are doing – you must be very hot in Leicester.
Try and get here for Saturday if at all possible as I cannot wait any longer.
I love you.
Elizabeth.

After some further exchanges of telephone calls, there had still been no opportunity to meet. Leave passes were getting a bit like hens' teeth. Some letter exchanges had become a little terse and rather to the point; the following in response to a telephone conversation the previous evening:

4th July 1941.
My darling Elizabeth,
Contrary to your belief, I had not forgotten the third anniversary, but as you know, I always regard it as being the first Saturday in the month. The happiest Saturday of my life.
I am terrifically disappointed at not being with you tomorrow, and I think that you will agree that in my own undemonstrative way

PRUNES FOR BREAKFAST

there is nothing I prefer than to be with you. However, there is a war on, and we have been very lucky.

Darling, I shall be thinking of you always, even when I am mounting the Guard at 9 o'clock on Saturday morning and turning it out at 2 o'clock on Monday morning.

Every bit of love, my Sweet.

Edward x.

PS. Have I any laundry?

Did not everyone send their personal laundry back home in the middle of the war?

A couple of weeks later, I managed to arrange a day pass out, and Elizabeth was going to meet me in Leicester city centre. I expected that we should be spending a good part of it in Marshall & Snelgrove, the large department store, Leicester's finest. I hoped that she remembered to bring my laundry, otherwise I thought that it was going to be chasing me around these shire counties for quite some time. It seemed that the Regiment was actually starting to fulfil orders from on high, and this meant that we should be moving out of barracks, to undertake operations in the field, so to speak. I had to break the news to Elizabeth.

It was probably also the best time to break the news that the MG would not be going back with her, but moving on to the base with me. I believed that she actually enjoyed driving her father's big Austin 6-Light anyway, as it had more space and softer springing. He did not seem to be bothered that she had not taken a driving test, and on a couple of occasions she had driven him all the way from Ripley to Blackpool in it, for him to stay in his usual hotel on the north shore promenade to take the famed bracing air, then fetching him back a fortnight later.

In the event, she took the news rather well and the MG came to live with me on the base.

15th July 1941.
XVII Leicestershire Regiment, Glen Parva Barracks, South Wigston, Leicester.
My darling,
I am glad you got home safely, and thank you for the parcel. I have some rather sad news for you. On Thursday morning I am moving to Holt in Norfolk with the 8th Bn. I am not sure if this is a good show or a bad show. The CO was very affable this lunch time and said that it was a very good Bn. and that he thought I ought to do very well.
Can you phone me at 1.30 p.m. my pet?
All my love
Edward.

It actually took until the 17th July 1941 before my transfer papers were received and I was formally posted to the 8th Battalion The Leicestershire Regiment, at that time stationed at Holt.

All was now packed up and I was finally on my way from the barracks at Glen Parva and heading for the East Coast in the MG. All that I had been told so far was that I should be on VP duty. VP's, as I was to find out soon enough, were Vulnerable Points, and I had been told that our services would be required at such disparate venues as ports, beaches and airfields, as well as the giving of general aid to the civil powers. In addition to all of that, as though it was not enough, we were to be tasked with defending and strengthening the defences of the East Coast from possible invasion. It seemed that the whole of this coastline was to be fortified and protected against enemy assault by parachutists or even the possibility of a full scale German invasion. I couldn't see that happening, myself.

PRUNES FOR BREAKFAST

We arrived safely after many vicissitudes – punctures and trucks failing to restart – and were billeted at Gresham Holt School. Wives were allowed to visit but a police permit would have to be obtained, so I wrote to Elizabeth suggesting she wait a few days. I was reunited with a friendly face, John Dickinson from Ashby, so that cheered me up no end.

7

East Coast Shuttle

It would seem that I had no sooner arrived and settled in at Holt than I was to be on my way 15 miles up the coast to Holkham, right on the sea. As a junior officer, I was rapidly learning that one could be switched from pillar to post, from one Unit to another, and one's daily duties could vary between digging holes to doing the paperwork of those more senior. I found it all a bit trying.

20th July 1941.
C Company, 8th Bn. The Leicestershire Regiment, Victoria Hotel, Holkham, Norfolk.
My darling,
 Only 30 minutes or so after posting my last letter to you I was posted to this spot. It is two miles from Wells and forms part of the Earl of Leicester's Estate, a small seaside village with not one shop and only this one hotel, which is rather like 'The Bridge' at Ingleton.
 My work so far has consisted of paying the men on Friday afternoon, standing them to at 11 p.m. to 12 p.m. and 4 a.m. to 5 a.m. Playing cricket Saturday evening, standing men to at 11 and 4 and watching 'em dig this morning, Sunday. Tonight I turn 'em out again at 11 and 4, but this time I have to patrol the line for an hour each time.
 Monday, Tuesday and Wednesday my platoon takes over the lines and for three days I shall not take off my clothes or boots. The outlook is healthy but bloody.

PRUNES FOR BREAKFAST

We only stay here until the 30th when we move elsewhere to somewhere equally bloody. I do not appreciate the position at all and propose to create a stink!!!

I think I had better have laundry sent also alarm clock and my watch if done. Yours will be ruined in this sand etc. Miles and miles and miles of sand.

At the moment I think that you had better stay put if you are alright, but I will phone you on Thursday at 7 o'clock when I come off duty.

I hope that your mother is quite well and everything going OK. All my love, Sweet.
Edward.
PS. Dominoes!!!

We had been told that heavy bombing raids were to be expected along this stretch of coastline, with the outside possibility that airborne troops might be landed. The word now seemed to be that it wouldn't be an invasion force, but more likely a small operation either to test local defences, or to land enemy spies well away from any built-up areas. Certainly no full scale invasion yet. Yet another rumour doing the rounds was that some special German forces might be landed from a submarine off the coast in order to snatch some unknown bigwig staying in the area for a war conference. It seemed a bit far-fetched.

Near to Wells-next-the-Sea there was a very nice, long, shallow beach, which had been identified by the staff planners as perfect for those supposed amphibious German landings, and so it had to be fortified and defended. My Unit was tasked with building the emplacements for some long range guns, and we spent days levelling out some dunes, concreting over new foundations, and then lugging the guns up from the beach road to the top of said dunes, to be placed on the newly prepared reinforced concrete emplacements, their barrels traversed out to sea. It was hard manual work, and not quite what I had been expecting. The weather was good, though, and the men all worked stripped to the waist.

Undated.
C Company, 8th Bn. The Leicestershire Regiment, Victoria Hotel, Holkham, Norfolk.
My darling Sweetie,

Life is 'B' grim isn't it? We have spent all day lugging a 3 ton gun turret up some beach steps and then up a cliff and to everyone's amazement managed to complete the job. Tonight I am sleeping in the line yet again, one of my blokes having a weekend leave.

We leave here on Wednesday and go to Blakeney. What life will have in store there I do not know.

I placed a bloke on a charge on Thursday for being asleep on sentry duty. He got 10 days field punishment, so I expect he will feel like shooting me in the back.

Tomorrow I am to attend a Court of Enquiry, called to give evidence on behalf of one of my blokes.

The officers here are a very happy lot and I think that we have a much better time together here than they do in the Bn. at Holt.

I am getting laundry done here locally, I think it will save time and trouble.

I must close, my pet, take care and remember that I love you and will try and find a billet as soon as I get to Blakeney.
Love,
Edward.

I didn't bother to mention to her that the MG was already doing sterling service, ferrying me between these various places in deepest Norfolk. It really was proving to be a boon; there was nothing like that feeling of turning up somewhere at one's own convenience, with the wind in my (sadly, receding) hair. I could also pop off to a local golf course, or pub even, without too many people being any the wiser.

PRUNES FOR BREAKFAST

Elizabeth had been a constant supplier of a stream of letters. I was unfortunately rather the opposite, partly because I was so infernally busy, partly because I hardly knew where I was and where I might be tomorrow, and partly because all of our letters were now more carefully censored. It meant that I was often unable to tell Elizabeth exactly where I was, and certainly not what I was doing. Who knew, the army kept telling us all, what the Hun might be doing to gain information from careless whispers. Letter writing had never come easily to me, especially the soppy stuff. But I did try, I really did.

3rd August 1941. (Sunday)
Station Mess, Willems Barracks, Aldershot.
My darling Sweet,
Isn't life just too bloody!! We moved from Blakeney on Wednesday. On Thursday at 12 o'clock I was called in to see the Adjutant, and he told me agitatedly that I should have been here on Monday to attend a Messing Course, so can I catch the 2.20 p.m. train from Holt, which I did, getting to Aldershot at 10 p.m.
We are not allowed to travel anywhere by public conveyance, so I cannot even trot up to London.
I shall be going back to Blakeney next Saturday and I propose to fix up for you to come down next Monday. I am leaving the MG here whilst I am away.
Anyway, I will phone you on Tuesday at 7 o'clock all being well and we'll talk about it then.
All my love, darling.
Edward.

I couldn't find out exactly how or why my name got put on the list for a cookery course. I hated cooking, unless it was the sort of cooking where you emptied a tin into a pan and then heated it up. I supposed that the level of my skills in that department left a lot to be desired. After grumbling and complaining about it, trying to wriggle out of the posting, I found out a bit more. In fact, this Messing Course meant that I was going to have training on how to run an Officers' Mess if called upon to do so, sourcing and calling up the daily food requirements, how they were to be cooked, and learning costings for how much should be paid for produce. Officers had to eat well. The CO would come down like a ton of bricks if the old-fashioned levels of quality food and service were not maintained in the Mess. The army had a list for absolutely everything, including the menus for lunch and dinner.

Nevertheless, I really did hope that no actual cookery was going to be required of me personally. It was right at the bottom of my list of skills and interests.

During all this time, I had been exchanging information and news with my father about the running of the building firm, as well as keeping in touch on a family level. My original notion of my mind as a blank canvas, leaving all thoughts of the family business behind, turned out, inevitably, to be naïve in the extreme. One could not just forget a major part of one's life, even if called to war.

Business had inevitably declined a little by then, mostly due to the uncertainties of the war in everyone's minds. How long would it last? How many men would the business lose to active service? How many people would want to buy new houses when there was a war on, or renovate their existing ones? Importantly, would local councils still want to develop commercial building sites that they had in their respective land banks?

That last point was the one that had set me a-thinking all those long months ago. I had phoned a few people that I knew in the building trade. Indeed, some were on active service with me. I had been couching my queries to them in what I prayed was a very low key manner. I had had three basic questions:

What were the long terms plans of local councils before the war started, in respect of building and development?

PRUNES FOR BREAKFAST

What were the plans of competitor builders and contractors before the war brought things to a halt?

What interest had we received from the private sector in building or development?

These three had been rattling about in my head for quite some months now. I had, from time to time, batted them backwards and forwards with my father. The older generation, I thought, was very conservative in outlook. I supposed that before the war started, his and my ideas were pretty much as one, but this war just shook things up a lot, and you started to see things, and think of things, that simply would not have occurred to you in peace time.

Father had got one of the men in the office to go around to various interested parties, slipping in an innocuous question over a quiet drink in the pub, and the answers were beginning to come in.

Meanwhile, I was still always on the lookout for opportunities to better myself, and moving about between battalions, where there were shortages, seemed to me to be a way of putting myself forward, perhaps for promotion.

13th August 1941. (Wednesday)
My darling,

When you receive this, I shall be on my way to Peterborough, to join the 70th Bn. Life is one constant travel isn't it? I heard that an officer was wanted and volunteered to go. Some people say that I am a fool, others do not seem to know whether I am a fool or not.

Anyway, the 8th Bn. was certainly an absolute dead end and it appears to me that this cannot be any more monotonous or soul destroying.

Well, my Sweet, I must complete this and get my Batman to take it to the post, otherwise I can see that I shall have to send you a wire, and that would never do, would it.

East Coast Shuttle

How are you getting on? I expect that I shall not hear from you for awhile since I suppose that you will have written to me at Blakeney.

All my love, Sweet.

Edward. x.

8

The Four Airfields

Just two weeks later, I found myself transferred away from further East Coast duties. The battalion had relocated under cover of night to a more permanent location at RAF Collyweston, a few miles away from Stamford. It had taken a number of days for the logistics of the move to be prepared, and then for the move itself. We were still seriously understrength and awaiting a number of specialists to complete our ranks. It seemed that, as in civilian life, you just couldn't get good staff nowadays.

Nevertheless, it still took a long convoy of those newly issued Bedfords, huffing and puffing, to get us and our engineering hardware to our latest destination, with the rest of the troops straggling along as best they could. Collyweston was a grass-strip airfield, the base for a couple of fighter squadrons.

We had been promised improvements to our living arrangements once we were moved to this more permanent base. Despite all the assurances, our lot was to be billeted under canvas. Not a happy arrival at Collyweston, resulting in all of us spending the first couple of days getting settled in and being half drowned in the process.

The nearest telephone available to me was on the adjoining base, RAF Wittering, and so for the time being all that I could do was cycle over there, introduce myself, and ask politely. Or, of course, have further recourse to pen and paper…

The Four Airfields

Undated. (Sunday)
E Coy, 70th Bn. The Leicestershire Regiment. RAF Station Collyweston, Northants.

Darling,

I have never known a girl complain so much, after all you are getting twice as many letters now as you did last year and yet you ask if I love you. You know that I hate writing anyway.

Well, don't we get about the country. I have now reached this spot, which is on the main road between Leicester and Northampton. We expect to be here for a number of months. When I heard that we were guarding an Aerodrome I expected something quite palatial. Imagine then my surprise when I found that we were sleeping under canvas and that the Officers Mess is an old Farm House that we share with about 20 RAF officers, and has no running water. Lavatory arrangements are of a very primitive bucket type, and I wash in my canvas basin, having shaved for the last 2 days without a mirror.

The food is good, plenty to drink, no tobacco, plenty of fresh air, not too long hours, earwigs in your trousers every time you put them on. The nearest pub is 1 3/4 miles away, the nearest town (Stamford) is 4 1/2 miles, and it rains every day.

It has not stopped raining ever since our arrival, and as a result, everything that I have is saturated. I am really concerned that, with my feet problems, I shall end up with trench foot.

How are you getting on? Are you missing me dreadfully? What news can you give me about the family? Is all well at home?

Now that we are here for a lengthy stay, I am allowed to put my location on to this letter, so that you will be able to write to me. Please write regularly to keep me in touch with back home. I will try to telephone you as soon as possible, so please do stay in during the evenings. I cannot give you a time because there are so many of us wanting to call back home.

All my love, Sweet.
E. x.

PRUNES FOR BREAKFAST

Her letters kept chasing me round a number of counties, and I never ceased to be amazed at how efficient the postal service still was. There must have been a huge amount of disruption, particularly in and around London, but the system appeared to continue to work on well-oiled wheels. I had been depending on telephone calls with Elizabeth to keep up with where I was, but it seemed that a bundle of letters, well overdue to me from my last few postings, was now waiting for me. The content left me in a sour mood.

Undated. (Monday)
E Coy, 70th Bn. The Leicestershire Regiment. RAF Station Collyweston, Northants.
Darling,
    You seem to grow purposely more and more annoying every time you write. I was expecting to see you at Holkham, at Blakeney and here at Collyweston. It is now a month since you wrote me to say that you could not come for three weeks. Even so, it would have been a fairly simple matter for you to have caught a train from Nottingham to Stamford for half a day. Leave and sleeping out passes are a difficult matter, after all we are supposed to be a defensive unit and on duty all the time. I should get seven days in the next month.
    Your letters tell me nothing of yourself, and you are able to write in comfort, I should think.
    The weather has been terrible for the last two or three days, tents have been dripping all over the place.
    Saturday and most of Sunday I spent in bed (lumbago). I am just going into Peterborough to have trench mouth attended to.
    It's a rum life, and you do not make it any easier, my sweet. Perhaps you will let me know what you would like to do.
    All my love, darling,
    Edward.

The Four Airfields

I found it so difficult sometimes to rein in my temper. Elizabeth was sleeping in a house with a warm bed and surrounded by her family. She wanted for nothing, as far as I could see. She had the continual use of her father's car to get about, and I was sending her a cheque each month. I, on the other hand, was sleeping in a tent, or rather a marquee with a number of others, with little or no privacy, and I was half drowned every day whilst trying to do my duty. I didn't think that she really appreciated the dramatic differences in our lives.

Undated.
E Coy, 70th Bn. The Leicestershire Regiment. RAF Station Collyweston, Northants.
Darling,
 Fortunately my tent is now pitched on a fairly dry piece of ground and apart from the fact that it is cold about 3 in the morning, it is not too bad.
 I shall be unable to get a sleeping out pass but of course I can stay out fairly late. I do not expect to get leave until the 20th of next month.
 Trench mouth is clearing up and you will be relieved that no teeth have dropped out.
 I think that if we are going to stay here, it will be as well if you forwarded sleeping bag also riding 'britches', travel clock and any grey socks that may be at Ripley, a pillow and two cases.
 I am sorry you are miserable, my sweet, and I do miss you very much, and I am waiting for the day you can get over.
 All my love, Sweet.
 Edward. x.

I felt absolutely bloody with what they called trench mouth. I was not sure exactly what it was, and nor was the MO, but it was playing havoc with my gums, and all my teeth thought that they were about to fall out every time I bit on something hard. The local dentist was worse than useless, and so I was depending on the MO to cure it.

PRUNES FOR BREAKFAST

He had given me some perfectly vile paste to rub on my gums three times a day after each meal, and told me not to bite on anything hard for a couple of days. The only plus side was that I was henceforth going to increase my daily calorie count in the form of beer.

> Undated. (Saturday)
> Officers Mess, RAF Wittering.
> Darling,
> The weekend is round again and next weekend will shortly be here thank goodness, and I have arranged not to be Orderly Officer.
> It has rained like the devil for the last two or three days and things have been rather miserable. I have visited the dentist three times and although he is a bit of a butcher I think he has nearly cleaned it up.
> I hope you are well and although I come in each morning and ask Corporal West if there is a letter for me, there has not been one.
> One of my blokes shot his (trigger) finger off deliberately this morning.
> I do not know whether you will be coming by car or train but I will write and let you know the trains.
> All my love, darling.
> Edward. x.

That business of one of the lads shooting off his trigger finger was getting a bit rife. I supposed that there would always be men who were not keen to do their duty for their country, for whatever reason, but shooting off your trigger finger, whilst extreme, only led everyone to realise that it had been done on purpose. Getting your trigger finger to the end of a .303 rifle required a certain gymnastic ability and it was completely obvious to anyone that it could not be done by mistake. I was not prepared to offer my services in defence when anyone did that. I did it just the once, and I looked a bloody fool.

The Four Airfields

Undated. (Wednesday)
Officers Mess, RAF Wittering.
Darling,

I think it will be as well if your visit is postponed until the following weekend. I have to go up to Leeds on Friday night to attend police court proceedings, one of my men having hit a policeman and removed a handset from a telephone box whilst he was away home on leave. I do not expect to be back before Saturday night, in addition to which the CO is going on leave on Friday and his 2 i/c does not believe in officers sleeping out.

I have had quite an interesting week. On Monday the Squadron shot down one Messerschmitt and damaged two. The RAF Squadron Leader has been posted to the Middle East and last night we celebrated his farewell, and all yesterday I was attending a Court of Enquiry concerning a bloke in my platoon who shot his finger off deliberately.

I was glad to get such a cheerful letter from you and to see that you were so full of beans. And to see that rationing in its various forms does not seem to be interfering too much with birthday celebrations.

Darling, do not feel too disappointed about the weekend, we will have a longer one next week.

All my love, Sweet,
Edward.

And away I was to go once again. In August I had been down in Aldershot in Hampshire for a course and now we were in October and I was to head back south once again, this time to Dorking in deepest Surrey. It would be yet another long train journey to get there, with many changes and delays, but hopefully providing an opportunity for Elizabeth to join me for a day or so down in London, if I could wangle it. Elizabeth had not been too well recently, so it depended rather on her state of health at the time.

PRUNES FOR BREAKFAST

27th October 1941.
Officers Mess, Eastern & South-Eastern Command, Weapon Training School, Anstie Grange, Holmwood, Nr. Dorking, Surrey.
Darling,
I am here on a 4 day Spigot Mortar Bombardment Course.
This is a god-forsaken spot, even more god-forsaken than Wittering. Who do you think I have met here? Norman Bond. I am very thankful that my Course is only until Wednesday – he is here for a fortnight.
We moved out of tents last Friday, at least the officers did, for which I am thankful. I have been Company Messing Officer and PMC, that is the chap that looks after the Messing.
I seem to have set in for a further attack of Trench Mouth, rather more violent than the last, but I shall visit the dentist tomorrow, DV.
I hope you are feeling OK and not worrying about going in Queen Mary's again.
I shall try and get another car as I come through London on Wednesday. I have my eye on a V8, a newer edition of our last, that I think might suit.
I am now preparing to go to bed before the Course starts tomorrow.
Give my love to your mother.
All my love, darling.
Edward. X.
PS. Will you ring me on Friday, Stamford 2251, Officers Mess, extension Collyweston.

My Unit was to remain there at Collyweston aerodrome, still just a grass airfield in the tight adjoining complex of local airfields comprising Easton-on-the-Hill, Wittering, and Kings Cliffe. There were fighter squadrons in training, others fully operational, and more recently some heavies, all scattered around the different fields, but they were no concern of mine. We were there to defend the area from any possible incursion or even invasion by enemy forces. What

The Four Airfields

was inside was no real concern of ours, just what happened on the outside from anyone wanting to get in.

When I arrived back at Collyweston base, however, I hardly recognised the place. It had, in the relatively short time that I had been away, been almost subsumed by Wittering. There were huge buildings mushrooming up from the churned-up earth. Pre-stressed concrete slabs were being erected in enormous sizes and volumes, and I could only dream of how they were manufactured. I wished that I could have laid my hands on some of them for our building business. All of the existing fighter plane hangars were being reinforced, and we were told that they would eventually be grassed over to provide camouflage. Clearly big moves were afoot in this small part of our world.

The noise was incessant from aeroplanes landing and taking off. In the middle of all that, the main Wittering runway was being doubled in length to accommodate the heavies, and ditches were being filled in and hedges torn down to make better perimeter roads and hard standings. They said that the runway would be all of 2 miles long when it was completed. What sort of aeroplane were we to expect that needed that length of runway?

Blocks of Nissen huts were being erected over on the far side of Wittering. Also, on the far side away from Collyweston more concrete foundations, for I knew not what, were being sunk in to the muddy earth. I was later told that they would be huge aviation fuel storage dumps.

It seemed that the idea was to turn Wittering into a major base for fighters and heavies, capable of supporting extensive traffic, not only by lengthening the main runway, but also by integrating and encroaching into the smaller grass strips surrounding it. Bomb-proof bunkers for the planes and their fuel (I hoped that they would be well separated!) were rising steadily from the surroundings, whilst all around were vast and highly visible concrete dispersal areas to keep planes well apart in the eventuality of enemy bombing.

PRUNES FOR BREAKFAST

Someone was going to have to dream up a method of 'aging' the new concrete because at the moment it was a highly visible magnet to any opposition planes. I did hear that they were going to spread animal manure on to the area in order to take the shine off it.

But there at Collyweston, my men were still to remain under canvas, and they were dug in around the perimeter so as to afford themselves protection against any unauthorised breaches of the defences. One of my jobs now was to do the night rounds of the perimeter, checking that the guards were on the alert, awake, and scanning for possible intruders. With this incessant rain, however, nobody could see very far in front of their noses.

It rained every day, all day. Oh, how it rained. Nobody could remember weather the like of it. It was the wettest autumn for years. All the work that we did, we had to do in waterproof clothing, where it was even available. Regardless, we were all saturated every day and I longed for a proper long deep hot bath like I could have when I went back home on leave.

That old run-down farmhouse on the edge of Easton-on-the-Hill, which was now almost part of Wittering since the runway extension had got under way, had been taken over by junior officers some while ago, and I was eventually lucky enough to find a spare space to bunk up there with them, on the basis of one out, one in. The farmhouse actually had a proper tiled roof which didn't leak, and, although there was no heating, it therefore promised that rarity, the opportunity of DRY CLOTHING!

And I could still cycle to 'work' in only a few minutes. It was not long before I found that I could stretch that on certain days by calling in on whatever project my men were working on at the time.

This was, for me, also a time of almost back-to-back courses. I no sooner seemed to have completed one than I was being shipped out on to another one. When it finally came to confronting the Hun face to face, I was determined not only to lead from the front, but to be as fully equipped as possible to do so, and in the best possible manner. My life would literally depend on it, and I was rather keen for it not to come to an overly abrupt end.

(Letter on Ellis-Fermor family crested notepaper)
Undated. (Thursday)
Darling,
    I was so happy to get your letter and I do hope that you do not have to stay in Queen Mary's longer than you expected.
    I have had rather an amusing week, with not quite such amusing consequences, but I will tell you all about that when I see you.
    I caught the train comfortably and had quite a pleasant run to Stamford, but it was pouring with rain when I got there, so I had to get the truck to run me up to Collyweston.
    I do not yet know whether I shall be able to come on Sunday, but I will try. We have Shellbrook, and Hodson away on Courses, and Lount will be away umpiring.
    However, darling, you know I will come if I possibly can, don't you. I love you very much, sweet.
    All my love, sweetheart.
    Edward.

My last course of the year meant that I was sent back to Norfolk yet again, this time to attend the 79th Division Battle School. Perhaps I was now being prepared by those above me for a move nearer to the front in the war? What had I seen of it so far? A few high flying planes, which others identified to me as Messerschmitt 109s (some of which provided superb AA practice for our chaps, and were shot down to rousing cheers and much drinking in the Mess afterwards with our RAF colleagues) and a couple of leaflet raids, which impressed nobody.

PRUNES FOR BREAKFAST

Undated. (Thursday)
My darling Sweet,
 I have managed to get Saturday evening out. There is a train at 1.10 arriving Leicester 2.23.
 We have been invited to Col. Loudoun's (some Hall or other) you to tea, me to tennis and tea. This train should bring you just about right.
 There is a dance tonight. I have spent all the afternoon trying to get some beer, but have failed dismally.
 Can you bring my blazer and cravat, also don't forget watch and tobacco pouch if you can find it. I think I put one in the top drawer of the desk in the library.
 All my love, darling.
 Edward.

I was on tenterhooks to hear back from Elizabeth as to whether or not she would be able to get over here for the weekend. She was not too keen on 'do's' like this, and meeting new people that she did not know and feel comfortable with.

In the event, she cried off, not feeling well. It was a great shame, because I was so looking forward to seeing her. I missed her dreadfully, all the time, but I didn't think that she was keen on taking so many trains by herself. With the Battle School over, I myself was quickly back on the train to Collyweston.

15th November 1941. (Saturday)
Officers Mess, RAF Station Collyweston. Northants.
Darling,
 I have received your wire and feel like a deflated balloon although I know that you would have come had you been able to. I looked forward so much to your coming and as I was the only officer left in the place I was proposing that we should have tea and supper here.
 Life is becoming very monotonous here, nothing but doing duty as Orderly Officer, drink and dominoes. I have just been invited to

The Four Airfields

go over to the Sgts. Mess to play Solo, so I should come back a little better off.

I can't understand this business of registration, surely they have not reached your group yet? If they have, describe yourself as a householder undertaking rent collection. In any case, my sweet, it will be years before they actually call up your group.

I have had a very dull week apart from Bretby's farewell on Monday. I have learned to drive a Bren Gun Carrier, which did not take very long.

Darling, until next weekend, which nothing on earth will stop. All my love, sweetheart.
Edward.

PS. Will you try to get some anti-freeze for the MG, and I will put it in over the weekend.

Elizabeth had got herself into a panic about being called up to help in some way with the war effort. One or two ominous letters had dropped through the letterbox recently. She was suffering greatly from the stress of the whole situation, as well as having to look after her parents, who were not getting any younger. I would have thought that her solicitor father could have wangled something for her to save her being sent off as a land girl or something. She collected property rents – there were some houses which were let to tenants in Ripley – and there were budgets to organise for me and occasionally decisions to be made about the farm in the Peak District, and she had two households to run now, as her mother was getting too frail to do much at The Woodlands. To cap it all, she told me on the telephone that some officious chaps had come one day, parked their drop-sided lorry in front of the house, and the next thing that she knew, all of their wrought-iron railings round the front of the house had disappeared, cut off and loaded on to the lorry.

'Sorry, love. Orders is orders. Needed for the war effort.' came the laconic response to her cries of outrage. You would have thought that there might have been a bit of warning. Or even a receipt? They could have just been anyone.

> 3rd March 1942.
> (Lettercard, postmarked Peterborough)
> Darling,
> *I suppose my last letter has gone astray, anyway, I have not heard from you. I am disgusted!*
> *Anyway, what about my pyjamas, I have bought two pairs, two pants, two socks and three collars, so my wardrobe is fairly complete.*
> *The Sgt. Major, whom you recall I defended, was found not guilty and has returned to the Company. The Squadron had a dance on Saturday evening, very beery.*
> *I saw the CO yesterday with not very good results.*
> *I am playing hockey tomorrow and Saturday to get my fat down. Can you bring my things with you Saturday lunchtime, boots, socks, shirt, stick and pads?*
> *Have you cashed in the coupons?*
> *Let me know what time at The Haycock.*
> *I shall be Orderly Officer on Thursday if you phone.*
> *Every bit of love,*
> *Edward.*

The battalion, like many others, was still short of proper army transport other than our allocated Bedfords; particularly the private army staff cars which were promised again and again, but never seemed to materialise. As a result, the MG had been really useful to me, time and time again. I really enjoyed it when I was posted somewhere and turned up at the main gate driving it, roof down if in fair weather, usually with my golf clubs propped up on the passenger seat. Sometimes when I drew up at the gatehouse of a new posting, the sentries' eyes popped out of their heads.

The Four Airfields

6th April 1942. Monday
Officers Mess, RAF Collyweston, Nr. Stamford.
Darling,

Have you had a good Easter? We worked Saturday and again today. I was OO yesterday and attended a Service in the morning after which I took 4s.2d. off the Padre at Rummy.

I had a fairly good run until I got to Melton Mowbray. Then I had a puncture and the jack would not work properly and I had to wait until someone came along and lent me one. This cost me over half an hour and I did not arrive back until 8.40.

I am sorry I make everyone miserable at Ripley. I have been thinking about it and decided it must be because I am not in my own house, consequently not being able to throw my weight about, order anyone about, and generally let off steam. But I do love you very, very much and it hurts like hell to think that I hurt you.

This is rather a long screed for me, isn't it? I have enclosed clothes coupons for Midland Drapery which I have meant to give you for some time.

We are not moving from this Aerodrome until 26th May, so we should be OK for another weekend or two. Be careful with the petrol coupons, you might think to have anti-freeze run off on your car. The worst frosts should be behind us now.

I must close now, darling and remember I love you always.
Edward.

9

Target Practice

I had not proved to be a very good shot when practicing on the firing ranges, thanks to a slight tremor in my right hand which seemed to kick in just about the time that I was lining up the shot and pulling the trigger. Nothing to be worried about, as the MO told me, something that afflicted quite a number of people, some a little, some quite a lot. I fell into the former category, but a wobbly trigger finger was not a great advantage.

The time had now arrived for the big one, something that I had been dreading. I was being transferred to the Small Arms Weapons Course at the home of shooting, Bisley, down in Surrey. It would be interesting to see how I would make out, and I admit that I was rather lacking in my usual confidence. But I was hopeful that it would lead to a few days' leave. The course would run from 26th May to 2nd July, quite a long one, so not only should I be pretty proficient at the end of it, but there would surely be the odd weekend for some relaxation with my wife.

26th May 1942. (Tuesday)
The Small Arms School, Hythe Wing, Bisley Camp, Brookwood, Surrey.
Darling,
    I am writing this after a really hot day, during which at many times I thought I should expire. However, after a shower, a gin and ginger beer at my side, I am sufficiently recovered to attend to my domestic affairs.

Target Practice

I have just phoned the Wheatsheaf Hotel to find that they cannot put you up a week on Friday, but Saturday/Monday is OK and if you like you can return on the Tuesday or Wednesday.

I think there is a fairly fast train from Derby at 10.20 a.m. and you then take a taxi to Waterloo where you can get a train to Woking about every half an hour. Then you can take a taxi to the Wheatsheaf where I shall be about 2.30 p.m. I should leave the car at Sanderson & Holmes in the centre of Derby.

Will you bring my pyjamas and any handkerchiefs, please?

This Course is not going to be too easy. The dashed instructors are not so easy to put it over as they were at OCTU. My performance with the bayonet, jumping over ditches etc. is not so good. Still, why worry, I have not stuck it in my foot yet or shot anyone.

I am proposing to start playing golf again tomorrow. Supper is now on my Sweet, so until a week next Saturday.

Every bit of love.

Edward. x.

Thank heavens for golf! Those clubs went everywhere with me – well, almost everywhere. And there was never a shortage of playing partners or opposition. Most of the officers that I had encountered so far had a liking for the game. I really could not have thought of a better way to break the ice when meeting new people in far off places.

Mid June 1942 (Friday)
The Small Arms School, Hythe Wing, Bisley Camp, Brookwood, Surrey.
Darling,

Your letter has arrived. I do like to hear that you have got back safely. I have felt rather brighter after your visit. It was a wonderful weekend. I have been troubled by mosquito bites and now have both arms bandaged from my wrists to above the elbows. I expect that it will clear up in a day or two.

PRUNES FOR BREAKFAST

We have now reached the half way mark, exams tomorrow, so I had better do a bit of swotting up tonight. We have thrown grenades today, fired the mortar yesterday, and the worst thing of the course, a dashed assault course, we did on Wednesday. I frankly funked the damn thing, but I did it. One bloke broke his ankle, I quite expected to kill myself when getting down from the 12 ft. wall with rifle and bayonet in one hand. I have managed to get a .45 pistol and 17 rounds, never been fired.

I lost my gold watch on the assault course but fortunately a party of fatigue men went out and found it. Huge sigh of relief.

Are you coming for the weekend again? Would your Mother like to come? If so, let me know by return as we shall have to stay at The Royal Albion in Brighton as The Wheatsheaf has only one room. You can get down to Brighton from Woking in about 2 hours if you would like to spend a day or two there. Don't bother about petrol, your need is greater than mine. Five gallons to Leicester and back is not too bad, 90 miles.

Every bit of love, darling.

Edward. x.

PS. Tell your Mother that having paid insurance for about 10 years, I don't intend to drop it now.

You know, I had rather taken to the Bren. I thought that it was the one weapon other than my trusty .303 that I was most proficient with. Before we were allowed to fire it – I didn't tell anyone that I had fired it quite extensively when on the local ranges at the back of Collyweston airfield – we had had to learn to strip it and put it back together again completely blindfold. I was seated next to the window during that particular lesson, and I supposed that my attention had wandered to what was going on outside.

I was brought back to the lesson with a bang when the Sergeant instructor told me to stand up and come to the front.

'Now then, Mr. Searancke, SIR,' he said, with heavy sarcasm. 'You seem to have it all off pat if you can afford to look out of the window for half the lesson. So I am sure that we shall all be delighted if you will give the class a demonstration of how to strip this Bren.'

And with that he shoved it into my grasp. I looked at him for a moment, and then glanced over to my colleagues in the class. Without further ado, and without even looking down, I stripped it well within the set target time, laying the separate parts carefully on the table in front of him. Then, having looked at him again, and without being asked, I really pushed my luck and proceeded to put it back together, again within the accepted timeframe. I clicked it back on to its front bipod, and then cocked it and dry fired it for safety. Then I put it down neatly, right there on the table in front of him.

'And thank YOU, Sergeant,' I said rather cheekily. Without another word passing between us, I moved back to my seat and sat down. Not another word was said and that instructor never picked on me again.

Undated. (Sunday)
The Small Arms School, Hythe Wing, Bisley Camp, Brookwood, Surrey.
How you can really expect a sweet letter, I do not know. I was very disappointed indeed. I had provisionally booked rooms and had arranged to have dinner in Ripley and go on to a dance at the High Pine Club, Weybridge.

I eventually made one of a party of eight, and although everything went swimmingly and very good indeed, I am afraid I did not enjoy it very much, you weren't there.

I was quite upset not hearing from you Thursday and Friday, even to the extent that it distracted my attention from my instructor, and when I did hear, it put me in a foul mood over the whole weekend. However, I have now recovered.

This weekend will not be too bright as I have to be on duty by Sunday teatime, so I think that you had better have the next weekend at Stamford.

PRUNES FOR BREAKFAST

You appear to have been quite busy and I hope that when you see the Labour Board you will stress that you cannot undertake anything, having my affairs to attend to. Darling, I will see you as soon as possible and in the meantime I hope that everything goes according to plan.
All my love,
Edward.

The other weapon that I was good at was what we all called a bazooka – a bit of an Americanism, I believe – a long green tube in two halves which you clicked together, and then, whilst it was over the shoulder, some other chap would load it up with a rocket from the back end. I would then aim it at a distant mock-up of a tank, and proceed, more often than not, to blast it to smithereens. There was virtually no kickback or recoil, because it was open ended at the rear. I reckoned that I quickly became quite good with that bit of kit, and hugely enjoyed showing off with it. I could project an image in my mind of its trajectory.

But with small arms, no, I was not so good. Finger wobble with a .303 bordered only on the acceptable and even with a .45, using the usual two-handed grip to stop my wrist being cracked from the recoil, I was still almost useless. Inner rings on the targets continued forever to elude me. Hey ho. You can't win them all.

Undated. (Wednesday)
The Small Arms School, Hythe Wing, Bisley Camp, Brookwood, Surrey.
Darling,
  Having waited 5 days for your promised letter, I thought it to be time to take up my pen. I am somehow feeling rather depressed, which is somewhat unusual for me. The Course has been rather a trial. Weapons are not my strong suit.
  I am leaving here early tomorrow morning to go to Easton-on-

the-Hill – A Company. Why, I do not know, and in truth am beyond caring. I had put in for 14 days before hearing from you and this had been granted so my leave should come a month hence.

I expect that I shall be Bn. Orderly Officer on Saturday as it is their usual trick which rather precludes you coming for the weekend, assuming you wished to come.

Darling, I wonder if you realize how much I hate not getting your letters when I expect them. You know that I have no trust in the people by whom you are surrounded. Looking back on the last year, I somehow feel that it has not been up to the standard of the three previous ones. Perhaps it is my fault, I do not know.

Darling, I love you always.
Edward. x.

At last it was time to pack up and go. Apart from the fact that the weather had been kind, it had not been much fun for me. I liked to do well at things that I had put my mind to. When I got back to Stamford, I made my way over to Easton-on-the-Hill to join a new company that was short of an officer. At least some of my friends were still part of the scene, though some others had been transferred, and I managed to get back my old billet. What could the morrow hold for me, I thought to myself.

Well, a bit of a transport problem, actually.

6th July 1942. (Monday)
Easton-on-the-Hill, Nr. Stamford.
Darling,

I am beginning to wonder whether I shall ever hear from you again. I arrived back at 0.15 Thursday. There was no transport to meet me, and I did not know the telephone number and the exchange refused to tell it me. So I slept the night in Burghley Park and on Friday went to Stone's Coy. at Easton. (Stone is away on a Company Commander Course). On Friday evening we entertained the CO and Adjutant and the local Lord of the Manor to a Dinner. A right royal time was had by all.

On Saturday morning I came off my bike and had to have a few stitches in my chin and be inoculated for tetanus.

I am very fed up. The Court Martial has not been held yet and I was expecting to see the new CO today to ask if I could not come home and then return for the Court Martial and he had no time to see me. So I shall see him tomorrow.

I have had a dozen oranges here for 10 days and sundry other things. They will go bad if I do not see you shortly. I enclose 4 Coupons which I should like you to take in tomorrow, though I think it may be too late. Did you cash the balance in?

Shellbrook is going into hospital, Ossie becomes Company Commander. If I don't get leave you must come this weekend.

I was Orderly Officer over the last weekend (dirty trick) and today have taken over duties of Bn. Weapon Training Officer. All very busy and rushed. Work until midnight tonight. We have no telephone otherwise I would have phoned you. I am dying to hear from you.

Every bit of love.

Edward. x.

Just because I had been on that bally course down at Bisley, some bright spark had taken the notion that I should be in charge of training the entire battalion on the use and safety of weapons. Battalion Weapons Training Officer sounded rather grand, I thought. All it meant was that I put batches of men through an abbreviated assimilations course for the various weapons that they would use. Safety was of course paramount, and it was astounding how many chaps I believed should never have been allowed to be in charge of a basic rifle, let alone a Bren or anything similarly high-powered or complicated. But the good news was that I was freed up, for weeks, from getting wet on picket duties and the like.

> Undated. (Sunday)
> Easton-on-the-Hill, Nr. Stamford.
> Darling
> I had a shock yesterday when I heard that day passes were to be discontinued owing to the increase in the number of absentees. However, I attended a conference in Peterborough this morning when the order was rescinded, so I shall be home this Wednesday after all, about 6.30 p.m. I imagine.
> I also gather that at the moment my application for transfer is not being considered and that we are likely to be in Easton for some time.
> Ernest Knight has taken a house in Stamford and has offered to let us have use of it when we want it, so things are not too bad, what.
> I expect to have the motor cycle ready for tomorrow but doubt whether I shall come home on it. That would shake you wouldn't it! I have had an offer of £8 for it, which is double what I paid for it.
> I don't like the way you dismiss my racing tips. I drew £5.2s.6d on Friday from the last 2 days but unfortunately lost £3.4s.0d yesterday.
> I am feeling rather tired at the moment. On Thursday morning I was up at 5.15 a.m. and on Friday at 4 a.m. for a practice dawn attack on Wittering, still, it is all helping to get me slim.
> Every bit of love, sweetheart.
> Edward.

We were going to do an exercise in Burghley Park. It was an immense place, Burghley. The house was a perfectly grand Elizabethan stately home, originally built for the Cecil family, I believe, and looked a bit like a cross between a chocolate box confection and one of the more outrageous French chateaux in the Loire. As you motored up the drive (or actually, to be more precise, in my case, cycled) and it came into view, it far surpassed places such as Highclere, and was quite on a par with Chatsworth for jaw-dropping amazement.

The park stretched as far as the eye could see, and all of the flat central part had become a sort of forces village, with row upon row of tents, and near to them, row upon row of more permanent prefabricated buildings. Metal and wooden tracking had been laid down in a vain attempt to protect what little parkland remained unsullied by the troops living and training there, or on temporary attachment for exercises. There was a vast shooting range off to one side, with an earthwork thrown up behind it the size of a small hill, in order to catch the spent ammunition before it could do any damage in the next county.

Undated. (Saturday)
Burghley Park, Stamford, Lincs.
Darling,

I arrived quite safely, cycled up, leaving the case at the station. Since then I have been in an absolute whirl. Wednesday I had to attend Peterborough Police Court, one of our blokes was in trouble, in the evening Co. Commander conference.

Thursday I was Co. Commander and had to act as advance guard on the Bn. Route March and in the afternoon had to pay the bally company, and on Friday the move to Burghley. All this on my own.

I had just got settled in on Friday when I was transferred to A Company, they had no officers and I became Co. Commander again. Capt. Melbourne returned this afternoon, so now I am CC no longer. Dashed shame isn't it.

I started this this afternoon and it is now 11 p.m. and I am sitting in the Orderly Room doing OO duties, waiting miserable and chilly for it to turn midnight when I can turn out the guard and turn into bed.

It has rained ever since we moved into Burghley and you never saw such a damp miserable dump (a word one of the troops used to describe it this morning). Everything is literally saturated.

Target Practice

I hope that you are feeling a lot better than when I saw you last. I hear that Brighton is closed, so I should try St. Annes at once. I expect to come on leave a week on Friday, but I think it would be as well if you came for the weekend next week, if you are feeling fit.

I trust all is well, and do let me have a letter by return of post.
Every bit of love, Sweet.
Edward. x.

The camp was laid out in the form of blocks that each held 500 men. Each block was sub-divided into tented villages holding about one hundred men. Pyramidal tents accommodated ten men, with some of the tents being set aside for the use of us commissioned and senior non-commissioned officers. New roads had had to be made in and around the camp. Later, when the roadways had been done, the tents had to be pitched and numbered, and the linking pathways had to be marked with posts and wire. Signs had to be erected so that visiting troops such as ourselves could find their way about the camp, night or day. The place was so big that it would be quite easy to get lost. Slit trenches had to be dug and numbered, so everyone knew where to go in the case of bombing raids or other emergencies. Vehicle hard standing had to be prepared all around the place. An entire camp organisation had to be set up including stores, cookhouses, dining tents and even an entertainment centre.

But thanks to the almost incessant rain, the place was much like a quagmire, and it was impossible to keep either oneself or one's machinery clean. Much as I would have liked to wangle a bed in the big house, I had to be under canvas. Despite all efforts, everywhere was soaking wet, and so were we. I'd be really glad when this was over and I could go back to Easton or Collyweston.

PRUNES FOR BREAKFAST

Undated. (Wednesday)
Officers Mess, RAF Wittering.
My darling Sweet,

Did you get home safely? I enjoyed every minute of your visit and was only sorry that it was so short.

We had rather an unfortunate accident a short while after you left. One of the Sergeants was killed when taking off and his machine wrecked. On Monday we had another crash, a machine was wrecked but the Sergeant escaped.

Yesterday I went to Peterborough to the dentist's, had a haircut, shampoo and a bath, ending at the pictures to see 'Miss Bishop'. Damned good show. I then went to the Peterborough Mess for the first time, and I must say that their capacity for ale is disappointing.

We shot down an ME 109 this afternoon and I gather that there will be some celebrating this evening.

I have got the oranges and now all I need is some brown paper and string. I don't think there is any further news and I only wait to see you again.

I have fixed a room at The George, Stamford and suggest you pick me up at the Mess either before lunch, say 12 o'clock or afternoon any time. I will wait until 1 p.m. and then go to lunch. I shall be able to sleep out.

All my love, Sweet.
Edward. x.

When I had a weekend pass, Elizabeth and I would meet up in Ripley or Ashby, or Elizabeth would come over and we would have a weekend to ourselves. The George at Stamford was a very nice hotel, one that I was pleased to be able to take Elizabeth to, and which was frequented by many of the senior officers. She and I stayed there on a number of occasions, and were very well looked after. The other hotel that we made use of was The

Target Practice

Haycock, also a grand place. They had, after the war ended, both gone on to be popular hotels, well known throughout the country.

⁂

The day passes caused more difficulties. They were a bit like hens' teeth, and when from time to time they would come my way, they could not be altered. There was not enough time for me to go to Elizabeth, so she had to come to me. One weekend I had fixed for the time off during the day, but had to be back to stand duty as Orderly Officer in the evening. When her parents decided to come with her and drive back the same day, it seemed a less appealing prospect, so I wrote to say it seemed a waste of petrol for such a short stay, and that it would be better for her to put it off for a few weeks when she could stay longer. I tried to remain pleasant about it, telling her she should do as she thought best, but I rather had the feeling that she was letting me down, and I descended into the slough of despond. I was even put out by the fact that she never bothered to thank me for those oranges that I had sent to her.

She said she still wanted to come, so I had been all geared up and ready for her arrival, complete with her parents. Then at the last minute I got a wire informing that they would not be coming after all. Perhaps it was not their idea of fun to wander round the town for a few hours whilst Elizabeth and I made ourselves scarce. It was still a little frowned upon to demonstrate much affection, even towards one's wife. I suppose that I could understand, but in the end it just meant a ruined weekend for me. Somewhat grumpily, I made other arrangements, and in fact had a very convivial afternoon playing bridge and dominoes before I had to be back on duty. If I remember correctly, I finished the afternoon handsomely in profit. Then on Monday I went into town and saw *Tropical Night*. Half a dozen of us laughed our way through it and afterwards we had a bit of a boozy time in a local pub before we wended our way back to the base, too late for any food in the Mess, much to my disgust, so I went to bed hungry.

> Undated. (Monday)
> Officers Mess, RAF Wittering.
> Darling,
> I was very sorry that you could not come over the weekend. I sent my wire before getting your letter and I would not have sent it had I known that you were not feeling up to it.
> We have had the Regimental Band here for a few days and are having an absolute riot of dances, dinners, drumhead services etc. I was Vice President at the Regimental Dinner on Thursday and was a guest of the CO and his wife at The George on Friday. I have been the CO's pet boy for about a week, but it will not last, the results having come in from Bisley, still he was quite nice about it. 'It was not good.'
> I am starting leave on Friday but I have just heard that Brighton is banned. I am wiring them and you should hear Tuesday morning. If it is not, I suggest we go Friday as I can get as free warrant. If the answer is OK, let me know what time you will arrive at St Pancras and I will meet you there. Otherwise I shall arrive at Derby about 11.45 a.m. on Friday morning.
> Every bit of love, darling.
> Edward.

It was a bit of a nuisance, that business of Brighton being banned to everyone. We had heard on the grapevine that there was some troop activity going on down there on the South Downs right behind the town, and that as a result the town and its surroundings had been declared a restricted district. Various rumours were doing the rounds as usual. A curfew on the inhabitants was to be imposed at once. It was a great pity as far as I was concerned, because Elizabeth and I enjoyed going to stay at the Royal Albion Hotel or the Queens Hotel, both nearly next door to each other on the seafront by the

Target Practice

Palace Pier, and had been going there, to one or the other, on and off, for a while.

Of course, the real news leaked out sooner rather than later, and it was in all the papers. Brighton beach had been mined because it had a long and fairly shallow pebble beach, even sandy when the tide was right out. It was therefore a prime candidate for any invasion force. What we had not been told was that Brighton was one of the towns on the South Coast, along with Shoreham and Newhaven, in and around which were billeted the Canadian troops that so gallantly were to lead the raid on Dieppe. On that beach on the other side of the Channel, so many of them perished as the Germans had late warning of the attack, and the Dieppe beaches could be so heavily and easily defended.

Of course, the dark shadows of these events were still unknown to us at the time.

And so, for my leave period, we booked to go north, visiting her parents at Ripley for a couple of nights and then going on to the delightful Clifton Arms Hotel on the seafront at Lytham in Lancashire. I could not get it out of my mind, though, that things were getting very serious if a Canadian attack was being planned from the South Coast. Would it be my turn next?

We checked in, leaving the car parked outside on the seafront, and went for a stroll along The Green, a sward that stretched for at least half a mile in either direction. We held hands and admired the 'captains' houses', a long row of lovely detached properties, so named because most of them had been owned by the owner/captains of the large boats that docked nearer to Preston, in the Ribble estuary. It was said that their wives could look out of their bedroom windows and, as soon as they saw their husband's boat coming up the estuary, hasten away their lovers.

Elizabeth seemed a bit tense, and so we made our way back to the hotel to change for dinner. Later, we had a drink in the cocktail bar and then went in to the elegant restaurant overlooking The

PRUNES FOR BREAKFAST

Green and the sea. She seemed to be getting ever more twitchy by the minute. Then, just before our dinner arrived, she reached over the table and took my hand, delivering the words: 'Dearest Edward, I believe that I am pregnant!'

After a moment to take it in, I stammered, 'Are you absolutely sure?'

And when she nodded, I leant over and kissed her, right there in front of the other diners. I think that some of them were rather shocked by such an open display of affection in public. I immediately called up a bottle of champagne and we had quite a merry evening, which I seem to remember passed in a bit of a blur for me.

10

Pip Pip!

In late summer, north Wales should be bathed in warm sunshine, a perfect place to spend some time even under harsh wartime training conditions, and I was rather looking forward to the change of scenery. It was August 1942 and starting on the 13th – another 13 – I was going to attend another course. At least there would be some hills to look at, instead of the unremitting flat countryside of Lincolnshire.

As to the weather, how wrong could one be? I was welcomed to north Wales by rain, followed by more rain, nearly every day. Rain, it appeared, was the order of the day in north Wales. And the course was as tough as anything I had been on so far. At the end of each day we ached all over and were too exhausted to do much other than sit around and swap stories of our lives in the army so far.

Undated.
Advanced School of Fieldcraft, Llanberis, Caernarvon.
Darling,

I have landed into it properly this time. There never was any Field Ranges Course, only the thing you see above, which is nothing more than a battle school. We worked until 5.30 p.m. yesterday and it poured throughout the day. To finish we ran a mile in full equipment. We double everywhere and I have nearly passed out on a number of occasions. The Course finishes on Sept. 3. We are billeted in quite a good hotel which is at the foot of Snowdon. Next

Sunday, we climb Snowdon. How about you coming for a week or so? It is very pleasant when it is not raining, which sadly is seldom.

I arrived with no battle dress or spare boots and was literally saturated on Friday crossing a stream and crawling through boggy grass, and the same on Saturday, so you can imagine how pleasant I have been feeling.

I hope you are OK and that you will decide to come for a few days, at least there are no sirens.

Every bit of love, darling.

Edward.

Undated. (Saturday)
Advanced School of Fieldcraft, Llanberis, Caernarvon.
Darling,

Your injunction to take care arrived too late. A quarter of an hour before opening your letter and parcel, I had a plaster put on my chin, a bandage on my knee, a bandage across all my knuckles. My unsplaterable [sic] glasses saved my eyes, but they are not much good now. I have been excused parades for 3 days and things are healing nicely. I had caught my foot on some rocky ground.

We were galloping along in the usual mad manner and I caught my foot on a rock and went down on some very rocky ground.

On the afternoon before, we had crawled on hands and knees on a tarmac road for 50 minutes. Absolute hell.

You could have stayed in the same hotel but unfortunately they are absolutely full and the other hotel is full, too, so it is just too bad. One can travel about without restriction and the weather is quite mild, although there is a lot of rain. In Llanberis we get low clouds that absolutely drench one.

The Course finishes a week next Wednesday and we are supposed to leave on the Thursday. I shall try and get to Ripley on the Wednesday evening and get an extra day.

Every bit of love, sweetheart.

Edward. x.

> *Undated. (Monday)*
> *Advanced School of Fieldcraft, Llanberis, Caernarvon.*
> Darling,
>   The Course is drawing rapidly to a close, we have only one more night operation, and then finish. My wounds are practically recovered, although I had a bad time in the big scheme on Thursday and had to crack up on the last 400 yards of the last leg.
>   I did not go up Snowdon on Sunday but did a climb almost as bad up the Devils Kitchen yesterday.
>   I expect to leave here Wednesday afternoon in which case I shall arrive late Wednesday, otherwise about mid-day Thursday, but in either case I will wire you.
>   Every bit of love until I see you.
>   Eddie.

Some of the things that we had been asked to do at that so called Advanced School of Field-craft were frankly outlandish, and I could not see how it might help in the future, unless I changed horses and joined a different part of the army. On the 1st October 1942, however, a month or so after I got back from north Wales, I attained another milestone. It turned out that I had received quite a good report from my time up there. That, coupled with the usual monitoring reports that went in at regular intervals to my CO, had led to the recommendation for me to be promoted to First Lieutenant.

As a result, I found myself running around even more, filling in for absentees and doing their duties as well as the new ones of my own that had been heaped upon me.

In addition, I seemed to have made a particular mark for my skills in court martials. I had been thrown in at the deep end a while previously, and when I had been defending blokes, I had got some of them off, but more importantly, had received some nice compliments from the presiding officers. As a result, people were now actually asking for me to defend them! I clearly had the gift of the gab for that sort of stuff, and perhaps some sense of gravitas for the occasion as well. I was to appear for the defence in a number of court martials during the war. Quite a feather in the cap.

However, all this extra work was quite getting me down, and trips to visit the MO or dentist were becoming more frequent. I never seemed to be completely free from aches and pains nowadays, particularly those associated with my flat feet and my mouth. I supposed that it was down to a combination of the pressure that we all were under, and the lousy weather.

> *2nd October 1942. (Friday)*
> *Darling,*
> *This has been the worst week I have ever spent. Whilst Norman has been away I have worked until 7 p.m. every evening including Saturday and Sunday and until 11 p.m. on Monday.*
> *I have had 4 Court Martials and 5 Summaries of Evidence. The place has gone absolutely crazy.*
> *I am supposed to be going on a weekend Course at Welwyn Garden City but I feel such a wreck I feel that I must put it off.*
> *I have got my 2 pips. All being well I shall take 48 hours next Saturday.*
> *How is everything, Sweet?*
> *Love,*
> *Edward. x.*

I was granted some leave last weekend as a result of getting that promotion, but unfortunately Elizabeth was not able to come over, despite us arranging beforehand that she would. I felt particularly aggrieved because promotion like that was a bit of a landmark. I had been part of the organisation for the Battalion Officers' Dance, and felt that I should attend all the same. I looked rather smart in my dress uniform and I had rather a good time, actually, what with the copious amount of beer that was available, and the presence of some fine specimens of the opposite sex with whom to dance. I did not feel like a wallflower at all!

> *Undated. (Monday)*
> *Darling,*
> *I am just finishing my day's work at 11.30 p.m. I was sorry you were not able to come for the Dance. It was quite good, the drink flowing fast and furiously. By the way, I have not got trench mouth but a touch of pyorrhea. I don't know if this is how you spell it. It is now cleared up.*
> *I hope your visits have been successful.*
> *We have lost 2 more officers to the 2/5th Bn. And it looks as though we shall not have any officers left shortly. By the way, I am a full Lieutenant now (did I tell you?) but don't put the pips up yet. I am working like stink, everything is getting organised at last.*
> *I played tennis several times last week, quite well for me.*
> *I am looking forward to seeing you this weekend and hope that the weather holds good.*
> *Every scrap of love.*
> *Edward.*

I had started to hear a rumour, and the word that kept coming up was 'Ireland'. Surely we couldn't be going to Ireland? What on earth for? I thought it was time for some sleuthing on my part, and it was later confirmed to me that, in the month of October, we would see part of 59 Division going over the water, and with them my chum Norman in 7 RN.

One morning, very early, I was pedalling along on my cycle from Collyweston to the main base at Wittering, working my way around the perimeter in order to check on my men who had been on duty overnight, when I looked up and saw, through the early morning mist, what appeared to be a lone German plane coming in to land. I nearly fell off into a ditch in my surprise and only managed to contain the wobble with difficulty. What was so strange was that there was no gunfire from the ack-ack batteries surrounding the airfield, as there had been in the past when a German raider came too close. We had actually downed one or two last year, followed by much merriment in the Mess which we shared with the RAF boys.

I pedalled along as fast as I could, and then, blow me, there was another one, wheels down, landing completely unmolested.

It was not long before I found out what was going on. During the past few months, under very close security, the RAF at Wittering (in one of those huge new grassed-over hangars) had been responsible for the formation of several specialised Units. The least known of these was responsible for putting together a new flight of enemy aircraft that had been captured, for the most part only lightly damaged. Eventually there were examples of most German planes, sufficient to form an almost complete flight which was later designated as 1426 EAC, which comprised Heinkel 111s, Junkers 88s, Messerschmitt ME 109s, and Fokke Wulf 190s, all newly overpainted with RAF roundels and proper number codes applied. The flight would travel from Wittering all around the country giving demonstrations and briefings, and so making it that much easier when it came to long range aircraft identification, particularly for the ack-ack boys.

It had been my good luck to see the very first one arriving, still in its German Luftwaffe livery. It was a sight burnt into my memory and something that I still remember as though it was only yesterday.

Much later, well after my time there at Wittering, it became the home of the first USAAF flights into the European theatre, with the 55th Fighter Squadron bringing with them their P38 Lightnings and P51 Mustangs.

But in the meantime, I was moving to Kingscliffe. I hoped Elizabeth would be able to get the car licenced and the weather would permit her to come soon, and then she could wire The Haycock for a room.

Undated.
Officers Mess, RAF Kingscliffe.
Darling,
I bet you thought I had forgotten you but you see! Life here is rather bloody. We are having to stand to every morning at dawn and if you do this without washing and breakfast you feel tired out by about 10 o'clock.

Also, our new Company Commander does not like the transport being used much so I am now cycling down every day to Collyweston and Wittering.

I was Orderly Officer last Sunday and also next Sunday, so I think the following weekend at The Haycock.

This Sunday I have to go to Oundle to demonstrate the Bombard to the Home Guard. I shall die of overwork.

The CSM's Court Martial is on Friday so that will soon be over, thank goodness. Stone returns on Monday so that is another good thing.

I think I enjoyed the last 7 days as much as I have had, and I love you more and more every day.

All my love.
Edward.

I had quite a happy time at Kingscliffe, responsible for the guarding of a much smaller aerodrome for a change, despite the unremitting rain. It was good to be under a proper roof and not under canvas. It really made so much difference having dry clothes, and not having the fear of awakening to find that one's bed was awash with rainwater that had come in through the roof in the night whilst asleep. However good those army tents might be, they still leaked. My intermittent visits to The Haycock with Elizabeth were a great boon, whether just for one night or more. I would have been very happy for her to have come over for just an afternoon, when I could wangle a few hours off, but I realised that, for either of us, that was not realistic. And it would have meant that her meagre allotment of fuel would have been used to very little purpose.

I had got myself into a good position at the airfields, and I was not having to work very hard. There was plenty of time off to play whatever sport was available, and in the evenings, when not on duty, I usually managed to augment my meagre pay with games of dominoes, bridge or rummy. I had this feeling, though, that things were now a bit too easy. Guarding those bally airfields was hardly the ultimate test, and I had been through enough courses to realise that my contribution to the war effort, though important so far, could be maximised elsewhere. I wanted to raise my game.

11

Ireland Beckons

Many Units of the 59th Division had already moved over to Ireland for some major exercise or other. What they were doing and why they needed to be over there was still anybody's guess for those of us left behind. That sort of information was well above my pay grade.

Perhaps they were just running out of space in England? I had heard, for example, that where the tank boys had been out on exercises, they had virtually destroyed nearly all the dry-stone walls in one northern county, bashing straight through them, taking no account of the sheep that were liberated, and so making themselves very unpopular with the local inhabitants.

There was a lot more empty space in Ireland, by all accounts, and it was, of course, that much further away from any pesky German spies. There was a lot of uninformed gossip doing the rounds because someone said that we had rounded up quite a number of them recently, and they were being held in some old converted manor house in the Lake District. Typical of our English sense of fair play, that. No doubt that they would be relaxing in the lap of luxury. I knew what I would be doing with them.

But as the Irish situation gathered momentum, lo and behold, I was being posted away on yet another damned course. There was a big plus this time, though. I was being sent to St. Albans, of all places, down in Hertfordshire. It meant that I might be able to spend some time with Elizabeth in London, which was not far away and would be easily accessible from there. I had to assume that we would all be getting some free time at weekends, and Elizabeth was still happy to travel down on the train as her pregnancy was not causing her any difficulties. She enjoyed visiting London, I knew.

It turned out that I and a couple of other officers were joining a joint training exercise with other Units whose designations were, at the time, subject to the blue pencil of the censor.

Undated. (Monday)
E Coy, The Oaks, London Rd, St. Albans.
Darling,
We have had a very busy day. This morning I gave a demonstration of platoon in attack à la Isle of Man. This afternoon I went shopping for the Mess and tonight we have a Night Op.
I am moving to Ossie's billet tomorrow as he is going in to hospital. I think they may be able to put you up, anyway you can stay at a hotel. I may be able to get some onions. Ossie has promised to try to get Turtle Oil and if he does I have told him that we will let him have 12 eggs.
Have you thought any more about London or Brighton?
Every bit of love, Sweet.
Edward.

This posting was a bit like going on holiday, but with new people that I did not know. I had to give a couple of lectures and demonstrations, and then I believed that I was in the frame to do some representations at court martials. In between there was not much to do other than to tap in to the local black market, trying to obtain either food or presents that were not available elsewhere.

Ireland Beckons

Undated. (Monday)
London Road, St Albans.
Darling,
　I have just finished a Court Martial in which I was defending officer for 3 accused men. I did quite well.
　I should license the car because I may be able to get some onions. This is a wonderful black market town. I had the promise of some oranges last night. Preparation for this Court Martial and PMC duties have kept me off training and I have got rather fatter. I am now eating much less and have cut out porridge and cheese, crumpets and things like that. I missed bacon and egg yesterday breakfast, steak for supper, bacon and steak today.
　As for my doings, Saturday afternoon we had our photograph taken and then I played snooker. In the evening we went to a couple of pubs and ended up playing solo with a bookmaker and his wife until midnight. Sunday morning I inspected billets, interviewed prisoners, played pontoon in the afternoon until about 8 p.m. then went to Queens and played pontoon until 10.30 p.m. and walked home. Miserable existence, isn't it?
　Quite a long scrawl for me isn't it. Not been to London or even the pictures.
　Glad to hear the anti-freeze has now arrived. Hope it is not too late.
　All my love, darling.
　Edward.

My exhortations for Elizabeth to take the fast train to London had met with no enthusiasm and so I had remained alone for the middle weekend of the course. That was not to say that I had not enjoyed my spare time there. St. Albans seemed to have so much more in the shops than was available in Stamford, or even Leicester. Perhaps it was the close proximity to London, but it was a veritable treasure trove by comparison, and a pleasure to walk around the place. The required shopping list for Elizabeth had been almost fulfilled, and I had managed to do some fancy bartering to boot, and so able to take some extra stuff back with me on the train to Stamford when I left in a couple of days' time. I had rather an exciting time on that train. I got on the wrong one. The Nottingham train came in first, so I got on it. Fortunately it stopped at Trent and my train was forty minutes late, so all was OK in the end.

It seemed almost definite that we should soon be on the move. The give-away was that the number of leave passes had suddenly accelerated. Everyone was in the queue to go home, perhaps for the last time. The lid was firmly on, however, and nothing further had filtered down to me. I could not even cajole any news out of Norman, because he was still in Ireland attached to Divisional HQ on temporary assignment, but I expected him back in England within the next few weeks.

Undated. (Wednesday)
XVII Leicestershire Regiment.
Darling,
You write the sweetest letters. I was sorry that you were unable to come for the weekend. Is the cold better? Sorry to hear about the increasing girth, but I warned you. I have been for my interview with C.M.P. (?) at York, got back into Peterborough at 1 a.m. Absolute waste of time. I turned it down. On Saturday I went for interview with C.R.E. (?) at Bedford and have now put in application for Royal Engineers, which I think in time will go through.

Wittering Dance was the most magnificent show I have been to. Every type of eatable imaginable, and all the drink you could wish for, all free, of course.

There has not been much doing for the last 3 or 4 days. We are sending people on leave as quickly as we can.

I shall be home on Saturday and expect to be in Derby at the

usual time. If you are not at the station I will come up on the bus, but I think that you might as well get a taxi.
Until Saturday, every bit of love.
Edward. x.

That spot of leave was just the ticket. Elizabeth and I had a great time, despite the third party starting to make his or her presence felt with the odd kick in her stomach. I was so sure that it was going to be a boy, though. Even my parents, when we visited them in Gresley, commented on how well Elizabeth was looking. She went out for half a day with my stepmother whilst my father and I held a directors' meeting. Things seemed to be holding up satisfactorily.

Undated. (Wednesday) (January or February 1943)
XVII Leicestershire Regiment.
Darling,

I agree that my letter writing is pretty putrid. But the intention is there.

I shall arrive at Derby unless I let you know differently at 11.45 – the train that you came back on.

Everyone except me is a little rattled because we have heard that the Bn. is going to be disbanded next month. However, this afternoon, things are a bit brighter as we now understand that we are likely to be formed into ITC for new intakes.

Life is quite full, beat Luffenham at hockey last week. All ranks dance last Saturday, working like the devil.

You appear to be having quite a good time but you had better get used to calling 'X' John.

Well, I must go to tea as I have to umpire a troops' hockey match at 5 p.m.

Lots of love.
Edward.

PRUNES FOR BREAKFAST

I seemed to have become rather popular as an umpire. That was good for my exercise because I had to run around almost as much as the players. The other thing about it was that it kept my mind off Elizabeth and 'X'. It would not be long before the big day.

Undated. (Sunday)
XV11 Leicestershire Regiment, Stamford.
Darling,
   London is visited and left, and no transfer to the RE's. They want young men who can be trained for bridging and dock work etc. for the 'Invasion'. In any case it would have been overseas service almost at once. I arrived in good time, changing in Nottingham. George Desford met me at the station and we all managed to get in at the Cumberland. He had also got tickets for the Bobbie Howes Show, which was quite good. Saturday morning to Golders Green and it was not until I came out that I realized it was actually the College Building which must have been taken over. After that I went to Bond Street and ordered a hat, and then back to Stamford at 5 p.m.
   Saturday night I spent with Norman and Margaret, afterwards to the Home Guard Dance.
   Sunday night I took my real farewell to Stamford when I walked up to the Crown about 9 p.m. The moon was shining and it was really beautiful.
   Sunday a quiet day with odd farewells and it is now 3 p.m. Monday, about to collect beer and sandwiches, and so to Ireland…
   I will see you, darling, as soon as you send for me. Norman is Godfather if it is a boy.
   Ever yours, with love.
   Edward. x.

Well, my application for posting back to the Royal Engineers had come to nought. Those on high had been burning the midnight oil and clearly had a plan for me for some time, as I was being posted

Ireland Beckons

away from 'our' airfields, as I had come to think of them after so long there, and was being sent to join another Unit within the Division. That Unit was to be the 7th Battalion The Royal Norfolk Regiment, and I was due to sign in with them on the 16th February 1943, at their location where they had been since last October: Northern Ireland.

I was not very happy about that; although Elizabeth had been having a relatively easy pregnancy so far, and was due to give birth in early March, her doctor had advised her that she should take a lot more rest than she had been doing. I really wanted to be a lot closer to hand in case of any unforeseen complications, without the problem of the Irish Sea in between us. It had never been my favourite stretch of water by a long chalk, and there was only about a month to go before I expected to become a father!

The MG had to go. It was time to have something more sensible, what with Elizabeth about to give birth, but it was going to be a real wrench parting with it; we had been through so much together. I would not have been able to get it over to Ireland, and it wouldn't be much use to me back here when I was over there.

Undated.
Darling,

Things are really hotting up now. Nearly time to go.

What a fluke! That chap over in Norfolk has just got back to me, wanting to buy the MG. You remember that he saw the car when I was based over there in Blakeney, and made some noises of interest. A farmer, I believe, so with pots of money. Anyway, he has just got back to me after all that time, wondering if I still have it. As we are almost about to leave here for Ireland, I snapped his hand off and said that he only had a day to get here and pay me. He came yesterday, as good as his word.

I got nearly £280 for the MG which will about cover the cost of those other 2 cars that I have made an offer for: the Wolseley 18 (only done 16,000 miles, £230, will pay to keep until after the war) Austin 10 (very reliable does nearly 40 to the gallon, which will do to run around in during the war, when I get back from Ireland, £65). The price for the MG nearly covers the cost of both. Have you had the new oil cap for it yet, and have Youngs of Lincoln sent fog lamp etc.? I told him that you would post them on when they came to hand. Will you do that please.

In great haste,
Edward. x.

It almost felt like letting go a part of me – but with a child due, what alternative was there than to let the MG go? It couldn't have worked out better: the bigger Wolseley for Elizabeth to take home and keep in the garage, and the little Austin 10 for me to rattle around in when I got back from Ireland. I made an arrangement for it to be stored in one of the big hangars on the base until my return.

12

Over the Water

Ireland looked to be a beautiful country, and, for a change, it was not raining as we pulled into the docks in Larne's harbour. The entire battalion had made the long journey up to Stranraer in order to take advantage of the shortest possible sea crossing. Larne was a bit like a very mini-Liverpool, there was so much military traffic going on, but without the heavy bomb damage that I had seen in Liverpool.

As usual, there was a convoy of heavily camouflaged trucks lined up ready and waiting for us to board. The rest of the 59th Division was currently in what was known as Zone B, the Belfast area, so there was not too far for us to go. Before we had been there long, however, my own Unit was moved further inland to the Dungannon and Summertown areas, on the far side of that big lough, to join with the Royal Engineers in Exercise Shovel, where we were going to practice road building. Someone on high had decreed that we should need this expertise once the Second Front was open and we were sent overseas, with the likelihood of having to repair some of the roads that our own troops would have blown to smithereens to hinder the Germans from either retreating or resupplying their troops.

Undated. (Wednesday)
7 RN. Home Forces.
Darling,
    Note the lack of address, letters of the 'blue pencil' variety, so there will not be a lot of news. We arrived about 5 p.m. on Tuesday

afternoon, having left Peterborough about 4 the previous day, travelling all night and embarking about 8 a.m. The seas were tremendous and I (in a goodly company) was very ill. I don't like that bit of sea. I was very tired by the time that we arrived.

At the moment I am on detachment. The officers seem quite a good crowd. One very good bit of news is that Fitz is coming here. He did not know when I left on Monday, but they have known here for a few days.

Being here seems miles away from you and I seem so helpless at the time when you could have done with me the most.

Since arriving I have been very busy. Each day I have had to visit the Dental Officer and he is 9 miles away (gum trouble again). Yesterday being a no-transport day I had to cycle and I shall have to do the same on Monday.

Night Ops on Thursday and generally they do not seem to expect to finish before 7 p.m.

I am OO today and Censor but I am managing to get a game of hockey this afternoon.

We are living on troop rations while we are here. I have only had one pint of beer and 6 bots of Guinness since Tuesday so I should soon be very fit indeed.

The troops had a cinema show last night – 'Seven Sinners' with Marlene Dietrich, but I did not attend.

This must seem a very dull letter, after many that I have seen when doing my spot of censoring. I can understand now what you would like me to write, but how the hell they think of it I cannot imagine.

I think that unless you wish me to come immediately on the event it would be better if I put it off 3 weeks or even a month. There is a special reason for this, connected with a new leave order. But I will come immediately you send for me.

I am thinking of you all the time, and am only waiting to hear that everything has gone off all right, which I know it will. I only live to hear that you and 'child' are both well. Be of good cheer and be brave.

I had a little time around the shops in Belfast while waiting for my train and I think there should be little difficulty in procuring cot sheets etc. Let me know everything that you want.

I hope that everything is going according to plan.
Love you always.
Edward. x.

The problem with the exercises was that they almost always took place deep in the countryside, as far away from prying eyes as possible. And that meant that it was difficult, sometimes impossible, to get away and back to any sort of civilization – in this case, Belfast, where there were shops in abundance. I was under strict orders from Elizabeth to obtain quantities of Irish lace. What the child would want with lace, particularly if it turned out to be a boy, was rather beyond my limited intellect.

26th February 1943. (Friday)
7 RN. Home Forces.
Darling,

I was delighted and relieved to get your letter on Tuesday. I am sorry that you had to go in to hospital earlier than you thought, but you will be well looked after.

Today has been a quiet day as we have reached the end of our 3 week Course. Tomorrow everyone has a day off. I think that I shall go in to the big city and try to get the cot sheets etc. that you want. There is also a good hockey match that I may watch.

I have been more energetic over here than I ever have before. Did I tell you that I played hockey last week against a neighbouring Unit? They have one or two officers that I knew quite well from Burton before the war. The ground was the worst I have ever played on and we lost 4 – 1.

In the evening I sawed some logs, otherwise there would have been no fire in the Mess. On Monday I cycled 9 miles to the dentist, and then 15 miles back to the Range. Spent 3 hours there and afterwards, a night Op. The teeth are clear now and I am a lot fitter than I have been for some time.

Last night we had a dance but I volunteered to stay behind although it grieved me to miss the 9 gallons of beer that I had managed to buy for them. Norman was given 14 days embarkation leave by the Spilsby crowd, but his CO got him off as they had not finished winding up. My CO, who I have liked very much, is going on a 6 month Course.

When I get back to HQ I shall ring to Gresley to try to find out how you are. I feel that I must have news of you. I suppose that it will be sometime before you can write.

Every bit of love, dearest.

Edward. x.

I received a phone message on the evening of the 8th March that Elizabeth had finally given birth in a wing of Derby Royal Infirmary the day before. It had been a long and difficult confinement. I was, at last, the father of a son, and we had agreed that we were going to call him John Edward if it was a boy. Any other names would have to wait. I was hoping to be able to speak directly to Elizabeth on the telephone, and perhaps to hear the lusty cries of the infant. It was not to be, however. All lines were down. I must wait for a letter with more information. Surely either Elizabeth or my father would write with the news?

Somebody suggested that the right thing to do would be for me to send her a congratulatory telegram on the morrow, the 9th. In the meantime, a number of my fellow officers, in the expectation of free drinks, I reckoned, were waiting in the Mess to congratulate me. I would want to do myself proud that evening, but I was feeling curiously deflated. The great geographical distance between us made it all feel so remote. I found it difficult to get excited about it. But that was the war, I supposed.

I sent the wire, but heard nothing back, so I put pen to paper as well.

11th March 1943. (Thursday)
7 RN. Home Forces, Ireland.
Darling,
    How do you feel now that it is all over? Was it worth it all?
    I am Bn. Duty Officer today and am writing this before I go on my rounds at 1645.
    I heard the news on Sunday evening about 2030 which was rather good I think. I promised to phone home last night, but I did not get in until 2300 which was of course too late.
    I had spent the day starting as an umpire and then spent the day digging out carriers. A day which compared with that awful night on the IOM.
    I come on a course on Monday March 22nd and I think I may ask for compassionate leave for 48 hours before joining, and then complete the end of the course which is April 6.
    I have bought an Irish Sweepstake Ticket, which I will make second present to the youngster. I put 'Edward' as a pseudonym but of course I should have put 'Young Edward'.
    Apart from my phone message, I have had no wire or anything about the event. Bad staff work on your Mother's part.
    Well darling, I hope that you are improving every day and that the infant is a lusty one.
    Every bit of love, Sweet.
    Edward. x.

That should do the trick, should it not?

In the meantime whilst we were over in Ireland, in addition to all of the hard work, there was inevitably time for R&R. We participated in most of the inter-Unit competitive sporting events, and I can remember that we held a boxing contest (not I for that one, thank you), a cross-country race (no, not I again), hockey (yes) and soccer matches, a treasure hunt (we nearly won that), tank and aircraft recognition (perhaps a premonition of my course on that latter one)

PRUNES FOR BREAKFAST

and a German speaking competition. There was even a one-act play competition. All of that brought a sense of fun and relaxation to the hard graft of the days of training, and kept our minds off other things.

15th March 1943.
7 RN. Home Forces, Ireland.
Darling,

A week has gone by and still I have had no official information that I have become a father. I have phoned Lou three times and have been kept fairly well posted. I have learned that young JE has dark hair, which I gather has thrilled Pop, but I still do not know how heavy he is. Notices have been put in The Times and the Burton paper, but I have not written to anyone, and expect that you will do that.

I shall be going to Ripon on Monday next and expect to be on leave on April 7 for 10 days. I hear you will not be leaving the Nursing Home until next weekend. You must be feeling very tired and fed up with it all, especially if you are having the wonderful weather that we are having.

We are situated in a lovely park with a beautiful lake, daffodils and primroses in profusion, it is all very beautiful at the moment.

What about the pram? The only thing I can get over here is pram pillow cases. To get Irish linen is more difficult than getting bananas in England.

Every bit of love, Sweetheart.
Edward. x.

Surely to heavens someone, and by that I meant my wife, could get in touch with me and tell me how she and the boy were. Did they not have a telephone in that hospital? Or writing paper? I was feeling very cut off, over there in Ireland, not knowing exactly how they both were. I had to just keep plugging on, I supposed, but I would have thought that the least that they could do would be to keep me updated on Elizabeth's and the lad's progress.

Still, I hardly had time to dwell on my feelings of vulnerability over the lack of information about my son when we commenced joint training with live ammunition. We had started a new regime of training techniques with battle drill, assault courses (I just hated that 12 foot wall, trying to get over with a rifle and a full pack) and being dumped into a very smelly flax pit. Everyone ended up in that stinking hole, much to the amusement of those senior officers present. It seemed to provide a rite of passage. I had suggested that officers should be exempt from that particular hazard, but I was promptly shoved right in it. We even had to do some sniper training, but I was useless at it, and was soon relieved. But that live firing of ammunition added a certain realism to the events and would surely pay handsome dividends in the future.

When some Americans moved in for joint training, they played by a completely different set of rules. We were in the middle of some joint exercise with the Yanks when they announced that they had captured one of our Generals! It turned out that the British General in question was actually off the exercise, and resting in his tent. We put that down as definitely not cricket.

There was something that entertained me, though, during a signalling and communications event. Orders were passed to and fro down the line either verbally or by signal. One such, which started out as *'Send reinforcements, we are going to advance,'* ended up with some wag at the far end passing it on as *'Send three and fourpence, we are going to a dance.'* The CO was not amused.

18th March 1943. (Thursday)
7 RN. Home Forces, Ireland.
Darling,

I am feeling quite distressed. Eleven days ago I became a father and still at the end of that time I do not know officially.

I have phoned Gresley for news 3 times last week and again last night, but I could not hear them but the operator asked (them) how you were and the answer came both well so I was a little more comfortable.

I have managed to get a pair of cot sheets made up and a pair of pram pillow cases.

I am in my last 2 or 3 days here as I proceed to the School of Military Engineering, Deverell Barracks, Ripon on Monday and come on leave on 6th April but before I see you I shall have some interesting news for you. I should think that you are now feeling much better and I hope the son is conforming to plan.

I am longing to see you and if I can steal only a few hours I shall do so.

Every bit of love, my Sweet.
Edward. x.

What with all of that which had been going on, I had managed to avoid Exercise Boonton which was designed to manage our movement from Northern Ireland to Kent. Both rail and private transport (yes, it was crazy, but we were still having to use some officers' private cars because of the transport shortage in the battalion) were to be laid on. As an administrative and practical exercise, it should stand the battalion in good stead for when real forward movement was required. I, of course, missed all that because I was to be off to another course, this time on Assault Engineering, one of my newly found but mainly unwanted specialities.

It would be nice to see the back of Ireland. Lovely countryside, but overall rather boggy and squelchy. And anyway, I wanted to see my son for the first time, and that was not going to happen if I was in Ireland, was it?

22nd March 1943. (Monday)
7 RN. Home Forces, Ireland.
Darling,

I was delighted to get your letter. It's a pity you can't have a child every week, at least I do get a few letters from you. I think that the Censor must have smiled when he read your last paragraph.

I find my great trouble to be that I am writing so often that I cannot remember what I put in the last one. Norman is coming here as a subaltern, and will not become Adj. We expect him this week.

I went to Belfast on Saturday, but shopping was most unsatisfactory, I could not get pillow cases or cot sheets. I could get a Moses basket and mattress in ordinary plain wickerwork if you would like them. I saw quite a number of frocks you might be interested in. I will try local shops for cot sheet on Sunday. Apart from that I had the first 2 decent meals since I arrived, and went to the Pictures ('All Through The Night' and 'Fingers At The Window'). Then a few beers and returned at 9.30 p.m.

I have enclosed an Airgraph I received from Capt. Jimmy Shellbrook, which I enclose. You will note reference to CSM's Court Martial and also Smith's visit to Collyweston.

I am thinking of you always.

Edward. x.

13

Building Bridges

My feet had almost literally not touched the ground in the last few days. Belfast to Larne, wait, boat to Stranraer, wait, then train to Leeds, wait overnight, change and arrive at Ripon, wait for lift… I arrived totally knackered, and only just got there in time by the skin of my teeth. I was in Ripon for the Assault Engineering course which started on the 23rd March 1943 and ran for two weeks until the 6th April. If I passed, then I would become a certified instructor for teaching my new skills.

There was a new-fangled bit of kit that was being demonstrated, called a Bailey bridge, about which everyone seemed to be talking at the moment. I suppose that they couldn't think of a better name, so called it after its inventor. The idea was that you made up some heavy duty bits of metal girder (I am paraphrasing this a bit), linked them together with some super new slotting system, and then slung them over a small river. The strength when assembled correctly was supposedly sufficient to bear the weight of even those new US tanks that we saw roaming over the moors on trial. They were heavier even than our own home grown Churchill, which was an apt name for a tank if ever I heard one!

25th March 1943. (Thursday)
Royal Engineers Mess, Deverell Barracks, Ripon, Yorkshire.
Darling,
I have tried to phone you twice without success and so rang the family at Gresley for them to pass on the number here. You will not

be able to come here because I am going to be fully occupied on this Course.

I had a very good crossing, sea like a millpond, and only saw 2 submarines. I arrived at Leeds at 1.30 in the morning and managed to get a room at the Queens Hotel and stayed in bed until midday. Marshall & Snelgrove in Leeds would make your mouth water, I have no doubt. The news I promised you! The Bn. will be on the South Coast when I re-join them and will be there for 2 or 3 months. How do you like that?

I managed to get the pram pillow cases and I can get the cot sheets made up if you like. I have enclosed a sample of linen 10s.1d. a yard, and I think it takes 1 and a half yards per sheet I can order them now if you like. Still, now that you are back at Ripley you will soon be blooming. Young JE´s cold is a nuisance and I am sure that it will soon be better. From your last letter he seems to be making quite a good start in life.

The work here is quite hard and I am looking forward to the time when I can be with you again, although I do not feel so far away now that I am back from Ireland. I hope that young JE does not get you up too often in the evening.

Every bit of love,
E. x.

It was necessary that somebody from my battalion had to do that Assault Engineering course, and at least I would be the main person properly qualified as a result of it. It was a really interesting subject, particularly that new bridging system, which I thought would come in pretty useful if they could get it right. I would reserve judgement until we had actually worked with it. Thank heavens, though, that most of it would be done by the heavy lifters.

When I actually saw it in the flesh, so to speak, that Bailey bridge system was fantastic! In the demonstration, the people in charge almost threw it together, they were so quick. I knew that they were well practiced, perhaps even showing off a little, but it was nevertheless an impressive display. Interlinked units were quickly put together and secured, and it seemed that, in virtually no time at all, a vehicle could then rumble across on the pre-set tracking. You could even use pre-made pontoons to link the longer stretches, so that quite a wide river could be crossed if necessary. It was still being developed all the time, but it was quite assuredly going to come in very useful when the Second Front got going. New machinery was needed to get the parts into place, but when they were all heaved into their rightful place – much more speedily than I thought would be possible – it turned out to be a very strong structure.

Surely it couldn't be long now before we were sent over the water to Europe? I had a little side bet that it would be France, but others were equally keen on the idea that the eventual landing could be in Belgium or even southern Italy. We would have to wait a bit longer.

Undated. (Sunday)
Royal Engineers Mess, Deverell Barracks, Ripon, Yorkshire.
Darling,

I was so pleased to hear from you on Friday. Had you been 3 minutes later, I would have been gone. It was a nuisance you not being able to come this weekend, but we did not finish laying mines (live mines) until 4.30 p.m. and then I had to attend a lecture on the battle of Alamein at 6 p.m., given by a Brigadier who was in the battle there and I think it was the finest I have ever listened to. Today I have had to plan and sketch the damned minefield, taking about 3 hours and I am thoroughly sick of it.

Work is hard and we have 3 night schemes a week, one next Monday starting at 3 a.m. Apart from these drawbacks the place is not too bad.

I was sorry to hear about young JE's cold and hope you were exaggerating when you talked about pneumonia. I was worried stiff all evening. I will put 2 adverts in The Times and Telegraph for a child nurse and see if they bear fruit. Have you thought about vaccinations, inoculations and all the other kindred items yet? I suppose that we shall have to have a Christening, too, during my leave.

How did you like the news about the move? I don't know exactly where we are going but I think it may be in the Hythe area. We are going at the right time of year, but against that there is the bombing nuisance.

Well, when you get this, I hope that your anxieties about JE will be over and that you are able to settle down into what will be almost a new existence.

I am thinking of you and loving you always.

Edward. x.

My part of the course was nearly over. We had all done the full course on Bailey bridges, and I had done a further mines course coupled with an active exercise out on the moors. Although I passed it successfully, and would henceforth be able to instruct others elsewhere, I and the other men were completely soaked through as a result of spending the night in the open; some of us were on the verge of hypothermia. Although mines were a necessary evil, I hated laying them almost as much as clearing them. They were so very unstable.

The final big exercise that was to bring everything together was cancelled at very short notice – perhaps because of the weather – and so the last day of the course found me almost with my feet up after enjoying a superb breakfast of cornflakes, eggs, toast and marmalade and coffee. I took the opportunity of re-reading the letters that Elizabeth had sent to me at Ripon, and pondered the fact that I would be going home on leave at the weekend.

Oh, it felt really wonderful to know that I would be going on leave at last. I had been granted seven days, and proposed to be on the very first suitable train that pulled out after I had packed my bags. The thought of seeing my son for the first time…

Meanwhile, there was a feeling amongst us that things nationally were by then building to some sort of a climax. All my co-officers on the course were going back to their individual Units, carrying with them the certainty that the Second Front, in some way, was now inevitable, and that our recent training, over in Ireland and elsewhere, had all been leading us specifically towards that one great momentous event.

Even the move from Ripon in the north to re-join my battalion at Hythe in Kent, from where it would be difficult to go any further south, seemed symbolic. It would be difficult to place us any nearer to France.

The entirety of 176 Brigade was, by then, on the move down to Kent, where we would be reunited with all the various scattered Units that were currently training, or on specialist courses, or simply still on guard at VP's, the likes of which I had been on for over two years.

The little Austin 10 that I had bought as a cheap run-around was still parked under a dustsheet in that hangar at the other end of the country. I had made good use of it for dashing about locally, and it had ferried me to the railway station a few times, but other than that it had been rather neglected. It was an absolute certainty, what with the way things were going, and my current posting, that I would not be going back to those airfields. I supposed that Elizabeth could have fetched it back home for me, but, in the end, I rang Collyweston Officers' Mess, and asked them to put a notice up on the board: for sale to the first offer over my purchase price.

It went within a week to one of the new young RAF officers that had just arrived on the station, despite the fact that it had slightly spongy brakes. One of the fitters finally found the time to do some work on it for me, and new brake pads and drums had been found from who knew where, and it looked like it was now raring to go. We split the repair cost between us and everyone was satisfied.

I was all packed up and ready to go, yet the powers that be decided there was time for me to slot in another course. So once again I found myself standing and waiting for a new travel warrant to be exchanged for a ticket to Hythe. Reaching there, I was immediately diverted to Clacton-on-Sea.

What was my destiny to be there, for a week from the 18th April 1943? It was an aircraft recognition course being held at one of the Anti-Aircraft Command schools. I failed to understand why on earth I might need this specialist type of knowledge, because I was not part of any ack-ack regiment. After all, when it was our turn and we actually got to fight the Hun (and I was looking forward to that, assuming that it was not all over by then) all I had to do was look up into the sky. If there was a plane coming at me with guns blazing, I really didn't care whether it was friendly fire or German – I and my men would be down in our slit trenches in the blink of an eye, without trying to identify the markings on the plane.

Undated. (Sunday)
7 RN. Attending AA & LMG School, 303 AA Wing GHQ, Clacton on Sea, Essex.
Darling,
How do you like this? Arrived here about 1500 today and I am billeted at the Grand Hotel and stay here until Saturday. I am really annoyed this time, if they had combed the Bn. through, they could not have found anyone less suitable to send on an aircraft recognition course. On my return I propose to put in an application to be relieved of my commission.
I had a reasonable journey here, with only five changes, still I arrived intact, but with rather less money than I anticipated, since the

PRUNES FOR BREAKFAST

ticket inspector insisted that my warrant was out of date and made me pay extra. So I used it from London to Hawkhurst. The RTO [Rail Transport Officer] at St. Pancras lent me his PV [Private Vehicle] to take me to Charing Cross.

The first thing I was greeted with was that I was going on another course so you can imagine that I felt rather bloody minded.

Hawkhurst is one of the nicest villages I have ever been in, and situated in lovely country. Kent at this time of the year is simply glorious. The Brigadier has given orders that wives will be allowed for a maximum of 3 days, but unfortunately you will be unable to avail yourself of this generosity because the Bn. moves to Rye about 2 days after I return – a sod is it not?

We have had a number of air raid warnings. I was just returning from the local and heard all the planes overhead, but did not know if they were coming or going. Most annoying.

How is JE? I hope he behaved himself while you were away. By the way, no sleeping in the same room. I expect he misses my comfort, still, he will get used to that.

Every bit of love, Sweetheart.

Edward. x.

P.S. I passed through Gt. Bentley on the train. It is only about 6 miles away, do you think I ought to take a walk over there one evening?

Crikey! Those results had just been announced from the Assault Engineering course that I had attended in Ripon, way back in April. I had forgotten about it because there was so much going on around me, and perhaps the paperwork had by then spent some considerable time chasing me around the country. It seemed that I passed the course with a recommendation entered on to my official War Record, and signed by someone at Brigade HQ, that I was now a suitable candidate to be named as a Unit Instructor. What deep hole was that going to drop me in, I wondered?

Undated. (Sunday)
Darling,

I am not at Rye yet, we move tomorrow, life seems one long move.

I left Clacton yesterday and arrived at Hawkhurst after a not too bad journey. I made about 15/- at pontoon. There was no supper to be had in the Mess, so I went down to the local and they gave me an excellent meal. The sight of a number of officers with their wives reminded me very much of our old weekends and tended to mar the enjoyment of the evening.

I am glad to hear that JE is growing at a satisfactory rate and that he has been good and not worrying you. All the observations about shape of head etc, are in my opinion, nonsense.

How about Smith, don't you think he would be better away?

I think a good day for the Christening would be Saturday May 29. I have suggested this to RWT Moore. The only snag may be if I go on some intensive training.

Clacton was not too bad and in the test I managed to identify 14 out of 30 planes. My section was top with an average of 21. One section had an average of only 10. Nobody was more surprised than I was, and the morning of the exam I offered 10 to 1 in half crowns that I shouldn't get 6 right. Nobody would take me on.

I don't think I shall get a very good Report, although I don't think I shall fail. I got quite a good Report from Ripon.

We have a few 'celebrities' on this Course and I usually got in last for breakfast with young Smisby. He seemed quite a decent lad, and of a sound mind.

We did not have a raid, the plane being brought down while we were in a lecture, so I did not see it.

I have sent you a claim for the gates and railings which I should get the Office to send in.

The 2/5th lost one officer killed and 5 missing when they were thrown in to stem the tide when the Americans broke. Chris Ticknall, who I succeeded as Intelligence Officer at Stamford is missing.

PRUNES FOR BREAKFAST

As for Rye, I think it is a little early for you to think of travelling. Anyway, I prefer to think of you safe in Ripley rather than in a dangerous area like Rye.
Every bit of love, darling.
Edward. x.
P.S. Please send my epaulettes for my shirts, which I took out of the box when I was on leave.

What a lovely old town was Rye. A thousand years ago it was probably right on the edge of the sea, but what with the marshes and the gradual silting of the river, it had become a delightful inland place to be. We were to be encamped right behind the town, but I decided that one of my first stops when we had settled in and made ourselves at home, so to speak, was to make a jaunt to the Mermaid Inn, which was historically a well-known landmark, a smugglers' inn of old, and would be sure to serve a good pint.

However, I was not expecting to be there for long. We had been told to expect a full turnout and inspection by our Corps Commander – a General no less – who was going to honour us with his presence in two days' time. As a result, everyone was running around sorting out the details for the parade and march-past. I was ensuring that vehicles were spick and span, others were frantically cleaning heavy armour, and just about everyone was pressing their battledress and blancoing their webbing. I even put some polish on my Sam Browne. Everything was really being beezed up. The downside of all that meant that I had to cancel my golf game.

The month of May saw us finally relieved of our long-standing anti-raid commitments, with the 38th Division taking over our role from us. Thus released, exercises had come pretty soon back into fashion. Exercise Snipe was an administrative one and then Exercise Gallop was undertaken, it having been devised to practice the Division's artillery in all normal battle tasks including cooperation with supporting infantry. In a few weeks we were to go to Salisbury Plain on a major exercise whose name had not yet been revealed.

Undated. (Early May 1943)
7 RN. Northiam, Nr Rye.
Darling,

Your letter, written Monday did not arrive until Wednesday, which delay I propose to report to the PMG.

The weather has been absolutely bloody, I thought all my tents and marquees would blow away. Fortunately we survived. The CO visited us for the first time on Monday at about 11.30 a.m. when it was raining like blazes and everywhere a sea of mud. He did not stay long.

Saturday afternoon I went to Hastings. The sleet and hail was so bad I had to stop the truck on the way. I had tea at some hotel on the front and then decided to see 'Mrs Miniver' (film). Unfortunately when I got out of the hotel I went the wrong way up the front and fighting in the teeth of a gale walked for 25 minutes before I realised that I must be nearly in St. Leonards. I took a bus back. Anyway, the film was very good. I then had a few beers and returned to find everything still standing.

I held a church parade on Sunday and on Monday availed myself of an invitation to have a bath at a place called Hoopers Court. Very pleasant too, the lady of the Court pressing me to about 3 gins, giving me 6 duck eggs and lending me a book 'All This And Heaven Too.' Have you read it?

JE seems to be going from strength to strength but you omitted to give latest weight in your last letter.

I can't say that Daisy's frequent visits please me too much. By the way, I take it that you do not sleep in the nursery? Sorry you were without Nurse for 3 days. Did you get any replies to my adverts?

The Christening date I cannot let you know yet definitely until my next letter. It is OK as far as I am concerned for Betty and Una to be godparents, but I had no idea that boys had Godmothers. Have you heard from RWT Moore? I wrote him when I was at Clacton. How do you like the news? It brings the Second Front closer.

Well, another fortnight and I shall be with you.

I love you always.

Edward. x.

P.S. Can you get me some name tapes marked Searancke?

In between all this tedium there was much enlivenment occasioned by the upcoming christening of our son, John Edward. My CO had agreed that I could take a week's leave to attend the grand event. Elizabeth was now feeling much better and stronger, and was taking to the preparations with relish. All well and good, said I, because there was little practical assistance that I could offer from down in Kent, nearly 300 miles to the south.

When I finally did go on leave next, I was going to spend the first couple of days closeted with my father in Church Gresley to get back up to speed with how the business was doing. There was only so much that could be achieved in exchanges of letters, and hurried telephone calls when others were standing in a lengthy queue behind one. I also wanted to know the full results – long overdue to my mind – of the enquiries that had been made months back about future building projects.

Undated. (Monday) (Early May 1943)
Darling,

I have arranged my leave from Thursday morning until the following Thursday, but in all probability I shall spend Thursday and most of Friday at Gresley as there is rather a lot to do.

I have raised the question of Betty and it is agreed that she must be invited to John's party.

If you fail to do anything in the matter of the coal, if you will let me know at Gresley, I will try to bring some.
I feel absolutely b——dy.
All my love.
Edward. x.

Undated.
Darling,
How are you bearing up having gone a whole week without me?
I had a letter from Champion enclosing a letter from the Secretary for War in which he stated that there was no trace of my application. So once more the wires are beginning to hum.
Your golf things are sold for £20.
I rather feel that you might need to get cracking straight away if you are going to get anything good for the party however we may be able to formulate a plan over the weekend…
Have you seen the coal man?
How is the domestic situation? Any new arrivals, and have you seen the manager of the Labour Exchange?
I do little other than play golf or badminton with an occasional deplorable exhibition game of billiards.
All my love, Sweetheart.
Edward. x.

There was always something rather nice about going back to the old family home where my parents lived, in Church Gresley, despite having my own house, Grantchester, on the Moira road just outside Ashby. My parents' home at Gresley was a rather old-fashioned three-bedroomed detached house, and lay in a street of similar houses, some semi-detached; as one travelled towards the pit, they became rows of terraced properties. Between the house and the pit were about three dozen houses, the old Drill Hall doing double duty for some wartime activity that escaped me, and the local church, hard by the pit. Church Gresley had started out in life as a mining community, and the pit was still active. Even at weekends when I was there I could see the pithead wheel winding gear in action. Soon after the war ended, the pithead stilled for ever, all activity so quickly forgotten by the next generation.

How nice it was to be able to sit quietly with my father and go through an update of what was going on in the business. The first day had been for our own discussions, and the next day for a meeting with the other directors (though one of them, Rushton, was unable to attend, having been posted overseas). That proved very interesting and fruitful, but for me, the planned arrival there the day afterwards of Elizabeth was rather taking my mind off all else. It would also be the final time for family discussion before the christening came around. The service was going to be held just down the road at our local church and then there would be a great 'do' at the family home afterwards.

It took place on the 29th May 1943. Despite the austerity of the war years, at least twenty of us had managed to come together for the service, conducted by my old friend Ron Moore. We all wore our Sunday best even though it was a Saturday. A couple of the more distant relatives from Chester wore what could only be described as outlandish hats, though they professed them to be *à la mode*. I suppose that Chester saw itself as one of the leaders in the fashion stakes. The family, on the other hand, were determinedly traditional.

It was a treat to see young JE wriggling about in the christening robe of Irish lace that I had managed to acquire when on my travels. He looked bright as a button and did not cry once during the service, even when he had water sploshed over his head. I hoped that he would grow up to take after me, but he currently had much of a look of his mother about him. Afterwards, we all walked back to my parents' house and enjoyed quite a boisterous party, surprising most of those present with the spread that we had managed to lay on, favours having been called in from everywhere. All in all, it was a thoroughly joyous occasion for all concerned. I was very proud, and Elizabeth was literally glowing.

Then, once the final goodbyes had been said to various relatives – some of whom we had not seen for years, and probably would not again for many years to come, if at all – it was time for Elizabeth and I to say our own private goodbyes also, and for her to return to Ripley and for me to get back down to Kent. Just when would we see each other again? And the boy, of course.

14

Salisbury Plain

My Unit had by now received imminent warning that we were to be on our way from our current base in Kent to take part in that major exercise on Salisbury Plain, the name of which was still subject to censorship, suggesting it must be a significant one. It was quite a distance to shift an entire battalion in full battle readiness with the heavy equipment needed. But it had been decreed, and so do it we must. As usual, I seemed to be required to be deeply involved in the planning stages, which had seriously disrupted my regular games of golf during the day and snooker in the evenings.

But before the starting gun went off and we departed for Salisbury Plain, there were a couple of interesting asides.

The first was that my dear friend – and now JE's godfather – Norman Tarry had a July posting to us once again. We had all been so sorry that he was *in absentia* from the christening. It was one thing for a father to get leave for such an occasion, but rather too much, even for Norman, to swing it with the powers that be, as just a godfather. I took a bit of cake away with me for him, but it would turn rather mouldy by the time that we next met up, though he soon was to join our crowd and take over as Adjutant, being made up to Captain. My betting was that he would not be roughing it under canvas like so many of us.

The second was that I was going to be attending yet another course, to be held just outside Folkestone. I had to go because my lot was then to be Unit Education Officer, amongst a plethora of other strange and useless job titles which I appeared for some unknown reason to have accumulated.

> Undated. (Sunday)
> 7 RN. Royal Engineers Depot, Shorncliffe, Nr. Folkestone, Kent.
> Darling,
> I was delighted to hear you on Thursday and afterwards to receive one of your sweetest letters.
> I am down here for 3 days, after which I return and for 10 days train the whole Bn. in mine clearance and assault engineering, followed by a 3 day Assault Exercise at Eastwell Park, near Maidstone.
> I may not get home until midnight as I have to see a specialist in London on the 22nd, but I hope with this to get an extra day's leave.
> We arrived here at 10.30 this morning and our first lecture started at 11.00 carrying through until 1800. Every day is a working day!
> You asked me if I remembered July 2 or the first Saturday in July as I remember it. Darling, I can only thank God that I enjoyed a year or two with you before it was all so abruptly changed. I can never express in words how much these years have meant to me, even since I joined the Army. I can only say thank you, you have made me happier than I ever imagined and in JE you have completed my happiness.
> One of Folkestone's big guns has just opened up, shaking the whole building. Rushton has just sent me an Airgraph, which I enclose.
> I have asked the MO about JE's weight and he suggests you cut down his feeds to 7.5 minutes.
> Every bit of love.
> Edward. x.

The long awaited day for us to get the entire battalion over to Salisbury Plain in short order for that damned exercise was steadily drawing closer. I was to play a big part in the event. Not only was I now a trained Instructor, but my role over the last few days at

Shorncliffe had been to train the troops there not only in assault engineering, but also in live mine clearance. I had done a number of courses on mines, both laying them and clearing them, but I could never get to the stage when I was comfortable around the bally things. They were too prone to go off in a random or haphazard way for my liking. I saw too many chaps with bits blown off them to ever operate comfortably in their vicinity. My main role was to be in charge of the battalion transport, getting everybody properly and on time to Salisbury Plain. When we got there, my other role would be one of co-ordination between our battalion and the various others taking part, particularly gunnery and armour.

Undated. (Saturday)
7 RN. Northiam, Nr. Rye, Sussex.
Darling,
 I know that I shall get a ferocious raspberry when you write me again although I think I am answering a little quicker now.
 I seem to have developed trouble with feet and ankles and eventually saw the MO who took me over to the Military Hospital. He recommended that I have massage each day and certain alterations to my boots and if that fails it looks as though I may be downgraded.
 A week last Friday I went to Shorncliffe in an m/c combination and to my intense chagrin lost my walking stick. The weekend was fairly pleasant had I not been feeling rotten. We had some m/c sports on Saturday and there were some really exciting spills. On Monday we had a cricket match, but I am afraid that I can raise little enthusiasm.
 On Wednesday I went to Shorncliffe, and you can tell how slowly I went, taking 1½ hours to do 33 miles. This time I lost my tobacco pouch.
 Thursday again to Shorncliffe, this time in the back of a truck to attend a one day Education Course as I am now Unit Education

Salisbury Plain

Officer. I think that the fumes must have poisoned me, because I have not been at all well since.

We are going on a 10 day Exercise on Salisbury Plain on Tuesday, sleeping by day and working by night, living mostly on iron rations and as far as I can see, no beer. I may survive but doubt it as I shall be riding a m/c two days, 10 hrs a day and part of the stint is 30 hrs. of digging. Ah well, we Searancke's are tough!

I shall try to write to you once or twice when opportunity permits but I may not get your letter(s) until I return.

Young JE certainly seems to be going from strength to strength and I shall expect him to say 'Dadda' when I come on leave.

This brings me to rather a bitter pill. My leave will not come until July 21 owing to many officers having to put off their leave until this damned Exercise is over. I am fearfully disappointed, sweetheart, but is just one of those things, and we have been very lucky.

Every bit of love, my Darling,
Edward. x

Well before the big day, and despite my relatively lowly rank, I felt cheeky enough to put in a request to suggest that I would come freshest to my various important duties if I rode there to Salisbury Plain in one of the staff cars. I was told that my newly issued motorcycle and sidecar would be quite adequate and that I could go along with my men at the head of the column, and that once there, I could also have the dubious honour of acting as the Battalion Traffic Officer to ensure that everyone got to exactly where they were needed. You see, never volunteer…

I suppose it came under the old heading of *'give a busy man another job…'* which I should take as a compliment, but I thought it just demonstrated how short of fully trained officers the battalion still remained.

PRUNES FOR BREAKFAST

Undated. (Monday)
7 RN. Salisbury Plain.
Darling,

I have not heard from you but that is not surprising considering present location and Exercise Fortescue under conditions of war. I propose to give you some idea in diary form of how the Army works. On Monday last I was frightfully busy preparing, especially as I was OC of the company. I made a bad start by overpaying someone £1 and having to make it good out of my own pocket.

Tuesday, Reveille at 0530, breakfast 0630, setting out at 1030 on my motor cycle. We went through Crawley, reminding me that had conditions been different, we might have been going to Brighton. We had a 10 minute halt every 2 hours and during one of those we had a haversack lunch. We arrived in Petersfield about 8 p.m. having covered about 112 miles. By this time I was what you might call 'saddle sore'. We bedded down in a wood and at about 11.30 p.m. had our next meal and two bottles of beer. On Wednesday, Reveille was 0500 and breakfast was a chicken roll and tinned veg.

I then set out with 2 Don R's for Lavington near Salisbury where I had to arrive at 0955 in time to act as traffic control for the whole of the Brigade Transport. I actually arrived at 0930 and was very pleased to have a bar of chocolate. Transport started coming through about 10 and continued until about 1530, me on my feet all the time and no food or drink. A bit of food about 6 p.m. After a couple of conferences etc., I got to bed at midnight with 4 bots beer.

Thursday, Reveille at 0430, breakfast as before, at 0545 recce of Salisbury Plain where the Bn. took up its battle positions for the next 3 days. Worked all day digging until 11 pm. Supper was at 12.30 a.m. and no beer.

Friday, up at 0430, breakfast 0500, worked until 10 a.m. We then bedded down for day, living on hard rations. In the evening I played a little Solo, 2 beers, 1 large whiskey (all very surreptitious).

Saturday we repeated the programme but in the evening I had to act as Brigade Traffic Control for a lot of traffic over a piece of road 3 miles long. This entailed riding my m/c up and down a shell cratered road without lights (only came off twice) until 0430 Sun morning.

Same next day, and came off 4 times.

When I got back to Bn. I could not find my bedding so slept in a truck until 0800 (now Monday), had a fairly restful day and got to bed about 10.30 p.m. with 5 whiskies.

On Tues Reveille at 0330 and we went by transport to Netheravon where we watched the artillery shoot up the defensive positions of the Division. There were (only) 6 casualties among the spectators. The Artillery fired 62,000 shells. Then we marched at 10.30 p.m. arriving at Borden nr. Farnham, at about 0700 hours. Breakfast and then to bed. I slept in an old bathing hut. The first time I have had a roof over my head since a week last Monday. Tonight we leave at 11 p.m. for Northiam and expect to arrive about 0800 hrs, which day I make out to be Monday. On the whole it has been a very good scheme but I am feeling a little tired and will appreciate being able to sit in a chair and feed in comfort off a plate instead of a mess tin. If anyone had told me 4 years ago that I could have done all this, I should have howled with derision!

Several days have elapsed since I started this letter and I hope that you are well and that JE is growing to look more like his father.

Every bit of love, darling,
Edward x
P.S. I think you had better forward this letter to Gresley because I cannot write all this lot all over again.

It was a great logistical exercise just to get us all to Exercise Fortescue where the battalion was scheduled to play a major part. Hundreds of us had to be moved by whatever transport could be dredged up, and we had to find somewhere for everyone to sleep overnight on the way there. That was the easy bit. Everyone camped in a large wood on the way. We found a suitable site just outside Petersfield. Food had to be arranged for upwards of 600 men, so mobile kitchens were travelling with us. Once they were set up and everyone had been fed, it was time to get our heads down for an early start the next morning.

Later the next day, when we finally got to our destination on Salisbury Plain, I took up my new role as battalion traffic control officer and arranged for everyone to be immediately dispersed to their designated positions. They were then instructed to set to, and dig slit trenches and gun pits and then lay themselves out in a fortress for imitation of a static warfare action. We were then all subjected to air reconnaissance and photography, which meant that we could not move from our positions at all during daylight, even for calls of nature. I slept quite well during that first day, and just got my head down and let the others get on with it. There was nothing left for me to do until later on. Afterwards, when that episode was completed, and when the evidence was mulled over by the brass, a fire plan was devised and put into operation. We then withdrew from the field, and watched from the side-lines, so to speak, as the Royal Artillery proceeded to plaster our previous positions, using everything that they had brought with them, ranging from heavy 18 inch pillbox-buster shells to smoke screens, and all with cooperation from the RAF. It made a fantastic scene to watch, but at the end of it all, when it was over and we walked back to survey the scenery at close quarters, the overall damage seemed to be a little on the modest side to me. *'Could do better,'* was my verdict.

The next day we played out a different scheme in a slightly different position. I had to organise the move of everyone from the first to the second position, causing all sorts of problems by arriving late due to the fact that I had injured myself when I came off my motorcycle in the dark. I think that I fell into a shell crater – my very first example of injury from 'friendly fire'! We did the same again, with variations, the next day. The thing that I remembered most about the whole thing was the acute pain when I came off my motorcycle several times in the dark, having had to ride down a long track between Units, without lights. I still have the scars from that exercise.

It had all been a hard, hard exercise. I ached all over and I was quite sure that I was not up for riding back to Kent as had been originally intended. I was going to pull a bit of a flanker and planned to hitch a lift back on one of the trucks, and they could take my motorcycle back with them too, because, as I said to my traffic sergeant, it seemed to have mysteriously broken down. As I was still Battalion Transport Officer, I could give the order for that and hopefully get away with it, as all the general staff officers had by then long departed back to the comfort of Brigade HQ for a de-briefing and, no doubt, tea and crumpets to follow.

15

Church Parade

I was really fast coming to the conclusion that there was to be no corner of this part of Kent in which I would not have pitched my tent at some time or another.

Undated. (Thursday)
7 RN. Brickwall Camp, Nr. Northiam, Sussex.
Darling,
    My stay in Rye has not been of protracted duration and I have now arrived at the above address. I set out yesterday afternoon at 1430 with 60 men and 5 sergeants, marching about 7 miles. We arrived at 1645 and had pitched tents by 1800.
    I have now run out of ink so will continue in pencil.
    We are here as an advance party to make roads etc. for the Bn. who will be moving in, in about a fortnight. I am happy in the fact that I am my own boss and am fairly safe from interference. I have got everything well in hand and after tomorrow do not expect to have to work for more than half a day each day. This morning I had everyone doing PT for 10 minutes at 0715 and then I went for a run before breakfast.
    There are 3 good pubs within one and a half miles but no cinema, the nearest being at Hastings, 9 miles away.
    I managed to get through the (Salisbury Plain) Exercise alright, covering about 200 miles on my m/c. I only managed about 6 hours sleep altogether, and was very tired at the end of it, but some of the 'tough guys' were worse.

Church Parade

I was very lucky on Saturday night, the owner of the park in which my Company was bivouacked invited 2 of us to have supper with him. It was 2230 before we were able to get there, but we found him living in his converted stables and supper was bacon, two eggs, rhubarb and fresh cream, cheese and farm butter, gin and 1qt beer, and then found us a bed to sleep on (rather better than the table top I had the next night!)

I hope that JE is growing more like his father every day. How are you, darling?

All my love.

Edward. x.

It came as a bit of a shock when I saw the notice that had been pinned up announcing that the entire Division was to be ready to mobilise within a month. That meant nine battalions with about 600 men in each; this was the first time that the entire Division had mobilised. It was the 27th June 1943.

In the full heat of summer the following month, we then undertook the imaginatively named Operation Eastwell. It was time for us to up sticks yet again and get over to Maidstone. I had wangled a room at Eastwell Park, some grandiose mansion set in wonderful parkland, and where the assault exercise drama was due to be played out. The object was to evolve further tactics between the Royal Engineers and the infantry by way of co-operation to take various fortified positions. I hoped that they didn't expect the parkland to be in the same condition when we left.

I was sorry, in many ways, to leave Northiam, having become quite accustomed to being 'Squire of the Park', the local inhabitants tolerating me with an almost affectionate regard, or so I felt. However, when we arrived at Herne Bay, Kent, it seemed one of the nicest seaside towns I had been in, very clean, with a cinema or two and excellent beer for a change. I was billeted in one of the nice hotels which was also the Mess – very convenient – sharing a room with an old pal, George Desford.

PRUNES FOR BREAKFAST

When I had last seen the CO, it appeared that AMGOT, the Allied Military Government of Occupied Territories, might be my destiny. It would be a month or two before I heard anything of my application. In the meantime, I dashed across the country for an overnight trip to Liverpool to discuss some business prospects for after the war.

The letters that I had been getting from Elizabeth recently were all about herself and the boy. It seemed as though he had taken over her whole life and that she had little or no interest left for me. I just supposed that it was a phase that new mothers went through. Anyway, I was by then so busy that I had no time to do anything about it, but I had made a mental note to definitely speak to her about it on my next leave, which should be due in a week's time – if it didn't get changed again. That was beginning to be rather the norm, though.

When I went on leave a year or two back, it had been mostly a happy-go-lucky time for us, whether we spent all or part of the time at Gresley, Ashby or Ripley. It was easier to banish the thoughts of war for two or three days – sometimes longer – when we were together. My mood only darkened as it drew near to the time that I had to take the train, or latterly the car, back to wherever I was stationed.

The unceasing training to which I was being subjected now, and the feeling all around us that the Second Front was actually going to happen sooner rather than later, meant that a dark cloud always seemed to hover over us when we were together. I suppose that I had so much more knowledge by then, had been trained to become a fighting soldier, so that my old life working in the family firm just seemed unreal.

Two years ago, I would have been glad to get away and go on leave. Nowadays, it all rather had the reverse effect, and I was quite glad to get back to my little corner of army life. Even to think that way made me sad, though, as I was missing out on my son beginning to grow.

Church Parade

7 RN. Herne Bay, Kent.
Darling,

We are more or less settled in, and my platoon has been doing painting, woodwork, plumbing etc. and I did a route march the day before last. I have had a game of snooker most evenings before supper and have been to the pictures twice, the first time I saw 'The Meanest Man Who Ever Lived' and the next 'The Man In Grey'. The first was quite amusing but the second one I thought overrated.

I should not worry about AMGOT yet, but no matter what one might like to think, it is almost certain that practically everyone in the Army will be abroad before the war is finally over.

My leave will start either Tuesday or Wednesday next, so let me know whether there is anything of a domestic nature you want from the shops here, which are rather well stocked.

I am glad the lad is recovered but I am afraid you are getting rather puffed with pride.

Every bit of love.

Edward. x.

11th July 1943. (Sunday)
7 RN. APO England.
Darling,

How delightful to receive two letters in one week, you are really surpassing yourself. I read them at least twice, the better to appreciate your caustic wit.

I have just finished off my Cadre which was quite a success. Today we have had a full Bn. Church Parade and after that I umpired a hockey match, chiefly to see how the new CO played. I am rather afraid that we may not get on too well, but Norman has explained to him that I usually take 2 to 3 months to get to know properly. This evening I am dining with Keith Answell and wife at Ruby's Café and should get some really good food.

PRUNES FOR BREAKFAST

I went to a Sgts. Mess Dance on Thursday and had quite a mellow evening. I won 2 x £1 bets by dancing with the Brigadier's wife and spent the last half hour talking with the Brig. I gather that I pitched in to him rather strongly, but nicely, and rather think that had he not been rather stinko! I might by now be wearing a bowler hat.

A bad blow. All 24 hour leaves have been stopped but I may be able to work something with Norman. I have managed to get the stockings (using my coupons) and have forwarded with 1 doz. oranges, 1 bot skin tonic and 1 pot Velva. The stockings were 9/6d. a pair, was I cut? I am getting fairly well stocked for the Second Front.

JE I think you will have to threaten with stern disciplinary action by his father unless he improves.

The weather has been marvellous recently. I could get some tennis in.

Darling, the war cannot last forever now, and when it is over I will make up for all the time that we have missed together.

Every bit of love.

Edward. x.

It was a wonderful church parade and service. I have never been able to sing in tune, but being able to sing with hundreds of other men really got me going. When it got to *'I Vow To Thee My Country'* there were quite a number of chaps around me that seemed to be shedding a tear, and when we finally reached the crescendo of our famous alternative national anthem, *'Land Of Hope And Glory'*, well, we sang the roof off amidst a flood of waterworks from most of those present.

But I had quite forgotten to explain to Elizabeth about the new APO address that we had all been allotted. Her last letter went astray initially and got a lot of blue pencil on the envelope by some jobsworth in the GPO or the army censorship office.

Church Parade

Undated. (Monday)
7 RN. APO England.
Darling,

I don't think you are at all sweet, and I am sure that you owe me at least 6 letters.

When I came back from the Course I saw the CO on Victoria Station, very miserable to be leaving us, but not half as miserable as I am at his leaving us. The new CO is quite young and appears to be fairly bright and intelligent, but I have an idea that I shall find him a little more difficult.

I joined the Bn. on Friday and roughed it until Monday morning. Sunday was rather tiring, as we were exercising all day, and was it hot! I managed to scrounge 6 eggs however.

We are starting day passes shortly. It would be difficult to get home, but I can manage a night in London, what do you think?

My passport photo has arrived and I had no idea I was so good looking!

Would you like me to send you some oranges? I have about 20.

Incidentally, I have found out that my calls have been costing me 8s.6d. owing to my making them before 6.30 p.m. we shall have to adjust timings.

How is the lad? I should think that he must be almost at the walking stage by now.

Try and be sweet and answer this letter. You have more to write about than I do.

All my love, darling.
Eddie. x.

The lad was all of four months old by then. Elizabeth was continuing to give me chapter and verse about him, but I had heard nothing about his weight and whether he was progressing satisfactorily. I would have to ring and ask whilst it was in my mind.

PRUNES FOR BREAKFAST

Undated. (Sunday)
7 RN. APO England.
Darling,

You will note from the address that we are now having to make use of these dashed new APO address designations. It is an internal addressing system for the Army to prevent snoopers from knowing about troop movements and where people are stationed. You have to use it from now on when you write to me, but I have no idea how it works. I suppose that somebody in London has created some huge great master plan, detailing every military post office location, and pinned it up on the wall in Whitehall.

As usual, in a most infernal rush, about to set off for the next 3 days until Wednesday.

I have fixed up Thursday and have written to the Cumberland Hotel and expect that there will not be any difficulty in getting in. Let me know which train you will be coming down on. I don't know whether I am on my head or my heels and am in a ferocious temper with everybody. If you can find a few cheap novels, they might do for my Second Front box for the troops.

All my love.
Edward. x.

I was really being unusually lucky at the moment in respect of getting leave granted. Mind you, it was in direct relation to the number of courses that I had been sent on. Each one got me a little bit of extra time that I could add on to a leave period. It was fairly easy to get the permission of the Adjutant (particularly since it was Norman who held the post) to extend the odd weekend after a course finished on a Friday. I did like the old Cumberland Hotel, just off Marble Arch. Old fashioned, but warm, comfortable and impersonal, and with lashings of hot water!

Church Parade

Undated (Friday)
7 RN. APO England.
Darling,

It seems an age since I phoned you, but it is only a few days.

For the last day or two my life has been that of a lotus eater, eating, drinking and sleeping, with a fair quantity of rummy and bridge and I am feeling in extraordinary good health and spirits.

How are you, bright and cheerful with the lad growing more lusty every day? I have very little news. I think in the next few months we shall be together to continue what was after all a rudely interrupted honeymoon. I have great confidence, and I want you to have the same.

We had the Corps and Divisional Commanders here yesterday, and all went well. Afterwards, Norman asked me to have tea with him and I found that the Brigadier and several other senior officers were present. All went well. Darling, you must not worry. I am making bets that the war will be over in 3 months, and believe me, we are doing far better than it appears on paper. So keep your chin up.

All my love, Sweet.
Edward. x.

Other than the planners and staff officers, everyone was far adrift in their thinking and knowledge of what was happening. We were pretty well insulated from reality and clearly not the slightest scrap of the bigger picture had filtered down to the likes of me. I was also doing everything that I could to bolster the mood of my dear wife by writing everything very low key. I really didn't want to put the wind up her, and if I were to say much at all, it would never get past the censor anyway.

16

Harlequin and Canute

Undated. (Monday)
7 RN. APO England.
Darling,
    I want to say how much I enjoyed my 26 hours with you in London. Looking back it seems incredible that one could have had such a pleasant time without the slightest hurry or fuss and yet with every moment occupied. As you know, it was life as I like it to be with you.
    I hope you had a good journey back and were met? Did the lad miss you?
    I called at the Royal Orthopaedic and they fixed me up very quickly and so my conscience was salved.
    I managed to catch the fast train from Cannon Street. We had another tea dance on Saturday which was quite pleasant and I dined at Ruby's on Sunday evening, otherwise little else to report.
    I will phone on Thursday at the usual time.
    All my love.
    Edward. x.

In late July 1943, I attended the Eighth Advanced Course on International Affairs at Chatham House in St. James Square in central London, the home of the Royal Institute of International Affairs. It was where many Allied officers were being sent to brush up on their knowledge and political awareness. We were expecting the announcement of a grand reshuffling of the battalion. I had heard that on the last day of the month, a new Corps, entitled X11 Corps, was to be established, and formally designated as the invasion follow-up Corps. A chap called Lieutenant General Neil Ritchie was to be the new OC.

Undated.
7 RN. APO England.
Dear Pop and Lou,
    I know that the last 2 years have been difficult for all of us…
    Have you thought any more about my proposal, which we discussed last weekend, to buy a number of plots and to create a 'Land Bank'? I think that what came out of our discussion was that all the various parties that we have put those feelers out to, are of the opinion that, once the war is over, there will be a frenzy of building taking place.
    For example, and I realise that it is not applicable to us, but London, Coventry and many other major cities will have to be rebuilt. This will have a knock on effect into our smaller centre of influence. New houses will be required, and local Councils will be looking for opportunities to spend money once it starts to flow into their coffers once again. It may be a slow process, but it is sure to happen.
    We talked of one particular example, if you remember. Swadlincote is in dire need of a new Fire Station. I think that we should buy some land on the outskirts of Swad, big enough for a new Fire Station, and present it almost as a fait accomplis to the Council. Even if they say no, and they won't, that plot of land, if carefully chosen, will be useful for another large commercial development, and we will have bought it cheaply.
    Some of those other plots of land that we discussed should be available to us for a good price, so I reckon that we should try to purchase. That big field half way down the hill in to Burton on the left hand side, which you can see from the far end of Brizlincote Lane,

should be another target. It must be ripe for planning permission, and the farmer just might be willing. I can only leave it to you...
    Affec.
    Eddie.

In September 1943 the entire battalion was to mobilize once again under the order of South Eastern Command in order to take part in Exercise Harlequin which had been devised as a rehearsal for invasion tactics, and would be used, on our particular part, to test marshalling and administrative organisation for future embarkation on the south coast for British and Canadian troops. Basically, it was to see if the plans dreamed up by the staffers would actually work. We had to pretend we were going to be embarked on an imaginary invasion flotilla force setting off from Dover. The men had to be kept in ignorance of the fact that it was just a dummy run. The exercise required us to march from our camp, accompanied by all the battalion vehicles, down into the town centre and then onwards, right on to the beach, forming up in lines to await the boats that would theoretically be there to take us over the water. But there were no boats of course, so after an hour or so, whilst the staff officers conferred amongst themselves and decided what the outcome could be, we received the order to about turn from the beach, and set off back to camp. We all just marched back up the beach, back on to the seafront, back through the town, and were bussed back to the camp.

    I, for one, felt a right Charlie, and from the bemused faces of the local townspeople as they clustered around us in small groups, watching our every move from start to finish, they were not too impressed either!

    But, in my own humble opinion, and from the limited amount that I could see from my own position in the wings, the new systems played out very smoothly and overall things went quite well, though a few tweaks would be of benefit come the real thing. I thought that some good lessons were learned. Were we getting there at last?

Harlequin and Canute

In October, HQ moved to winter quarters in Canterbury and we were all to be crammed in to the towns of Margate, Ramsgate and Broadstairs. The streets of those three towns for the next eight months or so, we had been told, would resemble Wembley on cup final day, there would be so many service men milling about. In the event, every boarding house and hotel was occupied, and I was lucky to get myself a room in a half decent hotel. Many more senior officers were not quite so fortunate.

I was going to be stuck in Margate, I thought – at the seaside – with winter coming on. But just a month after moving there, I was on my way back to Ripon at the same time as the Royal Engineers for a two-week course entitled Handling Bridging Equipment (Course 2) courtesy of the School of Mechanical Engineers. The design of the Bailey bridge had been refined, and it was by then so much easier to put together, and in much shorter a time. I got back to Margate afterwards with a real stinker of a cold.

Undated. (Monday)
7 RN. Margate, Kent.
Darling,

Just a line to let you know that I arrived back quite safely. The London train was only 2 minutes late, arriving at Cliftonville about 10 p.m., again being lucky to get a taxi.

The weather has been rough and cold and my impressions of Margate are not too good. The place now looks absolutely deserted in the torrential rain and has been knocked about quite a bit.

This morning I have defended a bloke on Court Martial at Herne Bay, getting me out of a rather cold motorcycle ride, as this morning we start on Exercise CANUTE and I shall be sleeping in the open for the next 8 days.

AMGOT has fallen through so I suppose they will try something else.

PRUNES FOR BREAKFAST

I hope JE behaved whilst having his photograph taken and that you got home OK. Now about to set off on the great adventure.

Every bit of love.

Edward. x.

Undated.
7 RN. Margate, Kent.
Darling,

We have just returned from 8 days purgatory. On the whole I remain quite cheerful and quite fit.

On Monday night we arrived in the harbour area. It commenced to rain immediately. I was fortunate to be able to bed down in the back of the MO's truck although it was a bit of a squeeze. This night I lost my gloves.

Tuesday, breakfast at 4.30 a.m. cold spam and biscuits and I was on my motorcycle leaving at 5.40 a.m.

We arrived at the new area about 7 p.m. and to help matters it turned very foggy. We had supper about 10 p.m. and I got 2 hours interrupted sleep in the front of my 3 tonner. At 1.30 a.m. we were off again for a nightmarish ride across mud tracks and a temporary bridge with no lights on. I managed to bed down on mother earth at 5.15 a.m. and slept till 7 a.m. Moved on again but about midday I got fed up with the motorcycle and handed it over to my sergeant. I managed to get to bed early at about 9 p.m. and it rained like stink and I got very wet, but a tot of rum when I got up warmed me. This was rather typical of the whole scheme, but one thing that I was extremely thankful for was my sleeping bag which saved me from the intense cold and discomfort that many officers suffered. However, all things come to an end and we were extremely grateful when the ceasefire to the Exercise sounded on Sunday morning. I rode back in a jeep and we made Margate about 6 p.m. and I was fortunate to get a bath.

George Desford has a compound fracture of the wrist and is on 2 month's sick leave. I was sorry not to hear from you during the week,

you appear to be slipping back again. Do you think you might make one of your super efforts? I hope the lad is not missing me too much.
　　Every bit of love.
　　Edward. x.

Exercise Canute, those eight days on the South Coast in November 1943 where our battalion and many others were deployed, was intended to provide false information, which it was hoped would be picked up by German spies or reconnaissance planes, to lead them to think that we were building up and preparing for the main thrust of the invasion forces to be in the Pas de Calais area of northern France. HQ told us that our activities would prepare us as well as possible for our role as a follow-up formation, and would give the Germans great cause for putting their thinking caps on once their aerial reconnaissance photographs had been interpreted by their High Command. We even catered for any spies operating locally by laying some trails of false information. After the war was over, we heard that there was nobody in the area anyway at that time who should not have been there, but you never really knew, and it was better to be safe than sorry.

　　Undated. (Tuesday)
　　Darling,
　　　You must have had a jolly busy day yesterday.
　　　Gresley was quite cheerful, will have the goose if OK but regret only one cake and little possibility of chocolate wafers.
　　　The eggs were well received and as I had to go into Coventry on a case of car stealing, combined business with business and took Mrs. T. to Leamington where I bought 5 books suitable for youngsters. I can also get one or two rag dolls, sets of furniture or other nonsense of that description. What do you think?
　　　I went to Bobby's but the only Jumper Suits they had were utility, turquoise blue. They are expecting more, and may be getting

PRUNES FOR BREAKFAST

some in in navy blue, yellow, or brown at 30/- the set. What about it? Let me have 5 coupons by return.

I now have some very good cigars. Rain and another of those blessed Court Martials have served to interfere with my golf arrangements today.

All my love.

Edward. x.

P.S. Tell the little B I will spank him when I return.

I was still regularly corresponding with my father, and he with me. My father had this dreadful scrawl which was difficult to decipher. I preferred the ones from Lou for general content and family information, particularly about my sisters, but it was the business orientated ones from my father that were more important. Between us, we batted back and forth a lot of updates on how the business was going, and I was continuing to play as supportive a part as I could whilst performing my army duties.

Did I remember that my mind should become a 'blank canvas'? Well, what a load of rubbish that was! How could I even have thought such a thing? Life had to go on, and there had to be a family firm still up and running at war's end. In part, it was up to me to see that it was indeed so.

There were contracts to be signed and returned, ready for exchange, and it had been pointed out to me by the army authorities that I should complete a power of attorney so that my father could continue to operate my side of the business and sign documents such as land transfers on my behalf. There was also the regular exchange of business cheques to be dealt with as I continued to play my full part in the running of the firm, or as much as my hectic schedule allowed. So far, I had yet to miss a month end, and that was very comforting for my father. He was dealing with the sale of a couple of plots of land for me and I was leaving him to do the negotiations. Last but not necessarily least, I wanted to remind him to keep sending me some tobacco (Wills Capstan Medium Strength) on the armed forces scheme which enabled him to place and pay for the order with a tobacconist, who would then arrange to send it on direct. To keep his spirits up, I told him that I had been on a successful exercise and managed to get an extra night in London on the way back to go to a show. He liked to know what I was doing.

Undated.
7 RN. APO England.
Dear Pop & Lou,
    Many thanks for all for all of your letters and I am pleased to hear that you are both well.
    The news is very good and I have made several bets that we shall be in Germany before the end of September.
    I have forwarded Pykitt's contract and I have signed it, although I feel that the repairs have nothing to do with the actual sale, and I should like you to check up on this and see that it is in order when perhaps you will forward it to Drewry & Newbold.
    I will be forwarding POA to you next week and then you will be able to sign the Deed. And also any land transfers that may transpire. I am also sending some other contracts for your signature.
    Love to all.
    Eddie.

Undated.
7 RN. APO England.
Dear Pop & Lou,
    I enclose a number of business cheques which I would like you to post on the dates that I have put on the envelopes. Also a form from Bourne & Co., which requires completion. Will you pay any other accounts that come to you, but check with the bank that funds have been transferred.

PRUNES FOR BREAKFAST

I shall be shortly engaged in this little incident. I have every confidence in our own ultimate victory and I am proud of the Unit and formation that I am with. We are fighting in a great cause and for a country and empire in which I have the greatest pride. Do not worry, and God bless you all.

My love to all.

Eddie.

As a result of efforts at both of our ends, business was holding up satisfactorily. Letters would fly about between solicitors and accountants, keeping them busy too. I liked to think that I was still managing to play an almost full part in what was happening, but I sometimes pondered that Elizabeth rather thought that my civilian work rather got in the way of my pandering to her every whim.

Undated. (Monday)
7 RN. Margate, Kent.
Darling,

I was delighted to hear from you this morning, together with the budget. I have written to Pop and Lou so they should be in a happier frame of mind now. I will write to Edith in a day or two. They should be very grateful to you, and I think they are.

JE appears to grow more like his father each day. I have not been to Bobby's yet as I was told to try another store in Canterbury first. I have tried to scrounge half a day but have been unsuccessful and will try and make a special effort next Saturday afternoon.

I have had an uneventful week apart from a spot of work with my cadre, a run with George Desford last Monday and been invited out to supper with Andrew and Norman last Tuesday. Magnificent steak and chips, black market of course, the usual rounds of Rummy and Solo and this week I am expecting to get in a game of badminton.

We have had a bit of enemy air activity, lot of ack-ack fire but the incendiaries were some distance away. Yesterday a Flying Fortress came down in the sea and bounced up on to the cliff, no one being killed.

I have not had my leave granted yet by the CO but if I cannot manage the 1st. it will be the weekend.

Well darling, I shall be hearing your dulcet tones on the phone before you probably receive this. I am looking forward with all my heart to seeing you.

All my love.
Edward. x.

I just hated going on runs, and indeed pretty much hated the regular PT sessions. Most I could get out of, pleading my officer duties, but occasionally I thought that it was appropriate to join in the 'fun' of staggering a few miles with a group of sweating and swearing men, so as to be seen to be leading from the front. Those runs played havoc with my dodgy feet, so much so that, on more than one occasion, I had been referred onward by the MO who was at a loss as to how to treat them further, and so yet again I was sent to the Royal Orthopaedic Hospital in London.

Undated. (November)
7 RN. Margate, Kent.
Darling,

You have been most unkind. Every morning I look for a letter and have been sure that one would then arrive with the second post, until in desperation I have to send you a wire and phone you. If you do not write in the week my imagination begins to run riot and I think that you must be ill or have fallen in love with someone else.

Cliftonville itself is most depressing and the weather has made it even more so. All the hotels are closed or taken over by the army and there are only about 4 pubs in the whole of Margate, Cliftonville and Westgate worth drinking in.

PRUNES FOR BREAKFAST

The first few nights after I returned I stayed in and played bridge and Saturday I decided to look the place over, but the result was most unsatisfactory and it looks as though I shall confine myself to the Mess.

Norman has just gone on 48 hours leave, prior to going on a Course, lucky chap!

We are repeating our Exercise starting a week on Thursday, but this time acting as the enemy.

I shall probably avoid the Exercise because I am going on a Chemical Warfare Course (gas) at Winterbourne (5 Dec) which finishes on Saturday 18th. And I think we might have our weekend then. You might like to think of having Esmé and Freda over and put in a bit of groundwork with Freda to see whether she will come and look after JE. I am glad to hear that the lad is in good form, if he gets obstreperous you had better warn him there will be trouble in store when I return.

We are doing rather better for eggs at the moment, so do not bother to send them.

I want you to be cheerful and have courage in the days ahead and be calm in the knowledge that before many months have elapsed, we shall all be together again.

Well, there is nothing more to tell you.

Every bit of love.

Edward. x

P.S. Try bottled Worthington in place of Guinness.

I knew that the Germans had a stockpile of chemical warfare stuff, including gas, which I believed that they used indiscriminately during the last war and people died horrible deaths as a result. I supposed that we had the same stuff, too, tucked away, just in case. The idea of the course was to train us in protection against all sorts of chemical warfare attack. I didn't like the idea of that sort of muck that I couldn't see.

There was a lot of classroom stuff and one day we were sent out, fully kitted up, on an hour's march, and then, without any warning, a Lysander (I think that it was one of those – I was never much good at aircraft recognition) flew over us and dropped a load of spray from a great big canister slung underneath it. Well, you had never seen anything like it! The idea was to check our reactions to getting our gas masks on but there were people milling around all over the place. Some put their masks on, others simply forgot, presuming that it was an enemy raid, and they buried themselves in the nearest ditch. It was a right hoot, I can tell you, particularly afterwards, when they actually recognised our own side's markings on the plane.

At the end, I was issued with all sorts of stuff, given some official looking bumph, told that I had passed and was therefore to be henceforth my Unit Instructor, and packed off back to Kent. How many Unit Instructors was I now? I'd lost count.

Undated. (Thursday)
Darling,
    Many thanks for the belt, although I doubt that it was necessary to register the same. I am ill, suffering from bronchitis, I went into my office for an hour this morning, but the MO has suggested that I retire to my quarters again this afternoon.
    Yesterday afternoon I drank 3 pints of hot orange which was very good indeed. I haven't had a smoke since Monday so it has been rather a cheap week. I think I shall continue to be teetotal.
    I am sorry to say that I shall probably be at home at Grantchester this weekend since my enquiry at the Orderly Room this morning brought forth the information that I was not on duty. Someone will probably kick and you will understand why.
    Needless to say, golf and all my other interesting sidelines have been out this week, consequently have done nothing with either car or frock.

PRUNES FOR BREAKFAST

I can only assume you exaggerate the boy's behaviour, however I have written him a letter, below, it may even do some good.

All my love.

Edward. x.

Dear John,

I am sorry to hear from Mummy that you have been a very naughty boy since I returned to Leamington. If you have not been a better boy when I come home, I shall take one of your big trains and give it back to Santa. Try and be a good boy.

Love,

Daddy.

17

We'll Meet Again

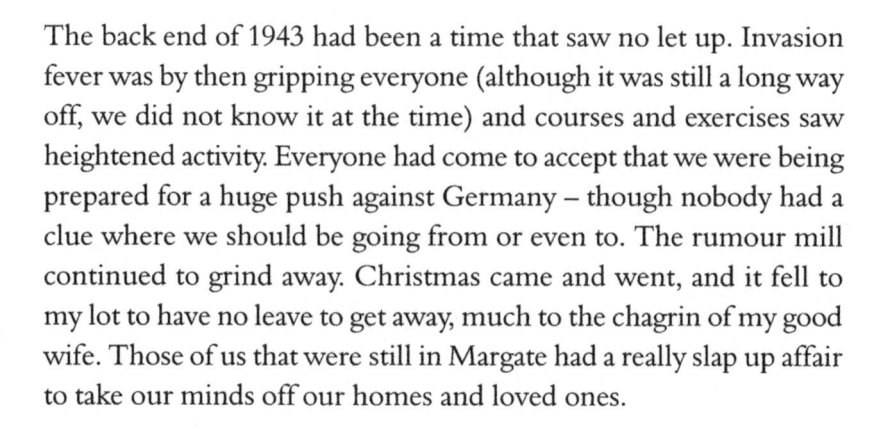

The back end of 1943 had been a time that saw no let up. Invasion fever was by then gripping everyone (although it was still a long way off, we did not know it at the time) and courses and exercises saw heightened activity. Everyone had come to accept that we were being prepared for a huge push against Germany – though nobody had a clue where we should be going from or even to. The rumour mill continued to grind away. Christmas came and went, and it fell to my lot to have no leave to get away, much to the chagrin of my good wife. Those of us that were still in Margate had a really slap up affair to take our minds off our homes and loved ones.

28th December 1943.
7 RN. Margate, Kent.
Darling,
The photographs were marvellous, sweetheart and I thought you were excellent. Most of the other officers said that you were far too good for me and some thought it a pity that there were no Courses up in Ripley so that they could ask for a date with you. I thought it was rather flattering to me and others told me that also. JE looked grand. They arrived Xmas day, so completing my best Army Christmas.
We entertained the Sgts. Mess on Xmas Eve and they had us a return visit on Xmas Day before lunch when they did their best to get me tight, but time was against them. We helped serve the troops their

lunches and I was in charge of the beer. Afterwards I played bridge and in the evening we had a concert (all our own artists). This was worth 7/6d at any time to see. One of the items was a beer drinking contest, to see who could drink a pint the quickest. I was hopelessly outclassed.

Afterwards I was invited to a party at our local, called The Wheatsheaf. On Sunday the officers played the Sgts. at soccer, and towards the end I took my coat off and joined in. On Monday we played all-in soccer at 50 a side, after which a few RE officers came to see me and took me back to their Mess where we had a hectic do, and that I think completes my chronicle.

I was glad you managed to get a goose, and as I told you, I have managed to get most of your Arden.

The family sent me a 15/- book token, Esmé some stamps, and Freda some tobacco. You did not send me the Rate Demand and if some Income Tax receipts have arrived will you forward them too.

I am waiting for the next month to pass quickly.

Every scrap of love.

Eddie. x.

8th January 1944.
7 RN. Margate, Kent.
Darling,

You have really taken my breath away with 2 letters in 3 days.

Life has pretty much proceeded according to plan with a night exercise last night to break the monotony. Apart from 2 Court Martials to defend, your letters have provided the only excitement.

I am sorry JE is so badly behaved, must have inherited it from his father. However, all being well, I shall make it home next weekend until the following Sunday when I have to go on a Camouflage Course in Tunbridge Wells.

I have all the Arden requirements except the lipstick, but I shall be getting this out of the next quota at the end of this month.

We'll Meet Again

Everyone seems to have been very kind this Christmas and I am not surprised that the photographs received so much approval.
Ever yours.
Edward. x.

Civilian life seemed so remote, even when I dipped back into it on my periods of leave.

And what a strange Christmas that had been, my fourth in the army. I had imagined Elizabeth, her family and young JE all sitting down together on Christmas Day and devouring that goose. Perhaps it was my son's first taste of goose. It could not have been more different to my day, where I was part of the age-old military custom of officers serving the troops their Christmas Day lunch. Apart from the strangeness of the situation (carrying platters of food and trays of beer, with my wobbly hand) and the fact that everyone was in uniform, the war could have been a million miles away. There had been a church parade in the morning, and then after the grand meal, the afternoon was taken up by chaps working it off with some soccer. I initiated a card game with some of the sergeants and carried on with the beer until the festivities of the evening took over.

Boxing Day – apart from the enormous game of soccer in which half the battalion seemed to be participating, all at the same time – was a quiet one for me. Duties were on hold and I absented myself, only to be found much later on in the Royal Engineers Mess. How I got there I could never remember.

Throbbing temples the next morning brought me back to reality and I returned to duty, Orderly Officer for the run up to the New Year. I had volunteered for the long stint in exchange for a longer leave, due a couple of weeks later.

I used my accrued leave to go back to see all of the family; staying at my own home, Grantchester at Ashby, and going over to Gresley to see my parents. It was an easy habit to get into, although I was

PRUNES FOR BREAKFAST

never sure that Elizabeth particularly wanted to go to Gresley. I suppose that she preferred to be queen of all that she surveyed, whether that be at Ripley or at Ashby. Sometimes she stayed behind at Grantchester in a bit of a sulk. JE, as I was still calling him, on the other hand, absolutely delighted in going to visit Pop and Lou, not just because of the cakes that had been made for him, but for all the exploratory trips that he could demand to make into the big barn behind my father's house. Stacks of wood and old bits of machinery seemed to fascinate him. Pop had even knocked him up a little toy wheelbarrow to put stuff in, and I could see that he could hardly wait to grow a bit bigger so as to manage to wheel bits of wood around in it. He just loved it over there.

All too soon my short spell of leave drew to a close. I kissed everyone goodbye and then, true to form, I was once again making use of my free travel warrant and the excellent train service down to London, and then onwards to Tunbridge Wells.

Undated. (Wednesday)
Darling
    Tunbridge Wells is not a bad spot, one might almost imagine that there is not a war on, other than for all the troops and the incendiary bombs that were dropped last Friday. I had a good journey, arriving only a little late in London, managed to get a pint of beer, and the train ran into Tunbridge Wells a little early, only the rain spoiling it.
    The billet is quite a good one, very convenient and very nice people that push out an early morning cup of tea and even a sandwich and cup of coffee at night.
    The Course is quite easy starting at 9.30 a.m. and finishing at 5.30 p.m., with quite a lot of notes. You did not give me the list of clothes that you required which is rather a pity as the shops here appear to be very well stocked. Please send me the razor blades that I left in my leather case.

I enjoyed my leave very much, darling, and I look at your photograph and quietly convince myself that the war must be over shortly.
All my love.
Edward. x.

I reckoned that my fellow officers in the battalion were beginning to think of me as some sort of casual visitor that popped in occasionally, I was so often away on those bally courses. Everyone seemed to be quite surprised each time I actually returned to base.

Undated. (Sunday). (Early March 1944).
Darling,
   Give JE all the wishes for his birthday that you know I would wish him if I could be with you. You know how proud I am of both of you and I only hope that in his next year he will bear out the fine promise he shows. I feel sure that he will be a source of great joy and comfort to you, darling. I know how proud you are. A very happy birthday to both of you.
   I got back quite safely, not forgetting to change at Trent, and took a taxi across London, but the train was rather slow getting to Margate. I am about to start another Mines Course on Thursday.
   I bought a Frankau on the way down, 'Woman on the Horizon'. I did not consider it one of his best. The eggs made everyone jealous on Sunday morning (two!).
   I have asked Norman to try and fix my leave on April 10. How will that suit? I will phone on Thursday but that does not absolve you from letter writing.
   Every bit of love.
   Edward. x.

PRUNES FOR BREAKFAST

7th May 1944. (Sunday)
7 RN. APO. England.
Darling,

The Bn. have gone out on exercise until Tuesday, leaving this morning and someone has stupidly taken the office 'censor' stamp with them, so I really don't know when you will receive this. Norman and I are serving on a Court Martial tomorrow, so will not be joining the Bn. until Monday evening. Good arrangement, what?

The chief news of the week so far is that I have taken a bet £10 to £7 that I do not touch alcohol for a month until 10.25 p.m. on June 5. So far I have gone 2 days and in that time have consumed more soft drinks than in the last 14 years. I should look marvellous when I see you.

I do not like the new CO and I fear the feeling may be mutual. My new Service Dress has arrived and is admired by all. I can now understand why people used to comment on the old one.

You are allowed to visit this celestial spot for 7 days and I am allowed to sleep out for 3 nights, but I personally had not considered that idea a healthy one. London I can arrange by conspiracy with the MO and Norman for 1 day and night, and I consider the chances of being bombed fairly remote. Dates available are any of the next 12 days, with the exception of the 14th to the 17th when we have an Exercise.

You may be a rotten writer, sweetheart, but your letters have improved by 200%. Have you been taking a correspondence course?

I am glad the lad's behaviour has improved but would suggest that that the curtains be drawn when I was on leave.

I forgot to mention that it might be a good thing if Kitty bought the few houses and you lent the balance of the purchase price at 4½%. Anthony would buy his then, I imagine. Tell Jones to get the lodgers out at once, the matter becomes serious.

All my love.
Edward. x.

I must by now have been the most over-qualified officer in the British Army. Once again I was hardly back in harness with my battalion after we had got most of the cold weather behind us, than news came that I was to go off on yet another course. This time I was to go to the Royal Army Ordnance Corps Training Establishment at Bramley to attend their Course 199, Care & Maintenance of Ammunition, in the middle of April. Who had put me up for that one, I would never know, which was probably a good thing.

In between times, we were still training hard; still doing a lot of marching, which played hell with my feet. Fortunately, I could usually arrange a lift in some vehicle or other for part of the way, pleading battalion transport difficulties to be sorted out. I kept a Transport Officer card over-stamped with our battalion details, just in case. It was quite surprising just how many 'just in case' problems there were! With all the training, we must by then have been well ahead of lots of other Units in our preparation for what was to lie ahead. I hoped that we could acquit ourselves properly, even if we were only to be first reserve, still without any actual battle experience to harden us up.

Unfortunately, it was still true to say that hardly anyone, other than the senior commanders and a few of the other non-commissioned officers, had seen action before. It was comforting that the new top brass had come to us directly from the North Africa campaign, and would be able to instil in their senior officers some of their experience with skills honed there.

I noticed that things they were a-changing. Those last few days had been remarkable for the amount of military traffic on the roads. Troops, guns, tanks and vehicles of every description had been going about their business doing what looked very much like final training and preparation: all part of the great master plan that I fervently hoped existed. I anticipated an invasion of Europe very soon now.

My Unit was kicking its heels, waiting for the big off – doing dummy runs to prepare us for all sorts of eventualities. One day we were loaded on to boats and then had to make an amphibious landing on some strange beach, God only knew where it was, because we were never told, though it was further to the north – I could work that one out for myself – away from prying foreign eyes.

It was a time of intense activity. It was now openly apparent that things were coming to a head. Endless army lists of requirements were now being printed and they came in a stack of booklets and documents. Each publication detailed absolutely everything that might be needed for an individual, for example a humble bar of soap (washing, for the use of) to others offering amazingly detailed information about traffic control from various troop and armoured bases to all ports of embarkation. There was one lengthy booklet detailing the way that each type of vehicle should be waterproofed against a sea crossing and possible landing on a wet foreshore, and yet another on the requirements for how casualty evacuation procedures should be instigated. Everything had been thoroughly thought through and was complete down to the minutest detail.

I took my hat off to those people who had put that lot together. It must have taken months for very keen analytical minds to work all those things out, and it was yet another example of the importance of the backroom boys in this war.

All leave had by now been stopped and censorship was more rigorously enforced than ever before. All civilian movement into the southern coastal areas had now been curtailed and closely monitored. Where we were in Kent, even wireless transmission limits had been imposed and individual Units were only allowed to go on the air at specific pre-agreed times. One lot of chaps had been sent off to beef up the guard at Manston, the Kent aerodrome a few miles away on the coast, with its long runway being the nearest to France.

And suddenly, there it was! The code word 'Overlord' began to appear at all Units stamped on the front cover of mammoth operational and administrative instructions. Vehicle loading trials had quickly begun and we all pulled hard to bring everything together as a well-oiled machine after those last four years of training. Time was running out.

After that, there was nothing more to do but to wait. No more exercises, drills, training reviews or parades. Finally, we reckoned, we were ready for the real thing.

28th May 1944.
7 RN. APO England.
Darling,
    Your letter was perfectly sweet and our phone conversations have been quietly stimulating, although I have been very unpopular with my snooker opponents.

I think the war news is fairly encouraging and it should not be long before it is over. The new radio controlled plane I am not so happy about, but I am thankful that you are so far away from the coast. I have no doubt that we shall find the answer soon.

I am fairly fit and well, prepared for most eventualities, with an ample stock of books, playing cards, dominoes, soap etc. I have enclosed clothing coupons which I should like you to hold until the end of the month as I am not quite sure how my a/c stands. I have also sent an authority to Barclays to pay you £20 a month.

I have decided to send home my service dress (you can always send it out to me) also 2 blankets and your Arden. A few balloons for the lad.

The books have arrived safely. My bet is still going strong, and finishes on Friday at 10.25 p.m. On Sunday I am throwing a dinner party to celebrate.

Every bit of love.
Edward. x.

Well, that just showed that I could do it! Which was a lot more than some others did. I had managed – quite easily as it turned out – to refrain from any alcoholic intake for the last month. Nobody thought that I would manage it and I had collected quite a bob or two as a result of the bets placed against my success. Mind you, it was rather paling into insignificance now that everything seemed to be gearing up for imminent action. I might never live long enough to spend it all.

That business of the V2 rockets was a bit worrying. During the summer of 1944 we had started to hear this funny noise high in the sky, coming in from the coast and making in the general direction of London. You could recognise what they were without actually seeing them because of the unmistakeable drone of their engines. Quite different to the V1 flying bombs that had blitzed London earlier. They appeared to pack quite a punch and I, for one, in a very selfish way, was grateful that they were not being targeted on us down there in Kent. Come to think of it, if there had been any spies about, and they had fed that information back to the Jerries who then targeted those rockets on to us, it would have likely scuppered any possibility of the Second Front completely.

I was firmly convinced that everyone was right when they gossiped that we were about to open the Second Front within the next few days. I still didn't know where, but my instincts told me that it must be France, and northern France at that. I could not believe that any of the longer sea journeys were even a remote possibility. Our battalion CO had actually known for some time now, but he was being very tight-lipped, more so than usual and nobody could wangle the destination out of him. Believe me, we tried.

There was not much more to be done. We had prepared and prepared, and everything was in place. The men were trained, all the machinery was oiled, checked and then checked again, and we entered into a period of hiatus. We were ready for the off and all we could do most evenings was to sit around wishing away the time until the moment came and we had the green light. The hit tune of the moment was *'We'll Meet Again'* by a lovely young lady by the name of Vera Lynn. That tune was on everyone's lips, and it seemed so very appropriate.

18

D-Day +

D-Day, the 6th June 1944, would never need any further introduction. I was sure that it was a date that had been instantly branded into the psyche of every single one of us for the rest of our lives, whether or not we were old enough to have played a part. It was a day that we in the Armed Services had together been working towards for all those long years since becoming enlisted.

Of course, we did not quite know the where or when at the time. We knew that something was coming and that it was going to be huge, an invasion, probably into France. Although everyone was taking bets on where, all other options had fallen by the wayside, in my opinion. You could get very long odds on Norway and the south of France, whether within the Mediterranean or nearer to Bordeaux. But why embark on a long sea crossing to land in Norway and then have to march all the way back across at least three other countries to reach what must become the main theatre? No, you could have a hundred-to-one against that in my book.

We talked amongst each other, of course we did. The local villagers knew as much as we – if not more, we often reckoned – because they saw who came and went, talked with us, and we shared what little information we had, though it was strictly forbidden on both sides. It was quite amazing to have a pint in the local village pub and openly be volunteered information about who was where and who was going where. There was nothing like village gossip. If only the Germans had latched on to that, they could have had a field

PRUNES FOR BREAKFAST

day. But no, we all concluded that it was going to be northern France.

We had taken part in all those joint exercises, all along the south coast of England, from Kent to Dorset. We knew from the millions of tents in all the new concentration areas that a huge number of us would be going to open the Second Front. You could hardly see a blade of grass left free-standing in the New Forest: it was covered with tents or tanks, or other paraphernalia of war. In Kent, the same applied, and towns and villages were filled to busting with service personnel. Including, of course, myself in 7 RN.

In our own camp, locked in behind the newly erected protective wire, we were now completely cut off from the outside world. That was to do with the major briefing we were to have. Senior commanders had been given theirs more than a couple of weeks ago, and now we battalion officers were to be thoroughly briefed.

There were special tents set up with map boards – one a huge wall map that I seem to remember had been made by Chad Valley, the jigsaw makers, together with large scale maps of the south of England. We then stood around mocked-up sand displays of a particular stretch of beach that we would be soon landing on. We knew the code name 'Overlord' for the invasion, the code name for every village and strongpoint inland from those target beaches. The only thing that we did not know was the country. We all guessed France, but there were no clues given, so speculation was still rife.

I bet those villagers knew by now, for certain, but we could no longer reach them beyond the camp wire. After the briefing was over, we were then kept in our sealed camp. No chance to wander down to the pub in the village, no opportunity again for leave to see loved ones. There was a special pay parade where each private soldier received, and had to sign for, 200 French francs, about £2 in old money. We reckoned that that was all a double bluff by the brass hats.

D-Day +

Then, to cap it all, as you might say, everyone was asked to accept 'a packet of three' – condoms, that was! I don't know who was more embarrassed, the recipient or the provider. Some men refused to take them on principle because they were Roman Catholics. That was the moment for the Corporal standing to one's side to whisper confidentially into one's ear, at full volume: *'Take them, laddie, and give them to a friend, whose need may be greater than yours.'* Oh, and as a parting gift from the army, for each of our kitbags we were supplied with a tin of foot powder. Those planners really had thought of everything.

Every highway and byway by then had their own clusters of signs at the side of the road; newly painted directional signs in army code with symbols such as pitheads, Britannia with her shield, bears and other animals, pointing to where battalions or full brigades were to congregate when moving to their designated marshalling area. The idea was to further confuse any operational German spies, if they had not already been mopped up and put into the bag.

German spies were on everyone's mind in those days. Whether you were a civilian or in the military, we all knew the mantra that *'walls have ears'*. It seemed inconceivable that the Germans would not have been able to work out where this great invasion force was going to land. There must have been so many pointers. Perhaps there just were not enough Germans over on our shores to feed back the information. Perhaps their High Command were not good at interpreting the clues.

As for us, it had been officially stated when we were amalgamated into X11 Corps that we would be held back in reserve and go over in the immediate follow-up. And so, instead of heading south to the coast, to Southampton, Portsmouth, Dover, or any of the stops in between, we were to head in the opposite direction. Our marshalling area was to be just outside the great commercial port of Tilbury on the north bank of the Thames. Bright and early on the 20th, we started the great move towards there, to be ready for our listed embarkation date of the 22nd.

Once encamped there, we were joined by other Units such as the Royal Tank Regiment and the Royal Artillery with their big guns. In all, with our support and medical groups, we made up all of the individual constituents of a small army of our own, ready and waiting. And waiting. And waiting.

Each day that we sat and waited for our own personal D-Day to come around, we watched, when there was fair weather, the endless waves of British and American bombers as they thundered out over the coast, their fuselages and plexiglas windows glinting shafts of silver in the sun. That was one of my predominant memories in those days: those huge lumbering bombers passing overhead – literally thousands of them – while the warm golden sun shone down on us as we stood and wondered at what it must mean, the pale blue skies of early summer over our heads.

Once or twice there was a false alarm when the battalion had stood to and paraded for departure, only later to be stood down again. There was little to do but lie back in the sun, or relax in our tents when it rained, and stuff ourselves full of huge meals supplied by the civilian cooks drafted in for our last supper.

And then the weather changed yet again. Not for the better. There would be more delay.

The original day proposed for D-Day had already been postponed because of the forecast high winds whipping up the Channel and rain clouds obscuring the moon. But delay could be critical because of the summer tides. Everything had to be just so, otherwise the

D-Day +

landings would likely be a failure. There was a mission critical window for it to happen. Eventually, so I heard later, and of course it was probably apocryphal, Eisenhower and Montgomery pressured the chief meteorological chappie to give an opinion on the weather for the next forty-eight hours. Slightly flummoxed, because his Atlantic charts showed nothing clear enough, he stuck his finger in the air and said the equivalent of 'go' and that was that. It was on. D-Day would be 6th June 1944.

And so it was, as we have heard so many times.

I pondered when it would be our turn to go. I remembered that, late in the night before D-Day, on 5 June, low above us came the snarling and growling of a horde of different aero engines. Huge numbers of red navigation lights passed overhead, very low in the sky, the planes moving out towards the sea, going due south in the direction of France. The black outlines of the bombers could scarcely be made out and their formations were soon lost in the darkness. Their noise faded away to nothing, leaving behind an eerie and ominous silence. By daybreak that day, the face of the world would have altered.

The greatest amphibious invasion that the world had ever seen was underway.

The world might well have altered, but for the civilians left behind in the south of England, things had suddenly become very quiet. Where there had been for weeks, sometimes months, tented camps and villages, there was suddenly nobody. Not a man left there. I heard, after the war was over, that villagers suddenly found that they had been deserted by the troops bivouacked nearby. They had stolen away in the night, disappeared, leaving behind the odd empty tent and other jetsam, the sole surviving proof of their passing. No khaki uniforms to be seen. No lines of camouflaged vehicles. No tanks. No artillery. One chap told me that he wandered round a camp the next day, to be greeted by utter silence, flapping tent door screens, empty coffee mugs and

PRUNES FOR BREAKFAST

he even saw a meal, half eaten, and then abandoned when the final movement call came in to get down to their allotted harbour and embark for France.

The road around Winchester which had become the temporary home for an armada of fighting vehicles was emptied overnight. Lines of tanks and other machinery parked in quiet streets had all made their way towards their embarkation points, leaving only the odd jerry can behind as witness of their previous tenancy. Church services were held up and down the land, as the news spread like wildfire, praying for their safe passage and eventual return.

As for us? Well, we still waited and waited. There were a number of sailings from Tilbury after the 6th June.

The tanks of our RTR friends went just before us. They had spent all their spare time in the marshalling area waterproofing their machines, and they could land, they reckoned, in up to 5 feet of sea water without conking out, provided that the LCTs, (or Landing Craft, Troops), managed to get to the beaches directly head-on. The tanks had been superbly waterproofed, but their steering mechanism was compromised by all the stuff wrapped around it, and it meant that they could only drive straight forwards until the waterproofing had been stripped away after the beach landing. In retrospect, we heard that a number of tanks were lost when their LCTs were caught by the waves and ended up being beached broadside in the shallows, with the result that the tanks could not be steered properly off the boats.

As with the tank boys, our motor transport technical Sergeant with REME (the Corps of The Royal Electrical and Mechanical Engineers) assistance had supervised the task of ensuring that every battalion vehicle could be driven into salt water, if the need arose, without any permanent damage, should they have to be driven

D-Day +

through the shallows instead of making it directly on to dry land. I was in charge of the battalion Vehicle Party and spent a lot of my time in the Marshalling Area outside Tilbury ensuring that proper waterproofing had been carried out.

Our departure date, as designated by the Marshals, was put back to the 22nd. Once all of the infantry party were fully prepared and all of the vehicles had been waterproofed, I had nothing much to do and so I used my time to write some letters. They might well be my last ever. One was to my wife's mother, also named Elizabeth, at The Woodlands, Ripley.

20th June 1944.
My dear Elizabeth,

Apart from my last letter to my wife, this is probably the last letter I shall write in this country, and only the second that I have written to you. I hope that you may forgive me. I should like to thank you now for the many kindnesses you have shown to me and the great comfort you have been to me in knowing that Elizabeth and JE have been with you while I have been away.

In a day or so I shall be set on an adventure rather different from any I have hitherto undertaken. I go in good heart, and with great confidence and in the hope that I shall not in any way let down those that I leave behind. The cause is a great one, and you know my pride in my country and empire. I expect to have dinner with you next Christmas.

Should anything untoward happen, and my plans be interfered with, I have the greatest favour to ask of you. Please get Elizabeth and JE away from Ripley. This will be hard on you but I hope you will see (sic) *with me.*

My love and may God bless you.
Eddie.

PRUNES FOR BREAKFAST

The weather was still not deemed good enough by the 22nd, and so whilst gales lashed the Channel, the entire 59th Division was stuck, delayed further because of the weather forecast.

We spent a lot of that extra time waterproofing, but were still making modifications and improvements right up to the 26th, our deferred embarkation date. It really was time for us to go by then, and not a moment too soon. Everyone was getting very twitchy, needing an escape valve from the enforced idling and being cooped up in our marshalling area. Strictly against standing orders, I sneaked out in the evening, hoping for a final taste of English beer before we left.

We had commenced boarding troops and vehicles straight after a snatched early breakfast, but it was to be almost twelve hours later before we finally cast off. Tilbury docks looked rather empty as our LCTs (Landing Craft, Troops) and other ships, everyone aboard at last, congregated into a motley fleet of sorts off Southend-on-Sea, shepherded by a flotilla of minesweepers and a destroyer, before nosing out of the Thames and into the open water of the great estuary, to form up with our defensive escorts into a long convoy.

I had just found time to pen one last letter to Elizabeth before we departed, having asked a dock-side worker to ensure that it got posted for me.

26th June 1944.
7 RN. APO England.
Darling,
    Two letters in 4 days is rather good going, aren't you lucky? I am writing this in the Officer's bar with a pint by my side. It is undecided whether to rain and everything is very gusty. I went to the local at 6 p.m. but found it closed, 'sold out'.
    Life has been very pleasant for the last few days, the weather good, and generally lazy.
    On Keith's birthday and the day after George's they had a daughter and son respectively. We had an enormous celebration party

D-Day +

on Friday lunch time. Saturday was much the same, but we met some Norfolk VADs who invited us to tennis and bridge on Sunday. We accepted with alacrity and had a most enjoyable time, very good tea and the odd gin.

Darling, on Saturday will be the anniversary of our wedding, or do you prefer July 2?

In case I am not able to send another greeting, darling, I am going to hope that we never miss another anniversary together and you may hold me to it, come what may.

God bless you, sweetheart.

All my love.

Edward. x.

It was evening as our snub-nosed craft butted out into clear water and headed east, the spindrift hazing away from the tops of the waves. I looked back: it was not a lovely landscape, even in the fading light, but after wondering briefly whether or not I would ever see my perfidious Albion again, I realised that I had never loved my country as truly as at that moment. I turned away, with a tear in my eye.

Pulling myself together, I cast my glance over the troops jam-packed onto that boat. I could see that I was far from being alone in having that wonderful feeling of belonging to a cause worth fighting for.

Down the Thames estuary and along the north Kentish coast we crept, maintaining silence and with lights dimmed, later to join up with another convoy going in the same direction, all of us pressed together in one of the designated cleared lanes, so close that we could have held a conversation between boats, had we been allowed. The weather was relatively calm, and for once I was not seasick. The moon peeped through the scudding clouds during the night as the southern coastline of Kent merged slowly into that of Sussex. Then finally we reached the great main convoy lane heading south from the Portsmouth area where yet more ships had congregated waiting for us to join them. With our strengthened defensive flotilla, we came together as a great armada, turned due south and we all watched the coastline of England slowly slipping away astern. There could be no turning back now. This was the real thing at last. We steamed in silence, our naval escorts using blinking Aldis lamps to communicate between themselves and trying to keep us safe from predatory German E-Boats.

Mid-Channel, there was a flurry of activity from our escorts, and through the gloom we could see that yet another armada of naval and civilian boats was on the move, this time going in the opposite direction, providing a continuous shuttle service backwards and forwards from the beaches of Normandy to their various home ports in southern England. They were carrying provisions and ammunition on the way out, and were full of wounded for their return. As the sky grew lighter and a watery sun poked its head above the horizon, we could see stretchers loaded with the wounded lined up on the decks. The occasional moans and cries of pain carried across the water to us and the mood on board turned grim. It was our first glimpse of what war could really be like.

The men started smoking a lot more heavily and gazed in silence as the scene unfolded. Nobody had seen anything like that before, and, in truth, nothing could have really prepared them.

We shuttled slowly in, past the huge warships that were still lying offshore, their deck guns all pointing southwards in to France. I was told that they were playing a defensive role against any German counter-measures and also lay broadside to the land in order to use their 15 inch guns to shell targets 7 or 8 miles inland, with quite devastating accuracy.

Whilst we were coming in towards land, I saw a lump of something floating in the water, and pointed it out to one of the officers. Was it a mine, or even a dreaded German U-boat about to send us direct to Davy Jones' Locker before we had even fired a shot in anger? The Captain and all the other officers had their binoculars trained on it in a trice, and everyone breathed a sigh of relief when they assured me that it was only some floating wreckage, probably washed offshore from the landing beaches. There seemed to be more and more of that wreckage the nearer we got inshore.

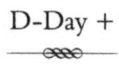

After having waited our turn, we finally arrived at our designated positions off the French beaches early that evening. The sun was still shining, the sea was relatively calm, and we could see that those beaches were a frenzied but well-ordered storm of activity. Altogether, we landed 1,147 officers and 21,575 ORs (other ranks) as the combat strength of 59th Division onto Juno Beach by the village of Graye sur Mer. Our orders – of course – were still to remain in reserve until further notice.

We had all heard about the terrible death and destruction that had been meted out on D-Day. It was quite a surprise, therefore, to see that the beaches were a hive of Allied activity, dealing quickly and efficiently with each boatload that reached the shore. No German guns were left on the dunes to bombard us, and no Luftwaffe planes were in the skies to strafe us. We were pleased not to lose a single vehicle as we got them on to the sands at half-tide. Our many hours of waterproofing had turned out to be a complete success. I was rather proud of that achievement.

One of the many DUKWs (a 6 wheeled amphibious vehicle universally known as a 'Duck') lurched and splashed through the small waves and deposited me on a patch of damp sand. We jumped out and our boots landed on French soil – Normandy, at last. Others, in boats with a deeper draught, had to wade ashore through the choppy waters, their rifles held aloft to protect them from the corrosive effect of briny water. The beach was a scene of astonishingly calm industry. The sun was still quite warm. Other landing craft were disembarking infantry, and yielding up their cargoes of vehicles and equipment. Beach Group personnel were everywhere, working in shirtsleeves, supervising the unloading and then the onward movement of infantry and vehicles off the beaches as quickly as possible. Metal road-strips had been laid from the beachhead through the flattened dunes and into the fields beyond. Barrage balloons were nodding aloft along the shoreline and heavy breakdown recovery vehicles were grinding slowly inland, their engines labouring under the strain of hauling vehicles that had got stuck in the sea water when their motors had seized.

Our arrival on French soil appeared to have been orchestrated to the sound of continuous rolling thunder as the huge guns on the larger warships further out to sea fired salvo after salvo of immense shells into the Normandy hinterland. I assumed that the navy guns had long been ranged on to the German positions, and were beating the merry daylights out of them. It was a good feeling to know that support like that was going to be on hand for us, when it came to our turn to fight.

Whilst my men were unloading the vehicles, I stood stock still, lit my pipe on the sands, and then had a good look around me. There were ships of all sizes coming and going, unloading their cargoes from England, and then preparing to take on board the wounded, lined up precariously on the beach, many unable to move from their stretchers. In between them were the hulks of sunken ships with great holes torn in them from aerial attack in the earlier days; some further out just poking their masts out of the water, whilst those closer to shore listed heavily in sad abandonment. Further out, there was a queue of those huge US-built LST ships with double decks, the lower one for tanks and heavy motorised equipment, and the upper one for the troops. One of them lay in the shallows further along the beach, toppled nearly upside down, having received a number of direct hits from the big German defensive guns, as though a giant hand from above had been playing with it and then dropped it back down through boredom. Beside it, an old steam tug lay on its side, a gaping hole visible just above the waterline.

19

Beachhead Salvoes

After a few minutes, I wandered over to where there was a flurry of activity. One of the RAF's Special Beach Units were assisting with the unloading from an LST. The sergeant told me that they were responsible for all RAF stores, aviation fuel, oil and ammunition, for getting all that off the various landing craft and then moving everything forward from the beachhead to forward dumps and thence to the first available, newly constructed, landing strip. This would allow our aircraft to land, refuel and rearm so that they could give our troops immediate air cover without having the need to return to England. I was much impressed by that.

The sergeant then leaned over towards me, winked, and confided to me that he had done it all before, during the similar Allied landings in Sicily. He reckoned that he and his team had practiced it so much they could do it all blindfold!

It really brought it home to me that we had, on our side, some of the greatest master planners that the world had ever seen. Who on earth had the foresight and skills to bring all that lot together to work in perfect harmony?

There I was, standing on one of those infamous beaches in northern France on a sunny evening, utterly amazed at the depth of planning that had gone into Operation Overlord to provide support through all three of the Services for the greatest amphibious invasion that the world had ever seen. I stood in awe and took my hat off to them all, those unseen backroom boys. It made me feel that I was a very small cog in a very big war machine.

PRUNES FOR BREAKFAST

Despite all that, I felt so sombre when I looked over to the far side of the beach, where the evacuation of the wounded was taking place. The lines of men and stretchers wound back from the shoreline right to the dunes. Just how many brave men had we lost on the front line? And when would I find myself, for the first time, on that front line? Would I live up to my own expectations and the hard training that I had been put through?

30th June 1944. (Friday)
7th Bn. The Royal Norfolk Regiment, British Western Expeditionary Force. (BWEF).
Darling,

Many thanks for your letters 1 and 2. My last letter, as you will have realised, was my last from England.

We boarded ship at 0830 Monday the 26th, leaving about 2030 the same evening. I was very proud of my country as I saw the last of it about 2310 the same evening.

The weather was exceedingly kind to us and we sighted the other coast about 1800 hours the next evening, and the following morning the scene was magnificent, reminding us of what I imagined Cowes to be like in regatta week. The trip was uneventful and we might have been on a pleasure cruise. We unloaded all our vehicles to Landing Craft and I must say the organization was magnificent. I have never seen anyone work so hard as the Sapper stevedores, and as I was the last officer to leave the ship I felt constrained to give them a tip of 200 Frs = £1.

The weather since arriving has been rather unkind, but the country around is very peaceful.

A further letter in a day or so.
All my love.
Edward. x.
PS. Have nothing to do with Tathams offer.

Beachhead Salvoes

Our very first job was to start the process of removing all of the waterproof sealing from our vehicles. There was a standard procedure for doing that – of course there was, it was in one of those manuals – dependent on the type of vehicle involved. Sometimes it was just a small bit of sticky stuff to be peeled away, whilst elsewhere you could see chaps frantically unwinding loop after loop of material to free up engines, transmissions, brakes and exhaust pipes. I did hear that the tank boys had found a novel use for those condoms that they had been issued with for completely different purposes: stretched tight over their injectors to protect them from salt, much to the consternation of the QMS who had to indent for extra supplies!

There were still a number of wrecked vehicles on the beach awaiting the heavy lifters to get around to them. Apart from the hustle and bustle of the resupply convoys being loaded and moving away from the beach area, all was eerily calm, though, apart from the whistling noise from shells passing close overhead when the warships used their heavy guns, blasting thunderous salvo after salvo away into the far distance, miles inland. But at least there were still no overhead aircraft to worry about. The Luftwaffe were singularly noticeable by their absence. And so we regrouped and moved in good order towards our designated Concentration Area, due to arrive there on the 29th.

We travelled inland throughout the afternoon, over the dunes, across the fields, and down some country lanes. When we finally reached Esquay-sur-Seulles, near Le Manoir, where we found our Army Group tactical HQ, we were able to watch a long column of infantry marching down the main street. There followed a long convoy of flail tanks, 'funnies' as we called them, with their massive steel chains dangling down from the great axles protruding in front from their hulls. They clattered along the centre of the highway, swirling up dust and scattering great clods of earth behind them. Everyone was, hearteningly, moving in an inland direction.

Some of the village inhabitants were waving and cheering as they went by, which was good to see; they obviously saw us as liberators and not another invasion force as they had the Germans. But not all of the French people were pleased to see us. Some looked on us as new invaders. In the countryside, they had by then become used to the German occupation. For the most part they had been left alone and had come to terms with it. And now there we were, about to wreck their villages and farms, and displace them from their homes, leaving them as little better than refugees in their own land.

We should never see the likes of all that again. Enormous quantities of men and materiel had been put ashore. Colossal masses of equipment were being stockpiled behind the battle lines, ready to be moved in support of those on the front line. It seemed, as we trundled on by, that the entire French countryside thereabouts must be packed to capacity with our men and armour.

The lanes that we marched or motored along still bore the German skull and crossbones notices denoting that the area had been mined, although our chaps had long since cleared a pathway through. The notices served to remind one that it was still dangerous to stray off the approved roads on to grassy verges that might yet have unknown enemy ordnance lurking below the surface.

The Division completed its assembly in the Creully area on the 1st July, preparing to move to the Forward Assembly Area at Colombey-sur-Theon, close to Anguerny. Surely things must start to hot up soon. Well, as a designated Reserve Division, our lot was still to wait, and wait.

1st July 1944. (Saturday)
7 RN. British Western Expeditionary Force.
Darling,
Six years ago today you took the biggest gamble of your life, why, I have never quite understood. I have been thinking back on our trip to Bournemouth and at the moment as I write I think we were about to eat at Newbury.

Beachhead Salvoes

(I have now been interrupted by my affiliated Sapper Platoon Commander and we have drunk a toast to us in an enamel mug in whisky and water).

I brought a magnificent desk, cum table, cum chest of drawers with me, containing 2 bottles of rum, 2 of whiskey, 3 packs of cards, 8 oz. tobacco, 600 cigarettes, 25 novels, dominoes and lots of other things, but of course chiefly it holds my official papers etc.

We are in pleasant country, much like the country we have just left and once more living the life of lotus eaters. I have been round visiting various other officers this morning, it was rather like a state walk, wearing an open neck shirt, no tunic, clean brown boots and carrying my stick. Norman, needless to say, is very comfortably billeted in a local chateau with the CO.

Last night, as a gesture, despite sleeping out in the open, I wore pyjamas. It rained but I was well covered and came to no harm, although rather shaken when there was an air raid warning, but I turned over and pretended that I had not heard it.

Earlier in the evening I saw a most magnificent air attack by our air force about 7 or 8 miles away. Several hundred bombers and not an enemy plane to be seen. I have not seen any enemy aircraft since we arrived. It is all very heartening and there must be good prospects of Christmas dinner at home. I make no apology for being the incurable optimist.

Jim Walker has just been into my office (a 3 tonner) and also drunk a toast and I have had my midday meal and I am finishing this waiting for the char (tea) to arrive.

I cannot remember much of what I wrote in my first letter, it was all very rushed. Thank you again for your 2 letters which greeted me on my arrival. I was glad to hear that your Mother would carry out my desires though it was a great request. Have nothing to do with Tatham's price, it is pouring money in to the drain.

I always thought the lad would grow up to be arrogant and anyway it is one of your latent qualities.

PRUNES FOR BREAKFAST

I am glad JE is going from strength to strength. I shall try and write to Rugby School in the next day or two.

Darling, this is far too long a letter and don't expect them too often.

All my love.

Edward. x.

After two days of reconnaissance patrols, the 6th July was a hell of a tiring day for everyone, though we were quite far behind the front line, and therefore in no immediate danger. In the morning, the entire battalion was briefed on a model, built by the Intelligence boys and laid out on the ground, of the terrain that would lie ahead. Later on, the battalion was mobilised in order to practice advancing through crops for tactical familiarisation before actually engaging into the battle ahead. During the day we were reminded to keep our heads down by the never-ending issue of salvo after salvo from the big naval guns lying off the coast. Their huge shells went whistling past us to annihilate some target far ahead, as did those of the nearby 25 pounders, manned by the Royal Artillery, practicing their ranging. We completely flattened a number of fields of ripe standing corn and wheat, no doubt much to the chagrin of the local farmers. Their annual crop had just gone for a burton, but of course, like other farmers throughout Normandy they would eventually be left to glean for the remains.

There were a couple of points that were drummed in to us about those cornfields, both of which were to serve us well in the weeks to come. The first was that green and inexperienced troops were likely as not to lie down when crossing a cornfield, should the enemy open fire on them. It was a natural reaction. However, it had been found from bitter experience that men who went to ground in such circumstances were a hell of a job to get upright and get going forward again. The trick was always to keep on going forward, even if bent double. The second point was to always keep in mind that the more experienced Germans would often cut swathes of corn in straight lines across a field of standing crops in order to provide them with sighted firing lines. Anyone coming across such should be very aware of the possibility of nearby Germans with machine guns dug in and ready to rain death and destruction on our infantry.

The area in which we were then situated was a mass of corn and wheat fields – all coming to a lovely golden yellow and nearly ripe for harvesting – or lush green fields, quite small, full of cattle and surrounded by hedges. This was not open rolling countryside, the type of terrain so much preferred by heavy armour. Infantry and armour spent the day traversing the fields, with specialist officers indicating where our infantry should take up defensive positions, where they should be ready to advance, and how they should move when in close support of our tanks. Those officers drummed into everyone once again that one could use a tank as a defensive shield, but that one should not get so close that the damned thing ran over you if it turned suddenly as it acquired a target. Most men were still not really aware that the forward vision of a tank driver was extremely limited, and that the sideways vision was almost non-existent, the only peripheral vision coming either from the commander poking his head out of the turret, or by using the small periscope.

Why was it only now, when we were actually in the field, that they realised we still needed training in close combat support with tanks? And vice versa, because the tank boys had absolutely no understanding of basic infantry warfare, and would simply overrun us in a trice. In their separate roles the infantry and the armour needed to support each other, and required an understanding of each other's needs in battle.

Slightly further away from our positions, another troop of RA support gunners were ranging their 25 pounders and firing practice rounds at a distant barn, reducing it quickly to a smouldering pile of rubble. My eardrums were beginning to ache.

Later on, pushing further forward, we slogged away along all those quaint country lanes, moving past field after field of artichokes standing tall on their dark green stems, the ripening heads swaying slightly in the freshening breeze. And this, of course, was camembert country, one of my favourite cheeses! Were they still making camembert around here, in all this devastation? I would have to find out.

We had done all that practising, of course, a number of times back in England, but it seemed very strange, and different, to be doing it over in France, in what had to be termed hostile territory. I think that we learned quite a lot from the day. I was fortunate enough to view much of it from the back of my sergeant's jeep, keeping both him and my signaller company, and a watchful eye over my men.

The cows in the nearby fields, those that were left, no longer exhibited much interest in us, unless a tank got quite close. The farmers, I was not so sure about. A few of them seemed to see us as saviours, but most appeared to think that we were little better than the *'Boche'* that had so recently vacated the area. I supposed that if I had had my entire yearly crop of cereals devastated by troop movements and shell holes, I might have thought the same, but I did wish that they could take a longer view of everything. After all, this was the second time that we had needed to come over there to rescue their benighted country, and we were still waiting for their 'thank you' for the first time!

Undated.
Darling,

The sun is just breaking through the rather heavy mist and I think it is going to be a very hot day. Incidentally, I have been getting a lot of cramp lately. Two blokes from the Intelligence section have just called with their map and the situation on our front is very encouraging. We have guns all around and I have a 25 pounder only 50 yds. from my hole, but one gets quite accustomed to them and cotton wool is not really necessary.

I have not spent a lot of time in slit trenches, although not everyone has been so lucky. I have not spoken to a French girl yet, except to buy camembert, and I think they put something in the tea which keeps one's mind off such things. I think I can manage the next 3 or 4 weeks (by which time it will all be over) without troubling about going off the rails.

I am glad JE is going from strength to strength and I shall try and write to Rugby School in the next day or two.

Every bit of love, and God bless.

Edward. x.

Late on the night of the 6th, we witnessed what I afterwards learned to be 443 Halifax and Lancaster heavy bombers dropping 2,276 tons of munitions a short distance ahead to soften up the enemy in their positions just northwest of the city of Caen. It was an amazing sight to see wave after wave of bombers, appearing so tantalisingly briefly between the clouds and dropping huge sticks of bombs on to the enemy, just after they had flown overhead. We could only watch in awe and cover our ears as the night lit up and lethal shrapnel whined far overhead, some of it clattering back through the trees ahead of us. The ground literally shook all around, and it all felt rather comforting to feel that the RAF were in there, doing their bit to soften up the opposition before we had to go hand-to-hand with them on the morrow.

Operation Charnwood was scheduled to commence the next day, the 7th. It was to be the major offensive leading up to the battle for the city. It would be the first time that our battalion had confronted the enemy head-on. General Montgomery had made the taking of Caen an imperative for the first few days of the invasion and even now it had yet to fall.

7th July 1944. (Friday)
7 RN. British Western Expeditionary Force.
Darling,
I have just received your letter (4) dated Sunday although I received a letter from Pop and Lou dated 3rd, yesterday. I understand now why people look forward to receiving letters. Without them one feels absolutely cut off from the world.

PRUNES FOR BREAKFAST

Our first week passed very quietly and I played bridge Sunday, Monday and Tuesday evenings under varying conditions and we made inroads into our limited supply of whiskey. We moved on Wednesday to another location and I think rather more strenuous times are ahead. I am very fit and feel tremendously confident. I feel that the Hun cannot now be long before he is on the run.

I have tried out my French and went into a shop the other day and asked 'Avez-vous du fromage camembert?' and I bought 4 at 11¼ francs each. Apart from this my efforts have been rather spasmodic and usually end with 'je ne comprends pas.'

I feel rather strange receiving letters, as though I was still in England.

I have not received any tobacco yet, although I am not short as I brought 12 oz. with me and since then we have had a NAAFI pack per man, and I get 8 oz. tobacco, 12 oz. sweets and other odds and ends, all this for about 28 frs = 3/-.

Could you send me a tablet of soap and a tin of Andrews about every 3 weeks.

I am glad you are all well. Keep your chin up, it will not be long.

All my love, God bless.

Edward. x.

Having reached our new forming up place, we found ourselves digging in on a reverse slope in cornfields clear of the woods that we knew had been ranged by enemy artillery. This was accomplished by first light on the 8th. The high standing corn would, so we were told, hide us from enemy observation ahead. Well, I hoped that they were right, but I had become quite accomplished in the digging of a slit trench, and then hunkering down in it, tin hat firmly on and gas cape over everything.

The crashing and banging from our own supporting artillery, as their guns let fly towards the enemy, the whistle of overhead shells still being fired by warships off the coast, and the incessant small arms fire meant that, once heads were down, they stayed down if their owners had any sense. I was not quite so lucky. It was my role to see what was going on, closely aided by my spotters who had been positioned a little way ahead. I had my signaller close by, and he was holding a running conversation, relaying to me all the constantly updated orders from battalion HQ.

H-Hour (the set time for the attack to commence) on the 8th was at 0420, just before dawn, and we got the signal to move forward. As we scrambled out from our trenches and holes, forming up into line in some sort of battle readiness, we prayed that our gunners to the rear kept moving their ranging targets forwards, so that we wouldn't run into our own shells as they rained down and exploded. It had happened before, to others. In all there were over 600 guns then aiming a constant barrage at the enemy. I kept a regular stream of information going back via my signaller, detailing almost every yard of our progress.

Enemy defensive shelling rained down on our positions as we pushed ahead. Men went down in the standing crops, where mortars and artillery then took a heavy toll. In the continuing smoke and haze, visibility was quickly reduced to less than 300 yards, and our tanks could neither see the enemy nor our own forward troops from their own start positions so far back.

As dawn eventually broke to reveal the beginning of what would turn out to be another hot and dusty day, we had actually advanced nearly 1¼ miles from the starting point, near Cambes. It took us over three hours to fight our way forward just over a mile. The objectives for the joint operation with 176 Bde. were the German-occupied villages of La Bijude and Epron, heavily defended by their armoured forces and with well dug-in infantry and artillery. Inevitably there was difficult ground between us and them, and with the constant enemy fire, our progress continued to be grindingly slow. I tried, at one stage, carefully concealed in a ditch, to raise a tin hat above the hedge to see what happened. Within moments it was riddled with holes. *Moral: always keep your head down.*

I was not sure at that stage that we would achieve the objective. We were pinned down by counter-fire, and until we got some armour up ahead of us to take out the heavily defended farm buildings on the edge of the village one field away and directly in front of us, we would be going nowhere. As we crouched down, all of us were very concerned about those Moaning Minnies, as they seemed to be universally known. The Jerries had a type of six-barrelled mortar which they called a *'Nebelwerfer'*, or fog mortar because they could also be used to lay smoke. When they were fired off in clusters, they gave off a sort of shrieking sound as they left their barrels and approached us. They had a multiple electrical firing mechanism to enable them to be sent off almost all together if required. The howling and wailing from those things, rising in pitch as they got closer and finally ending in multiple explosions all around us, was calculated to put fear in to the hearts of any opposition. And, truth be told, it most certainly did. If they started to land anywhere close, then it was the signal to hunker down in our slit trenches and pray for deliverance.

The Moaning Minnies were being fired, salvo after salvo, and they were getting closer and closer to our positions, as the Germans found their range and zeroed in on us. Either we were going to have to move, or we had to knock them out. Most of us were literally quaking in our boots at the thought that a direct hit would wipe us out regardless of trying to make ourselves as small as possible in our slit trenches. Clods of earth were actually beginning to rain down on our helmets and shoulders as the mortar rounds impacted nearby, inching ever closer with every salvo.

I got some of my lads to load up some tracer to see if we could pinpoint their origin. They just had to be taken out one way or another before we could do much else. Fortunately, now in close support behind us, hidden behind the hedgerow to our rear, we had a troop of Shermans and as soon as we were able to mark the battery positions for them with our tracer, they let loose and blew them to pieces, lethal hot shrapnel scattering everywhere, injuring or killing the unwary.

Once those Moaning Minnies were out of the way, we could see more clearly that directly ahead and facing our line, some 100 yards distant, were what we soon discovered to be Units of the German 12th SS Panzer Division *Hitlerjugend*. Their infantry was very well dug in; after all, they had had a number of days in which to prepare their defensive positions. All we could really see was a line of steel helmets accompanied by the muzzles of their rifles pointing directly towards us. Behind the infantry, their tanks had their barrels poking over earthwork berms, raised up in front of them as a defensive shield. How on earth, we thought, were we expected to overcome that lot?

There was no leeway in our orders however; they were to advance directly ahead, engage the enemy and push through to take the village. And so, on the next order, we all moved out of our hastily scrabbled foxholes or any other cover that we had found and pressed ahead, trying to keep our line stretched straight across our immediate front. There was ear-splitting noise as the Germans opened up on us with all that they had, the moment that we moved out in to the open. Men started to fall like ninepins, some killed outright by the rifle fire, others with body parts blown off from the impact of passing tank rounds, traversed low to take out the Shermans. The cries and moans were pitiful to hear, and we did our best to blank them out as we kept up the steady advance. Pace after pace, yard after yard. Grindingly slow, occasionally stumbling, but ever pressing on. Occasionally there was some sparse remaining cover to be had – a shattered tree stump, a clump of bushes, even a slight dip in the ground – and some men would huddle down for a moment to get their second wind. And then, with the vocal encouragement from their officers, up and onwards once again. Nearer and nearer we all got, paying a terrible price in men wounded or killed. I cast a quick glance behind me through the fog and chaos of the battle. Our tanks were rumbling up to support us, and, in between them, the stretcher parties were already hard at work clearing away the bodies of the fallen. Those parties would have some long carries that day.

Although their suspected HQ had just been bombed by the Americans, the Germans continued to fight on with great tenacity. Despite their having made a concerted counterattack mid-evening, it was not until about 2200 when the last Germans withdrew from the village in disorder, and we were able to storm into it and claim it as our own. La Bijude was ours, so leaving us breathless, dishevelled and so very sad at the loss of so many of our men.

We then moved on to clear Auberge, a small farming hamlet situated nearby on rising ground. It had been severely stonked and almost obliterated by our artillery and mortars. During that battle for La Bijude and Auberge, we in 7 RN lost 10 Officers and 142 ORs, with the battalion overall losing 45 officers and 648 ORs. It had been a bitter and bloody contest where the fortunes of war dictated that each French field and farm had to be fought over, one after the other. For each small advantage, so many men were lost on both sides. The Germans had been instructed to defend their line to the death if necessary, to prevent us from taking the strategic prize of the city of Caen.

That night, as I sat with a dozen others in a ruined cottage, roofless and with two walls missing, drinking a mug of tea and mulling over the events of the day, I resolved that what we had just been through should never be the sort of information for Elizabeth that I should touch on in any of my letters back home. Best not known by her, and best forgotten by me, too, if that was possible. Though I rather doubted it.

Only a hour or so later, my reveries were rudely shattered by a signal paper being thrust in to my hand, and my signaller then shouting in my ear, telling me that I was required to go back to see the CO in his command post, wherever that might be. I had no idea. I scrabbled backwards from my operational post in the cottage, crouching low and ran like stink across a field, diving head first into a ditch by the hedge at the side of the lane. In the lane there was a half-track Bren Carrier waiting for me, a phlegmatic private soldier leaning on the bonnet puffing away at a cigarette as though without a care in the world. I hopped in, and a few minutes later he delivered me safely to the command post. I ducked my head through the low entrance.

The CO's post had been speedily excavated by an RE armoured bulldozer (another of those 'funnies'), which was now parked to one side. They had created a large stout dugout, protected by comfortingly thick mounds of earth. I had time to notice that the roof had been shored up by the use of some salvaged wooden beams. A temporary safe haven it was, that shielded from the noise of battle as much as anything else, in a central position just behind the line. Inside were the CO, a couple of other officers, a couple of signallers and some other people that I did not recognise. The place was an absolute hive of activity, chaps running in and out every minute.

My newly acquired driver lounged against the side of his Bren Carrier and lit up once more, taking no interest in anything except his latest cigarette.

'At the moment we are going nowhere,' the CO said, after the briefest of salutes. Pointing to his map, he continued: 'We have got to get our vehicles and anti-tank guns along that road to Epron. It's the only way. I want you to take a platoon and clear the way of any mines for us. You have the most experience. Sorry about that. Good luck.' And without further ado he turned away, back to his map board, and a couple of moments later I was back in that Bren Carrier and was turfed out by the same ditch over which I had arrived.

I had to call a number of my more experienced men back from their duties, and discussed the requirements with them. It would not be easy, especially when the mines had been carefully dug in and hidden in a churned up road. I knew the method, and had practiced it many times, but never before had I actually had to do it whilst under enemy fire and being deafened into the bargain. Would my training on those mines courses now pay off?

20

Hell Alley

As soon as I got there and saw what lay ahead, I christened that lane 'Hell Alley'. The Germans had been in full and disordered retreat when they withdrew in panic along it under extreme pressure, back to the village buildings of Epron, in the hope of regrouping. Abandoned equipment lay everywhere. Dead soldiers, dead horses with their entrails hanging out, shattered light artillery, a couple of half-tracks and an upturned tank littered the lane. Amidst all that were broken wooden carts, used to ferry ammunition about. Loose piles of unused ammunition were everywhere. Retreating German tanks had, in their haste to get away, driven straight over some of the corpses, both human and animal, leaving a mulch of red and pink flesh, a sight too horrendous to believe. Through all that carnage we had to pick our way, hunting for those buried mines, pausing only to retch up our last meals and swat the blow flies away.

Clearing those mines was a slow process. We lost a man early on when he trod on one of them. It was a salutary lesson for all my squad. One, for a change, that I did not need to talk to them about. We worked out way forward in silence, quartering every inch of the road. My heart was in my mouth, and I could see that everyone felt the same. This was serious stuff, and I was responsible. Some mines had been concealed in the most disgusting of places, and it was a grindingly slow advance, moving forwards almost inch by inch, checking and re-checking for any anomaly or magnetic reaction. Once we reached the far end of the lane, my signaller called up a tank with a bulldozer blade on the front end, probably the same one that had been parked next to my CO's command post, and once it had driven the length of the lane and carved a wider path through all the mayhem, our vehicles and heavy anti-tank guns could roll forward, closely followed by the 7 RN infantry. I noticed that they all passed by with their eyes fixed firmly straight ahead.

At the time that 7 RN had crossed the start line on the 8th, pressing forward to the south, towards our first objective, we had been unaware of the strength of that enemy resistance in La Bijude. And so, it seemed, had our commanders. By the time that we had finally overcome the opposition, we were all well and truly blooded and bloodied.

So, what were we going to find on the way to Epron, the next battalion objective? It seemed so far away at the time, although I later realised that there was only about 600 yards between the two villages. And Epron was only a couple of miles from the outskirts of Caen. We were that close.

It had been a great comfort to everyone to see a high-winged Auster above us, regularly spotting for new intelligence and relaying back to HQ the position and movement of enemy troops. It buzzed along at about eighty knots, darting towards the enemy lines and then back overhead, waggling its high overhead wing as it zoomed past our positions. There were two on board, the pilot and his spotter, one behind the other in the cabin below that wing. It jigged about, agile as a firefly, to avoid enemy fire, and I really hoped that those two chaps stayed safe, as much for our benefit as theirs.

And so, moving forward from 'Hell Alley', I led a platoon and we came upon a huge – nearly 60 ton – German Panther tank, lying in a ditch, abandoned and desolate, with its mighty gun barrel poking skywards, still broodingly menacing despite its broken tracks

Hell Alley

and bogeys. Further along the road, trying to skirt around the village rather than make a full frontal assault, we passed an open field which was strewn with the charred hulls of brewed up British Shermans, their 17 pounder anti-tank guns pointed all cock-eyed heavenwards.

As we had been ordered, we plodded on wearily across those cratered fields, not really knowing exactly where we were going, except pushing forward to Epron. Always forward. We were no sooner out in the open than the chaos of battle quickly enveloped us. Enemy artillery was being brought down on us and we were being mortared by more Moaning Minnies, all desperate to get our range. Noise raged all around us, indescribable. It beat against all of our senses, until some of us had to hold our ears or stuff them with whatever we had to hand. We halted for a quick breather, and then our own gunners, somewhere behind us and to one side, let fly with a barrage of noise from their dug-in 25 pounders, their shells whistling overhead, and, in the brief lull, it was our turn to move forward yet again. Our tanks were providing devastating fire against the hedges and buildings of the village. Then it was up to us to start the attack.

The enemy was now so close in front that our own gunners were bringing down their fire almost on top of the infantry. The slightest incorrect calibration on the part of those gunners, or the slightest incorrect positioning of our men as we pressed on forward, didn't bear thinking about. My heart was in my mouth, because it was I who was shouting the positions back to control, via my signaller. If he misheard and transmitted something different, then we were all goners.

Suddenly, one of my men raised a hand, signalling us to halt the advance. I crawled forward and saw, poking out of a small copse nearly ahead, the 88 mm barrel of a dreaded German anti-tank gun. Just to look at it struck a chill into all of our hearts as we crouched behind that hedgerow, praying that its commander had not yet seen us. If he had, we were about to become mincemeat. My hand up went up and I sent a muffled signal for absolute silence.

PRUNES FOR BREAKFAST

We needed the heaviest of our armour-piercing shells to take a thing like that out. Nothing that we had with our own tanks came even close. Time for us to backtrack a little. We moved quietly off down a side line of the hedgerow behind us. All of us in single file. From time to time salvoes of mortar or heavy machine gun fire straddled our position, and men dropped to the deck in a flash. At first we thought that they had been hit, but moments later they were on their feet again.

I calculated that, for the last few days of almost unceasing fighting, we had not washed, shaven or taken our boots off. We had received no hot food, so we moodily chewed on whatever was left of our rations. Most of us had barely managed to get any sleep. Some men, like horses, seemingly had learned to sleep on their feet, or at any rate give a jolly good impression of it.

By late evening on the 9th, with a lot of support from others, the battalion had at last overrun and taken Epron, after very heavy fighting and with yet more losses to both sides. When we entered the village, we found nobody there other than a couple of snipers left behind to delay us. They did not delay us for long. Later on, after having sent out some reconnaissance patrols during the night, it was clear that the main body of Germans had withdrawn from contact. They had taken a terrific hammering. The dead left behind were an indicator of that. The battalion drew breath and stayed in the village for more than a day. In that time the battlefield was cleared and I recalled that a service of remembrance was held for the dead of both sides.

Some German prisoners had been captured earlier, and escorted rearwards through our line, most of them so very young, only 17 or 18, it seemed. Just whom had we been fighting?

I heard afterwards that some of those enemy troops we had been facing were elite German formations. Against us had stood some of the most feared of crack German troops: 1st SS Panzer Corps, including some Units of the 12th SS Panzer Division, made up of members of the *Hitlerjugend,* or Hitler Youth. That Division was one of only two that Adolf Hitler had allowed to carry his name in the war, so proud was he of them, and they of he. The other was the *Liebstandarte Adolf Hitler.*

The SS troops of this elite division had been recruited directly from the infamous Hitler Youth movement, and all of them had been completely indoctrinated to believe that Hitler was almost a god and that they were his chosen ones. With an average age of 18, they fought with the greatest of grit and determination. Despite being disarmed and bedraggled, they had strutted along, so very insolent towards us, their captors, and all with dead eyes staring forward. Nothing could shake their belief in an eventual German victory despite their capture. Terrifying, just terrifying, it was. They didn't seem to care whether they lived or died, those boys, so heavily had they been brainwashed to serve their Führer to the bitter end. As they were led away to a temporary holding unit nearer to the rear, their war was over, never to fight again.

As night fell on us, we lay back in our new trenches, some of them recently vacated by the opposition, for a little respite. We received a welcome message from Brigade HQ that another battalion was on the move forward to relieve us, and we were to be temporarily withdrawn from the fighting to one of the designated Rest Areas.

Much later, after the war was ended and there was time for proper recording of the events, I was very proud to have received a personal mention in the official War Story of 7 RN for my actions around La Bijude, Epron and Auberge.

Now that we had pulled back, I thought that I should write to Elizabeth to reassure her, just in case that action we had just been involved in should be reported in the newspapers back home. Those war correspondents were a keen lot. Still, I had resolved not to put anything too dramatic into my letters for fear of upsetting her. Some bits and pieces for her to believe in, but the gory details were best left unsaid, I thought. Time for all that later, if at all.

10th July 1944.
7 RN. British Western Expeditionary Force.
Darling,

I am writing this in a dug out, wearing my tin hat, in the evening at approximately 6 p.m. I have censored my men's letters and think I am still living and have a whole skin.

We have had our first taste of action and it was not too pleasant. I lost one or two of my best lads and was fortunate that they were my only casualties.

I find that my reactions to war are very satisfactory and I think that I acquitted myself with credit. I have seen the most horrible sights and the most incredible devastation but with all I manage to retain a sense of humour which is a great blessing.

We came in for some heavy shelling yesterday afternoon and believe me a slit trench is a great comfort. I have seen chaps who have never done a day's work since they joined the army dig a slit trench in an incredibly short time.

I have lost count of time in the last 2 or 3 days and last night I said in passing to my blokes 'What a lousy occupation digging slit trenches at 8 o'clock on a Saturday evening.' It took at least 3 of them to convince me it was Sunday.

I heard the news for the first time on Sunday evening for several days and I thought it all highly satisfactory.

How are you, my dear? Keeping fit and cheerful, I hope? The lad I take it grows more like his father every day, or doesn't he?

All my love.
Edward. x.

Hell Alley

After those few days of non-stop action, we welcomed the order for withdrawal rearwards for a rest and recuperation period, and moved to regroup at Couvre-Chef, not far away. I could still hear the rumble of the big guns in the far distance, but for a couple of days we were no longer a part of all that. We must re-provision, rearm, make repairs to our mechanised vehicles and do all of a hundred-and-one other things before we were called back to the front line. Oh, and in between all that, we were supposed to get some well-earned rest!

One of my duties was to be in charge of the pay parade. I had to indent for the amount of money that was required for my men, fetch it, check it, and then hand it out to them individually, in sealed envelopes. It usually happened on a Friday, but nobody, by then, bothered to even try to remember the day of the week – except when it was payday, of course. I was so pleased that I still had that old desk with me. I kept all sorts of bits and bobs in it, not just personal stuff like tobacco and whiskey, and it made the Friday pay parade a much easier exercise. I wondered what would eventually become of that desk because surely soon it would have to be left behind.

It seemed strange to see so many new faces in our midst. The battalion as a whole had lost a number of officers, killed or wounded, and quite a few ORs. Some of those joining us now were from other Units that had seen some fighting, which was a blessing for us. Everyone got called together by the CO for a pep talk. He reckoned that we had acquitted ourselves well and done 59 Div. proud.

I regularly made a special point of taking younger members of my platoons to one side and speaking to them confidentially. They were scared stiff, I could see it in their eyes. Un-blooded, they could just as likely freeze when the going got rough, and that could cause us all to be killed. So I was continually doing my best to pump some confidence and backbone in to them. Not that I had had any active service before then either, but it was up to me to show them

PRUNES FOR BREAKFAST

leadership and support. I think it served us all very well, and, if it saved some lives, then my time was well spent.

We were being tested like never before. It had robbed the younger ones in some sense of their childhood. We had all matured well beyond our given years, more rapidly and emotionally than any previous generation.

We had become hoarders of our rations of chocolate bars. We all had them, some of us more than others, but I was careful not to enquire too closely when I saw a haversack stuffed full with them. I expected that they would be bartered in due course for cigarettes, or even for cheese or eggs with the local population. Both of those two items had been sadly lacking from our diets recently, and would be a welcome addition.

The battalion was bivouacked that night adjacent to a stream, still running quite full. After I had searched about and found my pipe and tobacco, lit up and had a few puffs to get it going properly, I sat and idly watched a long column of men wending its way to a Mobile Bath Unit that had been towed along to us. Portable boilers had been hooked up to the stream and, through some strange system that had the better of me, could supply hot water within a marquee where showers had been rigged up. They looked grand, and I hoped I'd have time to get a shower myself.

But all too soon we would get the order to move forward again. And indeed, so we did, barely a couple of hours later. Another briefing, another target, and away we went, back in the direction of the rolling thunder that assaulted our ears the nearer that we got to the front line. I hoped that I was not getting too blasé when I cocked my ear and remarked to nobody in particular: 'I think we are going to be mortared again.' As though I might instead be reckoning on a change in the local weather.

Hell Alley

Before it got dark, there was our friendly Auster once again. It droned overhead, taking a zigzag course towards the enemy lines, and then dancing away before it got close enough for them to open up. They must have had a superb view of the terrain below from up there, even if they were a bit like sitting ducks in the sights of some sharpshooter. But I knew full well that we all benefited from the intelligence that those brave chaps were able to relay back to our command post.

We halted under cover of night and posted our sentries. There was always time for a brew – we were British after all! Having just arrived, one of our first jobs was to build a latrine. We did that in a slit trench at the side of a field, but in the rush to use it, it had not yet been encased. One just sat there without any screening, doing one's duty, as you might say, impervious by now to all going on around one. As the saying goes, *'If you need to go, you need to go…'*

Early next morning we received orders to advance again and found several knocked-out Panthers camouflaged at the edge of the nearby woods. Around them were quite large numbers of enemy dead – most of them very young men – and yet more others, wounded and moaning where they lay further back in the trees. Somebody had clearly got here just before us. We called up our stretcher bearers and got the wounded back behind the line. Their war was over too.

Our orders were to hold the new position, and we were very pleased to do so, knowing that those bloody great Panthers were no longer capable of aiming their big guns at us. The day ticked by as we waited for our next set of orders. Each time I got my signaller to call in asking for fresh orders, I was told just to stand by.

And so, in damp and dirty weapon slits close by those hedges, among the still un-harvested corn slashed flat by old tank tracks and pitted by shell craters, sheltered that ever-astounding being, the British soldier. Often to be seen in his shirt sleeves during daytime because of the heat, his battledress top rolled under his haversack straps, and with his sweaty steel helmet discarded contrary to strict standing orders. Regularly cleaning dust and earth from his rifle or oiling the bolt action or just gazing into space and thinking of home. Or snatching some sleep during a lull; ahead of him, two rifles loaded and mounted ready for instant use, his mate standing to, watching all around him for the slightest enemy movement or the glint of sun off a stray polished surface ahead, the tell-tale sign of enemy movement.

As for myself, I took the opportunity the following morning of stripping off naked and had a 'bath' in a canvas bucket, much to the consternation and amusement of my men. My feet were still playing me up, and I had not had my boots off for nearly two days. I rubbed myself vigorously and dried myself as best I could with what I could find to hand. This was no five star event, I mused, but, as I stood there with my feet in the mucky water, I still found time to admire the magnificent trees nearby and the golden yellow of the crops left standing.

New orders finally came in. Time to go again. I hoped that what was left of those half-flattened crops might offer us some protection.

Rifles at the ready, we waited for the minute hand to reach 1400 and on the second, 900 guns of various calibres, topped by the 15 inch broadsides from the distant warships lying off the beaches, spewed forth an inferno of aerial death. There was a continuous rolling thunder as different batches of our heavy artillery opened up. Near to us, the concealed 25 pounders of our artillery behind the hedges and in the fields on either side, released their armoured shells to whine over our heads and reap destruction upon our enemy.

We began the advance once again, this time under the cover of a smoke screen that had been laid down right across our line, not

Hell Alley

only to cover our own advance, but to prevent those Panthers from seeing our positions and knocking seven bells out of our dug-in 25 pounder artillery, busy blasting away at their last known positions. Then, overrunning the German positions as we continued the relentless slow advance, we passed by their dead. We looked on as they lay on their backs in the long grass, frozen in time where they had fallen, many still propped up on their haversacks, their blank eyes staring into the far distance, never to see home again.

Much as usual when in the white heat of battle, we were for the most part in bewildered ignorance of what was happening around us. I was being fed basic information on which way we should advance, what our objective was, and how long it should take us to achieve it. But it was just isolated information, generally denying the bigger picture. When we eventually dug in later on, the drizzling rain dripped into our slits and soon got down or necks and into our boots. We had had no hot food since the day before yesterday when we had left that last Rest Area. The bigger shells jarred us to the bone as they exploded nearby and splattered us with lumps of earth and grass. All around were the ghostly faces of the dead, still lying where they had fallen, ours and theirs, white in the gloom of the night, lit from time to time by the flashes from our heavy guns.

Throughout the night, one of our field regiments continued to rain shells into the darkness in a prolonged assault on the enemy line, keeping them at bay as we regrouped and rearmed. Nearby was parked under camouflaging tree branches one of those fearsome Crocodile flame-thrower tanks, off duty for a moment from spitting huge gouts of fire towards the enemy. I had seen them before, but not actually in action, and I was not sure that I actually wanted to see it launch its disgusting long tongue of flame, frying anyone in its path. I supposed that it was a necessary evil, clearing our way forward.

For reasons of morale and sanitation, both sides had the tacit agreement that the dead had to be got under ground as soon as practicable. Everyone tried to do that when they were able. Occasionally I volunteered to be a member of one of the burial parties. On one occasion I came across a man that I knew quite well. He was a Sergeant, stone dead with a bullet hole clean through his forehead. He had not been wearing his tin hat, or perhaps it had just fallen off. He lay propped against a hedge, huddled over, still clutching his Sten gun, with faint surprise registering on his face. His mates were nowhere to be seen.

A long shallow trench was quickly dug and bodies were brought along, either shrouded in a tarpaulin, or lying on a stretcher. We did our best to honour our fallen, to treat their bodies with the utmost respect, and to bury them with a quick prayer. There was no time for more.

21
Battle Lines

I received an immediate promotion to the rank of Captain on the 10th July. I liked to think that it was deserved because of my actions in the preceding days in the battle for Caen around Epron, La Bijude and Auberge. I thought that I had acquitted myself well in the face of the enemy, my first real action against the opposition. But perhaps it was because another Captain had been killed and they just needed to fill the gap? I supposed that I would never know.

We were then pulled off the front line again and the battalion retired to the designated Rest Area at Ryes, to equip ourselves anew with all that had been lost or broken in the previous week or so. We were there for a very welcome three days. It was back towards the beaches where we had landed, what seemed ages ago. When I had completed my paperwork and reports, I took some transport down there to have a look at what was going on. I could not help but gaze in total astonishment at the professionalism of the supply system, still then in full swing. But as my eye panned further away, I could see that there remained all that flotsam of war bobbing offshore to remind one of what had taken place just weeks before. Thankfully now, there were no bodies left on the beach or in the water.

'Mail up!' went the shout later on, after my return, and yes, there was one from Elizabeth! I never ceased to wonder exactly who was in charge of the logistics of getting a letter from Ripley in Derbyshire into my hands in a tent somewhere in Normandy, when even I did

not often know exactly where I was. I would have given the chap in charge of the Forces GPO an instant knighthood. It made for a very happy evening all round, made happier as my new Company all got together to sing a few songs in less than perfect harmony. I led them into *'Ten Green Bottles'*, followed by *'Green Grow The Rushes O'* and *'O Danny Boy'*. After a tot of rum all round, I think that we finished up with that old stalwart *'It's A Long Way To Tipperary'*. As I said, a very happy evening all round; and inevitably it was the lull before the next storm.

12th July 1944.
7 RN. British Western Expeditionary Force.
Darling,
    I was glad to get your letter yesterday, and so to know that you are receiving mine.

    We are now removed to a more comfortable spot from that in which I last wrote you. It is now about 8.50 p.m. and I am waiting for the boys to produce the supper, steak and kidney pie (tinned), onions and potatoes removed yesterday from a French garden. We also managed to get three lb. of honey from the same garden so this afternoon we had honey for tea, with bread, being the first bread we have had since leaving England. However, tinned food is very good.

    On the morning of the battle, I played rummy with Norris Hill while waiting for our attack to begin and lost 150 Frs. I gather however the CO was so impressed with my conduct that I am now 2 i/c A Coy (Capt.). I am very sorry to leave my Ptn. and they were rather upset at me leaving. It is not quite the job I would have chosen, but I have no option but to accept.

    I am so glad that you are cheerful, and thankful you are away from the flying b's. Your bet appears to have been a good one, but I don't think I would follow that stable too closely in future.

    I had no idea I was as popular as you make me out to be. Are you sure you are not pulling my leg?

Battle Lines

Tell John his Daddy often thinks of him.
Keep smiling, and God bless you.
Edward. x.

On the 16th, the battalion formed up again in the Concentration Area at Loucelles. A few days later (I think it was the 23rd) we learned that we were henceforth to be known as part of the British Liberation Army (BLA) rather than the British Western Expeditionary Force (BWEF) and to use that nomenclature on our correspondence home for identification purposes. I supposed that some big spark at general HQ had dreamed that one up.

The battalion moved as soon as everything was ready and joined in Operation Pomegranate, which was centred round the battle for Noyers. I was not there because A Company of 7 RN was held in reserve, whilst the remainder of 59 Div. was committed in the centre of the attacking force, under the general command of XXX Corps. Nevertheless, a couple of days filled with anguish as we learned of comrades that had been killed, and awaited the call to take their places in the line.

16th July 1944. (Sunday)
7 RN. British Liberation Army (BLA).
Darling,

I received your No 6 on Thursday also one from Lou and one from Freda all of which make me feel much nearer home. You will note the new heading, it does not mean I am now in another army it is still the same one fighting the same dour German who at the moment disputes every inch.

I have fallen asleep this afternoon, a most strange thing for me to do. I think it must be the effects of my new Coy. for there is little for me to do after the first half hour. However, I expect I shall be commanding the Coy. in another week or two, after all I did say when I purchased my new service dress that I should be a major within a month of landing in France.

PRUNES FOR BREAKFAST

Unfortunately I have had to leave the desk-box behind for the time being but the Assault Platoon have promised to look after it for me.

I have been thinking of things I may require, sweets certainly not, I am almost suffering from chocolate and sweet diabetes. Two handkerchiefs, a few razor blades and half a bottle of rum a month, I suggest.

I was very annoyed this afternoon when I missed my first opportunity to have a proper bath since landing owing to an error by the signaller. However, I propose to have a complete wash down followed by a game of bridge, this followed by supper with the Assault Ptn. They were very cut up when I left them, but Newlands could not bring himself to leave them, so I now have a new batman.

I note that the lad calls all soldiers 'Dadda' and feel that after all he can hardly be blamed.

I think any idea of spending £200 on the Farm House should be cut out, anything more than £50 is uneconomical.

Don't worry about me, look after yourself.

All my love.

Edward. x.

The battalion found itself on the Allied frontline once again, at the village of Brettvillette. That area of Normandy, famous for its lush meadows and grazing cattle before the war, still contained some of those poor brutes, but with their innards hanging out, and all around them was the stench of putrefaction, as they lay, their legs in the air, stiff and swollen in death. I was not really surprised at the animosity of some farmers, who had lost their livelihoods to German or Allied bullets.

As we moved along silently in the night from hedgerow to field, to next hedgerow, the foul smell was always with us in our nostrils, making some of the lads physically sick. It was quite grotesque to see those dead cattle by whatever moonlight there was. Usually one or more legs had been blown off by blast or shrapnel. When they had been rotting in the fields for a few days, the stench was quite unbelievable and sapped morale; to have that overpowering stink in your nostrils whilst you were trying to avoid being killed by Germans was truly not helpful to one's concentration. Now, pits were being dug and they were being buried. Where a heavy machine gun had ripped through a whole group, then a bulldozer was sent forward to shovel them in all together. It was a strange necessity of that war that I had not even considered before.

But our chaps were now getting quite adept at catching the remaining uninjured cows. The beasts would plod mournfully towards us and stand there with their heads hung low, mooing mournfully. They were clearly distressed at having nobody to milk them, suffering from painfully engorged udders. The Leicestershire farmer lads amongst us were quick to go and scratch their foreheads before leaning down and tugging calmly on their udders, quite gently, with long smooth strokes, aiming the spurts of milk into billy cans or mess tins, with the result that our next brew was tasty beyond anything with the addition of some of the really fresh stuff.

19th July 1944. (Wednesday)
7 RN. BLA.
Darling,

    Just a line to let you know how sweet you are. I received a letter on Sunday and 2 parcels and a letter on Monday. I was horrified to see the chocolate and have asked the Mess Corporal to hold it until I can send it back to you. I have a large tin which I am hoping to send to you.

    I am having a quiet time at the moment, as I have been left out of the battle, a sort of first reserve and dodge about with a few chaps a mile or two behind the Bn. I said a quiet time, we have 3 medium guns within a hundred yards of us, literally ear splitting.

    I am very fit and thank you very much for sending everything. This is only a short letter as everyone is making a move and waiting impatiently for me.

    Every bit of love.
    Edward. x.

PRUNES FOR BREAKFAST

It had been nearly a week since I last wrote to Elizabeth. On the 22nd, we moved to the designated battalion Rest Area near Tessel for a breather and R&R. Now that was over, we had moved forward once again to the new front line near Bordel on the 25th, and I was constrained to put pen to paper once again. I had promised to keep Elizabeth informed of what I have been doing, but there was the official censor to be considered, let alone the censorship that had been self-imposed. I did not want her to learn the full horrors of the war. It would serve for nothing except pain and anguish.

26th July 1944. (Wednesday)
7 RN. BLA.
Darling,

    I received two letters from you on Monday, one written on Monday and the other on Thursday. We had a little delay in receiving letters last week due to the weather. I read them both whilst on 'stand to' the following morning between 5.15 and 6.15 a.m. I am constrained to think that absence makes the heart grow fonder, if possible.

    I went out to the front line on Monday, the CO wishing me to superintend the laying of a minefield, but we are out again now for a bit of renovation (sic). I have been going about today just as I would at Stamford, brown shoes, perfect creases, stick etc.

    I slept last night in an old schoolroom, being the first night under a roof since leaving England. The walls are very thick so I am risking any bombs or shells.

    I have been out this afternoon fetching money for the Coy, 26,000 Frs. sounds a terrible lot but is only in fact about £130. I have only spent 100 Frs. of my original 800, although I have given the Sapper stevedores 200, batman 100, bought 3 bots whiskey, 12 ozs tobacco, 70 cigarettes and 10 camembert cheeses. Not bad, I reckon on 100 Frs.

    I heard from Betty on Sunday and she told me of the evacuees. I have whilst writing received your letter No 10 posted Sunday, which is very good.

I am sorry to hear about the lad's teeth, but he will soon recover. How is his walking and talking by the way?

Darling, next time I write I will try and tell you something of the battle.

All my love, and God bless.

Edward. x.

When the opportunity arose, we had been digging up fresh potatoes in kitchen gardens as we passed through shattered farms and villages. It had been on standing orders that we were not supposed to do it, but I just could not bring myself to forbid my men, provided that they had checked for mines and booby traps. There was nobody left thereabouts to eat the stuff anyway, and it would just have rotted in the ground.

The tank boys had been learning from us, methinks. A column of tanks came past us from their overnight laager, on their way forward and almost all of them had boxes slung along the front of their machines. From those boxes came loud squawking noises. They had captured live hens, which were due, no doubt, to meet their makers at the next stop, and provide some tasty meals. The initiative of the British soldier was boundless.

From then on we always did some swaps whenever we could; our freshly dug potatoes in exchange for some of their chickens.

27th July 1944. (Thursday)
7 RN. BLA.
Darling,

I think this must be my No 9. I have received your No 10. I have heard from Pop and Esmé, but nothing from you for several days.

Are you short of money? As you know, I gave the Bank instructions to pay you £20 a month. As for the car, tell Anthony I will accept the best offer over £300. How is the Farm House getting on?

As for the battle, on Saturday July 8 we took the villages of La Bijude, Epron and Auberge in an action that will certainly go down

PRUNES FOR BREAKFAST

in the history of the war. As far as I was concerned I sent one section with a Rifle Coy. and the other section had to clear the road for vehicles to La Bijude.

I understood that the village had been taken by a Unit on our right and we moved off quite bravely, passing through some mortar concentrations. I got to within 150 yards of the village when I found that the other Unit had withdrawn and that I was well in advance of our own troops, snipers on either side, and with mortars coming down uncomfortably close. When I heard that a couple of Tiger tanks were only about 200 yards away I decided on an orderly withdrawal. Hence my reputation for being unpurturbable (sic) in battle. Believe me, I was far from unpurturbable and my language to the first little subaltern of a rifle Coy. that I saw was unprintable! Looking back, I think that with a little determination we could have taken the village and then been perhaps mentioned in the newspapers.

I went out with Norman yesterday and we found an officer's shop and spent quite a lot of money. Handkerchiefs are only 4d each so don't bother to send any more in future.

Norman has just been on the phone to inform me that SAOC 2nd Army (a big bug) has reported us for speeding, so just going across to see him!

All my love, darling.

Edward. x.

We had moved back to the reserve Rest Area designated for the battalion at Rauray, and I was going about my own business, after organising future troop movements on the afternoon of the 29th July, settling my men in and making sure that they got re-provisioned and rearmed, when some clown standing on the crossroads in the village, to all intentions giving a fair impression of the local bobby but in the blancoed khaki of an MP, tried to 'do' Norman for speeding! How could that happen in the middle of a war? What speed was speeding anyway, and why?

Norman was at the wheel of the HQ jeep, plastered with flags and banners. Despite trying to pull rank on the MP, he was told that he was going to be reported.

He called me back later on. 'Eddie, I have a bit of a problem with that speeding offence. Do you think that we might temporarily swap identities, and then I can say that it was you that was driving? If I'm on the charge form, it could land me in a bit of uncomfortably hot water here at HQ. If your name is on it, then it is unlikely to affect you, and anyway, I will pull a few strings from here to get it all cancelled. Brigade HQ just does not have the time to be bothered with such stupid minor incidents.'

And like a mug, I just said 'OK.'

Norman, of course, needed to keep a low profile, because he was attached to HQ and billeted in the local chateau with all the brass hats, so it was yours truly that was going to have to carry the can. I determined to go and give someone a piece of my mind if I was being put in the frame. All just too daft to have even made it up.

Meanwhile, our survival when on the front line seemed more a matter of luck than anything. We were being machine gunned from the air, shelled by artillery, mortared nightly, sniped at, machine gunned by ground forces, and then there were countless mines and booby traps which we had to circumvent, either by going around them or by digging them up and taking them away to be safely exploded elsewhere. And some damn fool was worried, in the midst of all that, about me speeding in a bloody jeep.

31st July 1944. (Monday)
7 RN. BLA.
Darling,
*   I was delighted to get your letter (Wednesday) and letter and parcel (Thursday). I know it is a constant worry for you. The newspapers are chiefly to blame because they exaggerate everything. Our recent withdrawal on the Caen front was only about 1000 yds.*

PRUNES FOR BREAKFAST

(I was not there) and it was chiefly a matter of policy. From the reading of the papers it seemed that we must be going backwards so fast that I hadn't time to put my boots on! It is ridiculous.

You have at least 2 letters on the way, but I am afraid that it is now taking a day or two longer for letters to arrive here.

For the last 5 or 6 days I have been living a life of ease and luxury, sleeping in a schoolroom, walls 18 inches thick. We have not been in a slit trench once although the Germans are only about 2000 yards away. We had a Church Service with the band in the orchard yesterday morning and a concert in the evening at which I contributed one or two of my stories.

I have a new hat and have been going about for the last 3 or 4 days more immaculately dressed than I did at Margate, calling forth some derision from my fellow officers. I only wear boots now and again.

All I need in future is the occasional tin of Andrews, everything else is in ample supply, and much cheaper. It was very sweet of you to send the rum. The tobacco has not arrived, but I am not worried about it and I have more than I can cope with. Rather a blow about my parcel. I have 2 x 4lb tins of chocolate and sweets to send, but at the moment it is forbidden, but I am having the matter taken up. Cheese has now gone on the rationed list, too bad.

Unsigned.

One of the famous names of the battle for Normandy was that of the town of Villers-Bocage, and I should therefore mention it, although I was not part of the battle to take the town from the Germans, who defended it extremely heavily. The town had been bombed time after time by the RAF and it was fair to say that it was a shambles, although pockets of German troops, including some tanks and the inevitable snipers still remained, hidden, often in churches in the hope that we would not attack them there. However, bombing was generally of an indiscriminatory nature, and many churches had been at least partially shattered, some just with their ruined towers or spires pointing upwards towards heaven, as though in silent beseechment of God to end all the slaughter.

176 Bde. had the secondary task of flushing out the remainder of the German defenders from the town, once the main force had gone in, and then to move forward to the banks of the River Orne, and to force a crossing if possible. So once again we in 7 RN were held back in reserve, though we eventually moved through the town on the 3rd August, most of the men hitching lifts on Churchill tanks of 9 RTR. I had never seen such utter devastation of a town that until very recently must have been so very attractive. The fortunes of war certainly hit that place very hard, albeit necessarily so.

We suddenly, without warning, found ourselves in a strangely different terrain: the *bocage*. It must still be one of the most famous – and misunderstood – words to have come out of the Normandy campaign. There was an extensive land area around, for example, that town of Villers-Bocage, where the farming land was split up in to small fields, surrounded by high hedges. The hedges were thick and dense, more so than back in England, and in between them were lanes to enable the movement of farming and other traffic. As in Devon and Somerset, those lanes had become sunken through the passage of time, worn away by the feet of numerous horses and people, the wheels of carts, tractors, and the like.

It was deeply unfortunate that nobody had passed this vital information back to the invasion planners. Aerial reconnaissance had not shown just how low those lanes had become, nor how high – and thick – were the hedges. I suppose that the French Resistance were so used to it that it seemed normal to them, and they had made no mention of it back to their control officers either.

When the invasion forces moved inland from the beachheads, traversing open fields and pastures dotted with farmhouses and villages, they quickly discovered that the Germans had learned to take advantage of the different type of terrain and how to use it against us. German tanks would position themselves at crossroads or bends in the road. They parked in the field behind the hedge, or, more often, dug themselves in. The hedge was so thick that the tank could not be seen. Only the gun barrel protruded through the thickness of the hedge, capable of traversing down the lane and blowing us to smithereens before we even knew that they were there. The lanes were too narrow for us to turn our vehicles or artillery around to beat a temporary tactical retreat, so all we could do was to blast our way backwards and hope that we could get away before the tank could reload. In most cases, there was not sufficient time.

Nor were we able to get away through the hedges, which were too thick for men to scrabble through. And the lanes were too low, the verges too high. The whole area provided, for a time, perfect killing fields for the Germans.

In time though, we learned how to combat the problem. We had to use extra reconnaissance and then employ our own armour to punch our way through so that we could use the same sort of tactics as the enemy was using on us. Our armoured friends also learned better where to place themselves to avoid being brewed up. In turn, when we discovered hidden enemy tanks in the *bocage*, we learned how to sneak up on them and blast them at very close range with a PIAT anti-tank gun from one of our specialist platoons. If the operator could hit the tank in one of weak spots, at close range, then a PIAT was a very formidable weapon. Nevertheless, the word *bocage* will remain in the memory of everyone who was there, for the rest of their lives. Far too many men were lost to us unnecessarily in that veritable maze of country lanes.

4th August 1944. (Friday)
7 RN. BLA.
Darling,
    Your letter, No. 12, reached me last night about 7 o'clock, just as I was setting out for fresh fields. It was very sweet and made me feel homesick. We left our comfortable schoolroom last night after 9

days peace and comparative comfort and found ourselves in the middle of a wheat field, when we arrived at our new destination. Unfortunately the field had not been occupied before, and so we had to dig and I dug for about 2 ½ hours with an interval for a little bully stew and I had a can of beer and a pipe at about 11 p.m. By this time I was barely 15 inches down, the ground being as rough as on Salisbury Plain. I decided that this was deep enough, and had my bed pushed into it and got down. I slept very well, apart from some vicious mosquitoes which proceeded to play hell with me, and 3 or 4 shells which fell quite harmlessly several hundred yards away.

I arose about 7 a.m. (Reveille was at 6) having previously awakened my batman by throwing stones at him. Breakfast would have been quite good, porridge, bacon and beans and now white bread and tea, had I got up immediately, but I was too lazy as it was so cold. However, wearing my Ashbeian sweater I sat on a box and decided that the world is very large, the grass very green and I am a very small person in the world.

After which comforting meditation I proceeded to complete my toilet and proceeded over to my Company Commander and commiserated with him on his mosquito bites. This done, and having materially raised the morale of HQ, I returned to my Unit, censored several letters, read yours for the second time, decided what a lucky fellow I am to have such a sweet wife, and thought I should write you immediately.

Unsigned.

PS. The dairy I should put slightly left of the stable facing south.

Our next major objective was to get the whole battalion across the River Orne as soon as possible. We pushed on through the countryside and eventually reached the river at a small village called Goupillieres. Through the dusty shambles of what remained of the outskirts we watched the progress of an enormous convoy crammed with Wehrmacht prisoners being herded back to an Allied prisoner pick-up point.

PRUNES FOR BREAKFAST

We entered the village so very carefully. We had been caught before. We inched forwards, halting on the outskirts and then clearing each house, one by one. Anywhere apart from the main street, which had obviously been cleared, was certain to have been booby trapped by the retreating Germans.

They always seemed to find the time to do that, even when *in extremis*. They appeared to have no respect for their fallen comrades, and we had come across quite a lot of cases where they had left a dead soldier lying at the side of the road. When we arrived and went to move him, he would explode, killing one or more of our men. The Germans had booby trapped their own men! Another of their ploys that we had come across more recently was to leave their dead where they fell. We had now got wise to that one, having heard that a couple of them jumped up and stuck their bayonets into some of our unsuspecting men after they had moved on past. We made sure that such was never going to happen to us. A quick bullet or bayonet…

It took us until the 5th August to find a nearly suitable crossing place. I was still leading A Company, which had been tasked with overcoming the problem, and so, under cover of darkness, I hand-picked some of my men and led them down to the river bank, a little way away from the village of Ouffieres, towards a place a little further north, where HQ had directed me should be possible for such a crossing to be made. Of course, the retreating German forces had blown the little bridge. Under normal circumstances, one would have passed on by and looked for somewhere more sensible, but this was war, and it was imperative for the whole battalion to cross that river in short order.

As well as that blown bridge, you could see that the Germans had been there before us. The ground was churned up to a muddy morass by tank tracks. I later learned that that particular area, with the village of Les Moutiers-en-Cinglais and the nearby Fôret de Grimbosq, had been the forward HQ of 1 SS Panzer Corps on the

6th June, the day of the invasion, held back by Hitler in reserve. The famous – or infamous – Sepp Dietrich was the commander of the Corps, and was to go down in history as one of the best German Panzer Corps commanders of the war.

I was beginning to get that odd feeling deep inside me that all was not going to go too well. Perhaps it's the benefit of hindsight. At the last O Group the orders issued meant that I and my Company were going to be right in the forefront of what appeared to be a pretty serious battle ahead. 7 RN were to spearhead part of the advance, and, because of my technical knowledge as an instructor, I would be leading a Pioneer platoon in the forming of the bridge over the river. We had less than a day to get ourselves ready and to accumulate all of the mechanised support that we thought would be needed.

On the other side of the river was a heavy concentration of crack German infantry, well dug in, and with artillery and in-depth armoured support concealed in the nearby forest. Were we going to be sitting ducks for them?

I thought it best to write a letter to Elizabeth before we really got going. I was not sure when the next opportunity might present itself. If at all.

6th August 1944. (Sunday)
7 RN. BLA. – in a Jeep at 11.40 hrs.
Darling,

26 hours have passed since I described 14 hours in the life of a soldier so as we are waiting on virgin ground in France I thought I would use the time and write to you. Break for 30 secs. while I re-light pipe. When and where I shall finish this letter I do not know since we are really looking for the Hun.

We left our last location at 5.30 pm Friday night, the troops riding on Churchills and self in a Jeep, but after an hour or so I had to join them, and what a dusty outing it was. It could have been no worse in Libya.

PRUNES FOR BREAKFAST

We travelled about 9 miles but the Jerry had apparently heard I was coming and had drawn out, leaving nothing but mines and destruction.

At 10 p.m. we called a halt and settled down to dig more slit trenches. It was hard going and it was not until 1.30 a.m. that I was satisfied that it would give reasonable protection if the Hun started any games. However, a big mug of tea, some bread and cheese, and a liberal rum (thank you very much) helped me along until our Order Group at 0200 hrs. I managed a little sleep under the 15 cwt. And woke at 4.45 and we had breakfast of porridge, sausage and beans and bread after which I washed and shaved…I then read an amusing letter from Esmé and Thursday's paper, both arriving too late to read last night.

Having discovered several fowls which I had kept alive and put in a box and inspected a cemetery containing approx. 120 good Jerry's, we moved off. We have now covered about 6 miles of country over which British troops have not previously travelled and have not come up against the Hun. Not a bad morning's work, we shall be in Paris before next weekend at this rate.

I am afraid I spoke too soon, someone has just started firing and also I think we are about to get moving in the direction from which it came. Like the Duke of Plaza Toro, I am well to the rear.

I forgot to mention that yesterday I censored about 40 letters, and calamity, had stolen from me a tin of tobacco, a pipe, and my best lighter. Be of good cheer, sweetie pie, all is well.

Your ever loving.
Edward. x.

Fancy somebody nicking my pipe! It could only have been one of our people. I supposed that I could get over that, but to have had taken my best lighter was just one step too far. That lighter had been with me for years; all over the place in England, Ireland, Wales, the Isle of Man, and now France. It was a really nice quality one, given to me by Elizabeth when we first went out courting together, and she had arranged for it to be engraved with my initials on the bottom left hand corner. I was particularly fond of it because it had a big wind protector around the flame especially for pipe smokers. My eyes were going to be peeled extremely carefully from now on when anyone close by was to light up.

We started that night of the 6th to form the bridgehead, which we did by initially fording the river opposite the village of Grimbosq. We got ourselves totally saturated in the process, whilst becoming quickly petrified by the hail of German fire over our position. They had quickly worked out that we were an advance party intent on reconnoitring the area for a possible river crossing. Despite the strong German defensive position, by 0800 the next morning, the 7th, a bridge had been formed near Le Bas. It had been a hard night, with the enemy repeatedly trying to dislodge our forces from the fledgling bridgehead.

Later that same day we captured Grimbosq village itself and also the nearby hamlet of Le Bas, which after the war became known as Grimbosq Halte, and occupied them.

I was later proud that, in the official War Story of 7 RN, I received a particular mention for helping to deliver that objective. The main opposition to us came from 1 SS Panzer Corps. Various Divisions had been left behind when they advanced to other objectives. One such turned out to be some Units of the 12th SS Panzer Division *Hitlerjugend* which attacked again and again with about forty-four tanks supported by infantry and artillery. They threw everything that they had at us, and the battle raged on for a couple of days, with both sides gaining and losing ground; but we never got pushed back into the Orne. By then supporting troops had also established a strengthened and wider bridgehead, some 3 km in length and 1½ km in depth, and then we were there to stay.

The fighting was very heavy and the battalion continued to hold the bridgehead, but then yet another German offensive retook the village of Grimbosq. Fifty-four Mitchell medium bombers were sent but German flak was so effective that thirty-six of them were hit, some too damaged to return to England. German casualties were minimal but defence of this bridgehead was to cost 7 RN forty-two killed, 111 wounded and seventy-three missing. One of my fellow officers, Captain David Jamieson, was awarded a VC for his part in the fighting. His actions were quickly reported in various newspapers along these lines:

> *On the night of the 6th/7th, Captain Jamieson was in charge of a company of 7 RN that had been instrumental in establishing a bridgehead over the River Orne, near to the village of Grimbosq. For nearly thirty-six hours of heavy and continuous fighting, he led his men from the front, despite having been wounded twice, calling down artillery fire on to the opposing German positions, and so helped to maintain the bridgehead and repulsing seven counterattacks. At times his position seemed hopeless, but on each occasion it was saved by his coolness and determination under tremendous enemy fire. Contrary to orders he refused to leave his men, despite his wounds.*

Although I knew Jamieson, and was fighting close nearby, I was not next to him on that night, but felt extremely proud that a member of the Regiment should be so honoured and be in receipt of what has always been acknowledged to be the ultimate accolade for valour. The citation was granted on the 27th October 1944.

On the 8th, during that very heavy German counterattack, the battalion had been fighting continuously by then for over three days and nights, almost all of us without any sleep worthy of mention, and only one hot meal, brought forward on jeeps. We were holding the line with the greatest of difficulty against numerically superior enemy forces supported by heavy tanks. As a result, the battalion as a whole was severely mauled and weakened.

My own position on that fateful day was that I and my men found ourselves almost encircled by German infantry, with nowhere left to go. They tried to move around us, to the right, but we kept them off with accurate 2 inch mortar and Bren fire. We were holed up in a small orchard situated on a slight uphill gradient. Around that orchard, on three sides, was a low wall, some 4 or 5 feet high. Beyond the wall was a huge cornfield, where the un-harvested, over-ripe corn stood as high as the wall.

As dawn broke, the enemy made another concerted counterattack, this time directly from the front, through the standing corn. They quickly overran 9 Platoon, who only had eight men left standing, and then they came for us. There was no way that we could have seen those Germans coming our way. They wriggled through the field, getting closer and closer, until we were greeted by a sea of helmets rising up above the waving corn. Below those helmets appeared a long row of German soldiers, with their rifles and machine guns trained on our position. We were stunned. We were completely cut off, almost encircled, and by then we had run out of ammunition. We had been sending frantic messages overnight for resupply but, for whatever reason, nothing had been able to reach us. Most of my men too were already dead or wounded, lying scattered around the periphery of the orchard, and there was nothing further left that the few of us remaining could do.

We were unceremoniously rounded up at the points of their bayonets, and led away. We asked about medical aid for our wounded, and were told that they would be dealt with properly and correctly, and that it was no longer any further concern of ours. Those of us that were left upright, and there were precious few of us in 8 Platoon left alive that morning, were led away, we knew not where.

PRUNES FOR BREAKFAST

And so my fighting in the war ended that morning, in an apple orchard in Normandy, in the glorious sunshine of another beautiful day, as the heat of the sun started to clear away the swirling morning mist.

22

Cattle Trucks

My God, but it was hot in that truck! Hotter than hell. And boy, did it stink! After we had been put in the bag, we were moved behind the German lines and loaded up into ammunition lorries, whilst others were shoved into old cattle trucks, which appeared to have been commandeered from the local French farmers.

We were all sweltering in the August heat. I nearly said dying of heat, but that would have been too near to the bone for comfort. A chap called Graham Belmont died and it looked as though another might go the same way pretty soon; he was almost unconscious, but still upright, held only by the press of bodies around him. Four of the forty of us had perished in similar fashion since we were herded like cattle onto that truck. Nobody had slept for the last few days, well, not proper sleep, just dozing on our feet. It was all that we could do.

I felt so claustrophobic and yet so alone. Surrounded by heaving sweaty humanity, I knew hardly one of my fellow travellers, the only common factors our uniforms and our language. Nobody talked much anyway; what was there to say? We just stood there and endured the journey, hoping that it must end before too long. We were part of a small convoy, its miserable cargo the losers on the battlefield of Normandy.

I had been examining my feelings as I stood in the truck, swaying in line with the motion as it careered around bends in the road, the driver doing all that he could to avoid the cratered shell holes but caring less about his cargo. But there was nothing that could be done to avoid the cannon fire that we could suddenly hear above us. We were being strafed by our own side! Bloody hell! It finally dawned on me that we were in an old ammunition supply truck, and of course it carried no Red Cross markings to show that they were bearing British prisoners away from the battlefield.

When that little episode was over, our German captors pulled over to the side of the road to assess the situation. A couple of the trucks were damaged too much to be able to continue, and a number of men, both German and English, had died in the strafing. Those still living from the broken trucks were pushed in with the rest of us, and we proceeded on our way. I couldn't see if anyone was left behind to bury the dead. Our guards did not stop again for our relief until much later on in the day. They were treating us not much better than animals, I knew not why. Perhaps they were trying to assert their authority over us as members of the "master race".

And that smell, oh that smell! It was truly awful. Human excrement and urine, left where it dropped, was instantly buzzing with flies which then crawled all over us, attacking us at every orifice. Even as we drove along, we could not be rid of it: it travelled with us. Those of us that could shuffle about in the very limited space vacated by the dead were treading it into the floor, but most of it seemed to stick to the soles of our boots. Not for about another four hours would we be let out to stretch our legs and do what some of us had already unavoidably done. Our diet, such as it was, meant that we couldn't control what was going on in our stomachs and our bowels. I tried to put it all to the back of my mind and stared out into the distance through the small split in the tarpaulin flapping at the side of the lorry. I had used my increasingly sharp elbows to maintain my position by that gap, so that I could gain just a tiny idea of where we might be heading, and in what general direction.

I knew that we had been heading away from the battlefield. We had been through Versailles and presumably therefore were on the road into Paris. It got more and more built up, and then I spotted the famous tower, surrounded by barrage balloons. Some wag came out with the comment that we seemed to be a long way from his native Blackpool, so this one must be the inferior copy in Paris. It raised a bit of a laugh, which everyone needed. From my vantage point at that split in the tarpaulin, I could just see its outline against the star-studded night sky. Soon thereafter, our now slightly shorter convoy turned in to some great railway station and we parked in some freight marshalling yards for the night.

We were still there the next day. We were allowed out from the trucks, and met up with hundreds of other Allied prisoners in the same boat as ourselves. The marshalling yard was wired off and there was no way out of it, particularly with the guards being posted at close intervals to ensure that nobody bothered to try. Instead, somebody came up with the idea that we should have some sort of open-air church service in order to give thanks for our lives being spared. It seemed quite a good idea to me, and I offered to be part of the organisation committee. How very odd it was to be organising a church service in a goods yard in Paris. I reckoned that there were about 500 chaps there for it – voluntary absence was, of course, not an option under the guns of the Jerries – and the greater number of us were Yanks who had been captured when pushing in from Omaha and the Cotentin.

We stayed there again that night, sleeping in the open instead of in the filthy trucks. The following day there were some comings and goings as our captors shuffled us about, presumably to get the latest arrivals onto the correct transport for our final destinations. By then yet more prisoners had joined our motley ranks. Eventually, they found enough trucks for all of us, we were loaded up, and off we went, who knew where.

Oh how that good luck of mine had deserted me. It must have been about two days later after leaving Paris behind us, and my only clue was that, provided that the sun still set in the west as it always had done, then we seemed to be going roughly the other way. There were very few signs along the roadside, all the newer ones in German, but just occasionally I saw old and faded ones in French that had escaped the eye and the paint brush of the German censor. I believed that we must still be in eastern France, although not knowing exactly where I was felt quite unnerving.

By that time, we were exchanging information between ourselves as to our Units, where we had been fighting, how we had come to be captured, and any information as to the bigger picture, if anyone knew what that was. When it came to my turn, I related my own experiences to anyone that was interested enough to listen to me, shouting over the noise of the truck as we rattled our way along. I told them how my legendary luck had completely, utterly, and finally run out on the 8th of August. I started my story with my landing in Normandy, and how I had led what a number of my men and fellow officers had described to me as a charmed life. Bombs and bullets had passed close by, but seldom close enough to disturb my equanimity. Had it really only been in late June that we had all so enthusiastically set foot on the soil of France?

As a Captain in 7 RN of the British Liberation Army, I regaled them with the fighting at La Bijude and Epron during the battle to take Caen, followed by my leading a number of platoons from my battalion as we pushed forward through the infamous *bocage* and eventually reached the area just north of Thury-Harcourt, that small but strategically important town on the banks of the River Orne. I told of how my platoons, decimated to less than a quarter of their original strength, had no option, after we had fired our last shot, but to yield or die a pointless death where we stood, hopelessly outnumbered. My story took quite a while to relate to my captive audience who asked a lot of pertinent questions about tactics and strategy. There was plenty of sympathy for me because many others had found themselves in much the same predicament before joining

Cattle Trucks

the wretched convoy. Nearly all, including some more senior officers, had had their positions overrun and had to yield.

It didn't occur to me at the time, but if the Germans had infiltrated a man onto one of the trucks, they could have learned a hell of a lot of information. Although a battlefield was generally a very fluid place, with each side constantly moving forwards, backwards, breaking through or consolidating a new position, there would still have been much of interest to aid the enemy.

But my story, told to my new friends, was by then over a week old. Since that time, we had all continued to be locked into that old German transport truck which had seen better days. A lot of better days, and probably even more worse ones, because one of my fellow captives, an RTR lieutenant who could speak a smattering of German, had learned that our heap of mobile wreckage first saw duty on the Russian Front at Stalingrad, laden with ammunition boxes, and then was used to ferry troops back to France in support of a Heavy Panzer Regiment as it made the headlong dash back to Normandy to intercept us British and, as dear Adolf was so often wont to say, push us back into the sea.

It seemed all so long ago, and, dulled by the steady roar of the engine, interspersed with the creaks and crashes of the suspension as we fell into yet another of the endless French potholes gouged out by the equally endless military traffic, my memory started to flit between my time in France, and my home back in England. I suppose that it was some sort of delayed reaction, and I fell once again in to a reverie.

My dreams during those long days were of the home life that I had left behind all those years ago, and of my wife and new-born son, and what their life would be like with me behind German bars for the foreseeable future. Would JE even remember his father when I eventually got home after the war? Probably not. I could remember clearly when he posed on my knee for a photograph on my last leave. I had on my best new uniform; Elizabeth looked lovely. I wished that I had a copy of that picture with me. I would gladly have exchanged it for that damned shaving mirror that I had managed to hang on to. Then I remembered our home in Ashby, and our walks over the fields to the next village, Blackfordby. I remembered the happy days that we had spent in what I still call to this day 'God's Own Country', beautiful north Derbyshire, in the heart of the Peak District. I recalled how we had enjoyed a picnic in the shadow of Thorpe Cloud and then, on the way back to the car, I had slipped off one of the stepping stones over the Dove in Dovedale one Sunday afternoon and got both of my shoes and feet wet. Oh, how we had laughed in those more carefree days. I tried to concentrate on anything positive and sunny. It was not easy, under those circumstances.

23

Border Crossing

Through the crack in the tarpaulin, I glimpsed one of those old stone roadside signs that had not been painted over by the occupying forces and still bore the legend Chalons-sur-Marne. Where the hell were we? I had never heard of the place. Where was the River Marne?

It had been nearly two weeks on this rattletrap of a lorry now. In that first week of captivity we had had to stop quite often and take cover when we heard the drone of fighter engines high in the sky above us, particularly on the road towards Paris. There were still no Red Cross markings on our convoy, and we were all terrified of being lined up in Allied gun-sights and becoming casualties of friendly fire. During that second week, as we had pulled away further across eastern France, there had been no further incidents, though a few scares when the convoy would just suddenly stop at shouted commands. These happened quite frequently, often for some hours, so progress was slow. Perhaps it was the Resistance?

I really did hope so. I had some rudimentary knowledge of the work that various cells of French partisans were doing behind the lines: harrying the Germans at every opportunity, changing road signs to point in the wrong direction, and blowing up sections of railway lines, tunnels, and the like. If we encountered one of those groups, then I might have been able to get away from our captors. But it was not to be. Nothing so exciting materialised on our trip. And, fortunately for us, I suppose that the Allied planes didn't have the range to reach out to us by then, despite the fact that the Luftwaffe had virtually no remaining planes left in the skies to harass them. We appeared to own the skies above that part of France, wherever it was, and that could only augur well.

Chalons-sur-Marne must have been some sort of a staging post. We tumbled out of the trucks and found that we were in a goods yard, hard by the main railway station. There were hundreds of us there, brought in from different places, and we were slowly herded into various groups, each group being isolated by German soldiers dressed in the field grey of the Wehrmacht. Thank God it was not those ghastly men in their black uniforms! Chalons was a dismal place from what little we saw of it in its funereal wartime plumage, and we were marched away and locked up into a huge old French barracks that had clearly seen better days.

And there we stayed for nearly two weeks, sleeping each night on foul old rotting horse blankets which stank of ammonia. During the day we were interrogated repeatedly, and, if our answers were deemed not to be satisfactory, then it was quick march into solitary confinement. I was sent off to do a couple of spells in jankers, as military punishment was known, but I really had nothing of importance to impart to them. The Germans obviously did not believe in the Geneva Convention rule about only providing one's name, rank and number. They wanted troop numbers and concentrations, not realising that we were not privy to that sort of information, certainly at my level on what had been a wildly fluctuating battlefield.

There was no chance of escape from the Chalons barracks, even if any of us had the strength after the fortnight on those trucks with a very poor diet. When it came to the time for our departure, destination Lord knew where, an ever-present circle of guns ensured that we toed the line. We shuffled aboard a lengthy group of railway goods wagons where we did our best to find some comfort. I reckoned that we were all glad to be leaving that place. I felt ashamed and degraded as we carried along our ingrained smells with us, now heightened by an extra whiff of ammonia. There had been no opportunity to properly cleanse our battledress or ourselves.

The only highlight of our stay at Chalons was that the Red Cross put in an appearance. How, or why, I had no idea. They asked us if we were being treated properly and, instead of going into some long diatribe about our appalling conditions, I persuaded one of them to accept a hastily handwritten note for Elizabeth. Suddenly, everyone was begging for scraps of paper. Whether it would ever get through was another matter.

20th August 1944. (Sunday)
POW (somewhere in France). 193377.
Darling,

I hope that by now you will have heard that I have been taken prisoner. It is with mixed feelings that I have to make the admission, but I have no doubt that you will be fairly content.

It is a little over a fortnight that I wrote, and I must admit that becoming a POW was the one thing that had never entered my head.

Continuing my last letter, we advanced to the banks of the R. Orne and the following night, Sunday, it was decided to make an attack across the river to the forest of Grimbosque (sic). We crossed the river, wading, shortly after midnight and pushed forward towards our objective which we reached without opposition. The fun then commenced, the enemy appeared from all sides and A Coy. were completely surrounded and although we fought on until 8.15, by this time our ammunition was gone, all the other officers wounded, I decided that there was no other option but to surrender. Over 2/3rds of my men were killed or wounded.

Since that time I have made a general progress towards Germany across France. I had a good look at Versailles and Paris from the transport truck nearly a week ago. I was very fortunate when captured as I had my small pack with me containing my washing gear. My mirror is in great demand.

PRUNES FOR BREAKFAST

Last Sunday I held a Church Service which I conducted, an American Colonel reading the Lesson. Nearly 500 men and officers attended, mainly Americans. My wardrobe consists of the clothes I was wearing and it is quite a problem arranging the laundry.

Darling, I am quite fit and I hope you have not worried too much. I cannot give you a permanent address yet. How is the boy? Please phone Gresley and give them my love. Every bit of love, sweetheart.

Edward x. John E x.

P.S. Don't worry.

A railway goods wagon was wonderful transport when compared to the truck that had been our home for the previous weeks of our travels. It had never occurred to me just how comfortable the ride could be on relatively smooth steel railway lines and, as we pulled out of Chalons early in the morning, we were lulled by the metallic clickety-clack, clickety-clack of the wheels over the steel rail joints. My companions were different now. We were all officers and had been segregated from most of the others that we had come to know so intimately those last couple of weeks.

Some bright spark then came up with the idea that we were going to be sent to one of those concentration camps that we had heard so many rumours about. If it was possible to feel more depressed about our enforced incarceration, then that rumour really took the biscuit as everyone's minds flitted back and forth over the terrible mental images that they had of those places. The rest of the day was spent in moody silence as we all pondered our possible fates.

I was not so sure, though. We were, after all, now being treated better than we had been during our lorry journey. Food was more plentiful on the train, even regular, and stops were made each few hours for what one might call humanitarian reasons. But, oh, how I wished for a change of attire. I had been nearly four weeks now in the same clothes and underwear. And those horse blankets at Chalons had done nothing to help the situation. We all stank to high heaven.

Border Crossing

We ground to a halt somewhere or other and were told to get down from the wagons. It seemed that a small group of prisoners had managed to escape the previous night and as a result there was to be an extra roll call, and after it, our boots and braces were removed from us to discourage anyone from trying to imitate the absconders. We then had to hang around for hours whilst a search of the surrounding countryside was made, but, of course, they were long gone by then. I wished them luck in trying to get back to England. They would probably have to go via Spain, if they could contact the local Resistance. Others had achieved it before, so I knew that it was a possibility.

The next few days rattled slowly by as we wended our weary way, clearly using little-used branch lines to avoid clogging up the German war effort, twisting and turning, with long periods of inactivity whilst we waited for trains on the main line to thunder past on their way towards western France. I had never been on a train that stopped so many times. Not even the old 'stopper' that used to go from Burton to Ashby and then on to Leicester, halting at every village in between. Someone had suggested that other delays were probably the French Resistance mining the tracks up ahead, although sadly we saw none of that. Where were they? The countryside was getting hillier and we sensed a change of attitude amongst our guards. They seemed to be becoming more relaxed, and the occasional packet of cigarettes, tossed into our midst, would set off a mad scramble.

The next morning, we found out just why.

Welcome to the Third Reich, the Fatherland! Welcome to Germany!

Once we were over the border into Germany, you could see quite clearly that the civilian people were completely depressed. There were visible food and clothing shortages, and all the spirit had leached out of them. It must have been apparent to the entire population for a number of months that the war was on the verge of being lost, and they were just awaiting their fate. I know that the German papers continued to prop them up with unlikely propaganda, and our captors were quick to distribute some of those amongst us, hoping that there would be some German readers in our band who would spread the word. Fortunately, we knew better. Although I had departed this war in some haste, I knew perfectly well that the Allied forces had made sufficient advances that they would never now be pushed back into the English Channel, barring some momentous unforeseen calamity. We were established on the Continent now in such force, being strengthened every day with fresh troops and armour, that it was only a matter of time before we would finally prevail. Even if it took months more, the outcome was inevitable. And they knew it as well as we did.

A couple of days later, having made very slow progress because the Allies had bombed nearly every railway station that we passed through, we finally drew in to a station, and everyone was told to get out. It soon became evident that we were about to enter some sort of holding camp where we were going to be sorted out further, put through a de-lousing chamber, and then be sent on, once again, on our merry way, to who knows where. This interim place was a prisoner of war camp called Oflag X11B.

At least I had a chance to send a letter to Elizabeth and to my parents, advising them that, although I yet had no permanent address, I was still in the land of the living. I had to have faith that the letters would get through. We were assured that they would, and that there was some sort of humanitarian system in place, honoured by all sides – with the likely exception of the Russians.

Little did I know that others were writing to her about me.

18th August 1944.
Letter from Capt. N T Tarry, 7 RN. BLA.
Dear Elizabeth,
No time for lengthy letters at the moment, very busy. Can give

you no further news of Eddie. When I have time and 14 days has elapsed, I will write and tell you what happened to him.
Goodbye for now.
Yours ever.
Norman.

I learned much later that letters had flooded in to Elizabeth and to my parents. Friends and family put pen to paper urging her to be of good cheer and await further news of my situation. At that time, nobody actually knew whether I was alive or dead. It would be some time before that particular battlefield could be cleared of corpses and the wounded. Others might simply have disappeared, either blown to smithereens or wandered off, suffering from shell shock and completely disorientated.

My son's godmother, Una Ellis-Fermor, was one such to put pen to paper to my wife in Ripley. On the 23rd August, she wrote from her home at Abbey Road Mansions, NW8: '*I have just heard the most distressing news that Eddie is missing. I am very glad indeed that you have John to be a comfort to you.*'

Ron Moore also wrote a very kind letter on the 29th August from his address in Buxton. He had heard from my mother that I was missing in action. I did not know how they knew each other, but the friendship was sufficiently strong that he was to officiate at the first marriage of my son, John Edward, some thirty years later. By then he was a Canon of the Church of England.

She also received a number of more official types of letter.

20th September 1944.
War Memorial Social Institute, Ashby-de-la-Zouch.
Dear Mrs. Searancke,
   I am instructed by my Committee to tender to you our sympathy during the trying times that you are experiencing. I can assure you that our thoughts are with you and of the welfare of

your dear husband. We trust your suspense will soon be ended and that you will hear the news that we all hope for. Kindly inform me when official news is received to enable me to pass on to members who are most anxious to hear of our very popular trustee and friend.

 Yours sincerely,
 G.W.Poyser.
 Hon Sec.

My parents, too, were quick off the mark to write to Elizabeth, pressing the point that, at that stage, I was only listed as missing. There were always a lot more men posted as missing after an engagement than there were posted as killed in action. Later, the list of missing would go down as the system kicked in to trace them. All around, there seemed to be great hope that listed as missing might eventually turn into news that I had been found, safe and sound.

 For my part, I too had been quick to send a note to Elizabeth, but I had no way of knowing if the decaying German postal system had allowed it to get through. Nevertheless, I felt it to be important to keep writing, in the hope that at least one letter would get back home. She must be worried sick. Not having a permanent address at a camp left me in great doubt that my communications would be satisfactorily established, but I kept on plugging away with the letters anyway.

 Perhaps something would get through to me at Hadamar, this main transit camp.

29th August 1944. Stamped Oflag X11B.
Darling,
Just another line to let you know that I am feeling very well and in good spirits. Food with the aid of Red Cross parcels is very good. They are a godsend. Please donate £5 to them. You cannot reply to me yet

*but I hope to be able to let you have a more permanent address shortly.
I hope you are all well.*
   God bless you all.
   Edward.

24

Halfway House

We had pulled into the station at Hadamar and disgorged into some sort of a glorified transit camp. I hoped that this was not going to be a long stay because it looked, at first glance, to be a miserable place. Everyone was walking around looking lost – well you would, wouldn't you – and it was only slowly that the Germans processed each one of us. A few of their officers strutted about in their smart uniforms but most of the ordinary soldiers, the guards in the usual field grey, moved about like robots, just doing what had to be done. And nearly all of them, to be truthful, were old men, ready for their pensions, but pressed back into service by their Führer. Anyone younger would have been sent to the Front.

8th September 1944. Stamped Oflag X11B.
This is No. 3 of the present series. I am still unable to give you an address to which you may reply. I am very fit, considering the lack of exercise, but have plenty of food and sleep, and a reasonable quantity of tobacco. I spend most of my time playing bridge, solo or rummy, with slight success. The Red Cross parcels are the big event of the week. It seems years since I heard from you and I often wonder how you are and hope that you are not worrying too much.

We get a translation of the German news, and I think that it cannot be far from the end. I asked Norman to write to you should anything happen to me and I hope he did so. But that I should ever be a guest of the Reich is something I never ever considered.

Halfway House

How is the lad? Phone the family and tell them not to worry. I don't know how long this will take to arrive, so I wish you a happy birthday.
All my love, darling.
Edward. x.

Our captors at Oflag X11B were to treat us reasonably well. The camp food was not that good, but then again, with the shortages that there clearly were, it was to be expected. I wondered if all Germans lived on cabbage, turnips and potatoes. As long as those Red Cross parcels kept coming, we would survive in reasonable shape. I was just grateful to have somewhere to shower at last, even if it was cold and the water only came out in a dribble, so that I had to run around to get wet. That was not much fun either with a number of other chaps all competing at the same time for the same dribble of water.

The village, from what we could see of it, actually looked not too bad. There was even a great big castle on the top of a hill just outside the village. I was told that some of the most senior officers that had been captured had been billeted up there in an effort to seduce them into giving away their secrets.

Eventually, after a couple of weeks when we had been classified and graded, the system allowed us out on organised, but closely guarded, walks. Having given our word of honour that we would not try to escape whilst on one of those walks, we enjoyed them immensely, and they became the high spot of the week, since there was little or no space for extended exercise within the camp itself. I couldn't help wondering, however, how long we would be there for.

16th September 1944. Stamped Oflag X11B.
Darling,
My weekly effort to cheer the family hearth. How are you all? I am feeding well, sleeping well, and playing cards indifferently. I am

PRUNES FOR BREAKFAST

become quite an expert at laundering, but manage to farm out my darning for a few cigarettes. I find that I can make an excellent meal out of tins and German rations and one of the chaps in my room is an expert at making puddings out of stale bread and chocolate spread from cocoa and tinned milk. I have taken a number of bets on the date of the end of the war, and I think that my original date will not be far out. We have a side of pig tomorrow which we are having boiled. Jolly good, what! I washed my socks this morning and then walked for an hour without socks, consequently have developed a sore toe. Still at Oflag X11B, and still no final address to give you.

All my love and God bless.

Edward. x.

It was on one of those walks that an idea came to me. Those boxy houses in Hadamar had given me another idea about how to further the opportunities for the family firm once the war was over. Looking at the basic architecture of German housing, particularly the ones at the lower, or mass produced, end of the scale, it came to me that there was sure to be a requirement back in England once the country started to get back on its feet. Over there in the north of Germany, they appeared to plan and lay out the interiors of their houses in a different way, but that was not to say that it was worse, or better. Perhaps it was a result of the colder climate? The lifestyle of the people who lived there? I would have liked to get inside one to see how the internals were constructed, and how they sorted out the heating. I could only assume that the heating was more efficient, and the corresponding heat loss would be a lot less. I had also been able to see, looking through various windows, that a lot more wood was used than in England. Even I knew that wood would act as a good insulator, and look very good in to the bargain.

We already had those prefabricated houses in England, called 'Prefabs' by one and all, and I reckoned that it should not be too difficult to design something a lot better and more lasting. I must

Halfway House

see if I could scrounge some drawing paper and a pencil, so as to come up with something that had the best features of the German and the English, whilst shedding what I think were the less attractive or useful. I always liked a goal to try to achieve, even there in captivity, and so I was going to put myself to work.

A couple of weeks later – most of us had lost track of the actual date by then – a kindly guard with whom I had exchanged some very potent unfiltered Capstan Full Strength cigarettes for pipe tobacco led me to believe that we would very soon be off to our final destination, an Oflag camp specifically for officers. He assured us that we would be well treated, and we shook hands on it before we parted.

But yet another week had gone by and we were still behind the wire of the camp at Hadamar. There were new intakes almost daily, but our batches had all been classified by then and I think that they accepted that we were low risk. I know that it was ingrained in us that it was our duty to escape if we were caught, in order to harass the German military machine to the maximum, but it did seem to be a bit late in the day at that stage, when we knew perfectly well that the Allies were almost knocking on the Germans' front door. And by then, we had received our new identification papers – all in German, though – and we should therefore be moving on soon, I believed. There was an onward destination stamped on my new identity documents – Oflag 79.

Yet I was still there in Hadamar, another week later. It was another false alarm. We were, I had learned, near to Frankfurt, though I did not know the exact location, other than the name of the village. I was quite getting to like it there, what with those loosely supervised walks. The food was half decent, considering the circumstances, and the guards were, by and large, a lenient lot. They realised that, by then, the war was moving to its final stages, and that

PRUNES FOR BREAKFAST

Allied troops were now on the borders of Germany, moving ever closer, with the inevitable conclusion. Their own news, whilst still heavily doctored, must have substantially given the game away.

Nevertheless, I was very pleased, although apprehensive, when I learned that we were finally to move on to the Oflag 79 camp, supposedly a few hundred miles further to the north. Nobody knew what to expect of the place though our guards led me to believe that it might have better facilities for us. The Germans had told us that trucks would be here for us this week in order to get us to our final destination. That sounded rather ominous to me. The words 'final destination' had a nasty ring to them. I cast my mind back to those conversations that had taken place on the way there. It sent shivers down my spine.

A couple of days later, having said our goodbyes at Hadamar to new friends that we had made there, and even a couple of German guards that had been kind to us, off we set, ready for another long bumpy ride in a convoy of cattle trucks. There were sixty or so of us to a truck – though we were to travel for a change in some luxury as we had been provided with wood shavings for us to spread over the floors – and though we were crammed in all together, the mood was much lighter than it had been on any of our previous travels since our abrupt departure from Normandy.

25

POW Camp

A full day later, tired and even more dishevelled if that were possible, we finally arrived at the gates of Oflag 79. It turned out to be situated about 3 miles outside the north part of Brunswick, a larger town than Hadamar. We marched (if that was the right word for our stumbling progress) under close supervision – and rifles – from Brunswick train station to the camp. I wondered why the trucks could not have driven there directly. I supposed that there was some reason, but it escaped me. The difference in temperature that much further north was already apparent, although it was only just autumn. We were going to need overcoats, though where on earth they were going to come from was anybody's guess. How I wished that I still had my British Warm, left behind in somewhat of a hurry back in Normandy. I hoped that by now it had found a good home and would serve its new owner as well as it had me. Was it going to be a particularly cold winter, I pondered? We would just have to see, but things did not augur well.

The camp was nothing at all as I had imagined. We were told that it had been especially converted to take Allied prisoners, and that it had originally been the headquarters of a German Parachute Regiment. I could well believe that because it was sited just over the road from the defunct Hermann Goering aircraft engine factory. The place was absolutely vast, with large two-storey barrack blocks and a great central asphalted parade ground. I had imagined that, as had the rest of us, we would be billeted in draughty wooden makeshift huts, but there was even an upstairs to each block. I began to wonder if my charmed life had been resurrected and managed to follow along with me.

Well, we would have to see about that, and it was time to get settled in. There were roughly, I was informed, 3,000 Allied officers of various nationalities in the place, with the greater part of them being British. The SBO, (Senior British Officer) a full colonel by the name of Ferrers, ensured a strict pecking order with most elements of military discipline being rigorously maintained. If we were all going to be living cheek by jowl, it was pointed out that everyone must continue to follow strict army rules.

As with everyone else newly arrived, I was called in to see him. He had a small office allocated to him by the Germans, with quite an imposing desk, behind which he was seated in a smartly pressed uniform. I wondered exactly where he had got that from. When it was my turn, I marched in to his office and snapped off my smartest salute. Rather wearily, he returned it. He had a great long list in front of him, giving details of everyone in the camp from all of the three branches of the Services, and it was he that told me that there were one or two Royal Norfolk chaps already here, one from as far back as the debacle of Dunkirk. We had a friendly and informative chat that probably lasted less than five minutes, and then I marched out again.

Oflag 79. (3 Coy)
7th October 1944.
Darling,

At last I am able to write to you from a permanent address, to which you can write me. Considering everything, I am very fit, feeding well and sleeping swell. The complexion is now as normal as ever, still remarkably ruddy. There are one or two people here who recognise me. A young fellow from Woodville named Staunton and Calke's brother from Rolleston. The only other Norfolk's officer a Dunkirkite, has been very kind, inviting me to a meal last night, especially kind in view of the food shortage, however, he has built up

POW Camp

a reserve over the years, so all was well. He has also provided me with some clothing necessities. The tobacco situation has deteriorated this last week or two. Letters take about 3 weeks to reach here from England, I think. So I look forward to getting a budget from you in due course and hope that it will not be too long before you receive this. How are you all? How goes the boy? It is now more than 2 months since I last heard from you.
   All my love.
   Edward. x.

I was billeted in a proper room – upstairs! – although it looked as though each room, with doors letting off from a central corridor that ran the length of the building, was originally designed to hold four people and we were now having to put up with a head count of twelve to each room instead. You might be able to imagine that it was all somewhat crowded.

The buildings were all properly block-built using some bricks and mortar, but for the greater part using wood in the main construction. There even appeared to be a heating system, but of course it was not switched on. I supposed that there was no fuel for it either. So I could already imagine that everywhere was going to be bitterly cold that winter of 1944.

Taking a stroll about after I had been allocated my billet and put away my shaving mirror – yes, it was still with me – I could not help but notice that there were about seven large holes on the parade ground in the centre of the camp. They looked very like bomb craters with which I had become intimately acquainted back in Normandy. I soon gathered that they were the result of an air raid by the Allies on the 24th August, when the US Air Force came by. They dropped a marker almost overhead of the camp instead of over the adjacent airfield, and the results were a bit unpleasant for all concerned. As well as a few Germans killed in the attack, three prisoners were killed and a further fifty wounded. I was rather pleased to have been delayed in my arrival. As winter drew ever closer, those large craters across the parade ground slowly filled with rain water and later froze over, and one or two chaps could often be seen keeping fit by skating on the ice. I forget now what they had made their skates from, but they worked very well. Rather a nice touch, I thought at the time – an ice rink provided courtesy of our own side!

Away to one side of the camp sat the brooding presence of that immense factory, by that time a bombing target for the Allies, but previously under the control of Hermann Goering – an aircraft engine manufacturing and assembly plant for his dear Luftwaffe. The RAF were the next to pay it a visit, on the 2nd October, and we all stood and cheered as they thundered overhead in formation and then the ground literally shook under our feet, as sticks of bombs fell all around the target. A lot better aiming than those Yanks, back in August.

My luck had held once again. Such were the fortunes of war.

On Sunday the 15th October, the RAF were back again in some force. This time their target was the nearby town of Brunswick. We could see that the town was shooting up in flames for about twenty-four hours afterwards until the authorities got it all under control. We watched and saw vast columns of smoke rising skywards to about 10,000 feet. There was much cheering from all behind the wire, much to the chagrin of the Goons.

16th October 1944.
Darling,

Another short effort to let you know that I am fit and well and bearing up and quite cheerful. Am settling down here and finding the chaps in the room very kind and helpful and they have been extraordinarily generous with things like clothing, chocolate and cigarettes. I shall have to send off rather a lot of Stilton by way of thank you's when I return. There are a number of camp entertainments and I have attended the play 'Gaslight' which was very well done and a Gilbert & Sullivan concert. Apart from that I have been reading and playing the odd game of cards, so time passes quote quickly. How are you, sweetheart? And the lad? Not deteriorating from lack of paternal control?

We have a Solicitor in the room on the lookout for a junior partnership. You might ask Shepherd what he thinks of that? Then we might not have to take the business from them. I will write again in a day or two.

All my love.
Edward. x.

28th October 1944.
Darling,

Having just finished my breakfast of prunes, bread and butter and coffee, I feel impelled to let you know that all is still well. Today is our chief day of the week, Red Cross parcels being distributed. I got a sore throat 5/6 days ago, which I declared, and it has now turned into a nasty cold.

I wonder if you will please re-order The Builder and The Farmers Weekly so that I can read back on my return. I have also been wondering whether Anthony sold the V8? If not, ask him to get a set of new tyres for it. I have been attending horticultural lectures and am now an expert on gardening.

I Hope you are all well.
All my love.
Edward. x.

There was a chap in the camp that did caricatures for a living in between his press jobs for Allied Newspapers. I asked him if he would be prepared to do a likeness of me. I thought, afterwards, looking at it for the first time, that he had got my chin wrong and that I also appeared to be quite a bit shorter than I really was. I supposed, though, that such was the art of caricature? But he had done wonders in making it look as though I was still dressing in a smart uniform, instead of the hideous drab khaki battledress, worn through and patched in several places and completely past redemption, that was now my daily garb. I proposed to hang the picture on the wall next to my bunk bed where it took pride of place. I might even ferret it away back home to England eventually, if I could, as I was that much taken by it.

I was also spending quite a lot of time in the camp library. There were about 6,000 books there, donated by the Red Cross over the war years. There were regular courses and lectures put on each week. When you brought 3,000 chaps together under one roof, so to speak, there was inevitably an expert on hand for almost everything. Almost everybody could claim to be an expert in their own particular field, could they not? The good thing about that was that everyone was keen to share their knowledge, if only to alleviate their own boredom. It helped to keep our minds active and away from what might be happening at home, or to our wartime comrades still on the field of battle. I quickly put my name down and signed up for some of those courses on Business Administration because I was led to believe that you could actually gain some sort of qualifications whilst incarcerated. It would occupy my mind for a month or two.

2nd November 1944.
Darling,
I wonder whether you have received my letters yet? I have calculated that I should be hearing from you soon. I hope that everyone is well, and that the lad grows more like his father every day. I have often wondered how my father took the suspense.

I have shaken off my cold. If you think it worthwhile to send parcels (they take several months to arrive), will you send two large ones, half tobacco and half cigarettes, in each with a few 3 holes blades. Small parcels seem to go astray more easily. I have provisionally ordered 2 new cars as I expect it may be months after my return before

I can get delivery, so do not be alarmed if a letter arrives. I am becoming an expert gardener, so look out for radical changes when I get home. I am also studying farming very thoroughly, and so time goes very quickly.

It will not be long now, darling.

Edward. x.

The incoming postal service in the camp was pretty atrocious. If Elizabeth wrote to me at the previous camp at Hadamar, would they have bothered to send her letters onwards to me at Oflag 79? Did they even keep lists of where they sent prisoners? As likely as not, no, and as I had received nothing, I feared that they had not. I kept on writing to her and to my parents to give my news, in the hope that my own letters were getting through to them. Until I actually had a letter from any of them, I really would not know. Most chaps were in the same boat, other than the 'long stay' ones that had been in the camp from the early days of the war, and for them the system had worked quite well, until recently. Though it was ever extremely tardy.

11th November 1944.

Darling,

Today is Remembrance Day and we are having the traditional 2 minutes silence. I am hoping that during the next fortnight I shall hear from you. Dick Moss is in the camp and I also saw Tony Calke the other day. The siren is a constant nuisance and yesterday I had just heavily soaped my hair and was standing under the cold shower and the dashed water stopped. Imagine my language.

My hopes of Xmas dinner at home have receded a little I am afraid. How is everyone by now? I expect the lad is getting quite big, talking quite a lot and walking all over the place. I hope that the lack of parental control will not be too obvious 20 years hence.

PRUNES FOR BREAKFAST

Will you buy him an £8 Savings Book for me as a Christmas present.
God bless, sweetheart.
Edward. x.

The weather was getting absolutely freezing by November. Our potato ration had been cut back again and we were surviving, if that was the word, on totally insufficient calorific intake each day. And there was, of course, still no fuel to fire up the boilers for the dashed heating system. On the plus side, we had another batch of Red Cross parcels on the 14th, and the contents of those, when shared out, were what was keeping us going.

Things had certainly changed since I first got to Oflag 79 in the first week of October. At that date, there was plenty of food, almost more than enough, and people were swapping cocoa for cigarettes, for example. It was warm outside, and we enjoyed the outdoor concerts that had been put on by our fellow prisoners. But by the beginning of December, all our nerves were becoming frayed, what with the rations becoming less and less, the bitter cold that had set in, and the uncertainty of when the war would end. Nobody by then had much spare energy to do anything except to fight their own personal fight in order to continue to exist and stay alive. Things were getting a bit desperate.

2nd December 1944.
Darling,
How are you? Saturday evening and I am just contemplating a cold shower, having spent quite a busy day. Written up 4 sheets of foolscap notes, attended a lecture, and played Rummy until interrupted by an air raid warning.
A week or two of Ripley food will soon get me back to normal. Our hopes of being back for Xmas have now dwindled to zero.

POW Camp

I have just heard that the Bn. suffered very heavy losses the day I was captured and those left were rather scattered. Tomorrow I am expecting to have a change from work. There is a show 'Ladies in Retirement' in the afternoon and bridge in the evening. I have not heard from you yet, but look forward daily to so doing. I hope that the lad is behaving and conforming to pattern.

Every bit of love.

Edward. x.

It was at the show '*Ladies in Retirement*' – a really great show – that I first met an RTR Captain by the name of Stanhope, captured when his tank was incapacitated at Villers-Bocage after a very one-sided exchange with a 57 ton Tiger with armour so thick and strong that he said that his rounds just bounced off it, even though they had been fired at almost point blank range. He seemed a very nice chap, and had been one of the organisers of those musical events, singing contests, opera and, from what I understood, a symphony that he had written himself, due for an airing the following week. I made a note to go along, for they gave everyone so much pleasure and relief from the tedium of our existence. He was quite a talented chap for a tank driver! Oh, and 2,000 Red Cross parcels arrived the same day, so we were rescued from the brink of starvation for a while longer.

I was told that there had been at least a couple of dozen plays such as '*Blithe Spirit*', '*Ten Minute Alibi*' and '*HMS Pinafore*' put on by the camp amateur dramatics society in the two years or so before I had got here. They were drying up though, what with the cold and the lack of decent food. Nobody had much spare energy to do anything by then. It was a great shame for the rest of us who had to kick our heels to avoid the boredom.

There was a big musical contingent in the camp. I had absolutely no skills in that department, and couldn't play any instrument. Nor was I tempted to bother to try, because whatever instrument there was, there was someone there who could play it, if they had one to

PRUNES FOR BREAKFAST

play. We had enough talented people there to provide a couple of full scale orchestras, the only problem being the lack of most of the required instruments. One or two of the simpler ones had been fashioned from bits of old piping and other things, but we really could have done with someone dropping off a grand piano.

I was working up further interest in the building business and learning all that I could from other chaps. I thought that perhaps Elizabeth would be allowed to send me some trade magazines so that I could see what the up to date market position was. It would have been nice, but there still had been no letter from her.

I was doing my best to keep extremely busy, otherwise I would go stir crazy.

I woke up on the 11th December to find that the first snows of winter had fallen. It had settled deeply on the roofs of the barrack blocks, because there was no heat from within to melt it. It was overlying the sparse branches of the trees in the main compound, hiding any remaining green that there was left, and it had softened everything all around. The parade ground had gone white overnight. Sharp angles had been replaced by gentle curves and small drifts had built up along the sides of the blocks. Those with more imagination than I concluded that it made a rather fetching subject for a Christmas card. A few bright sparks found the energy to go outside and have a snowball fight. I stayed in, cooked some Red Cross prunes for my breakfast, and conserved my energy. I reckoned that it was going to be a very hard winter.

21st December 1944.
Darling,
I have delayed writing to you for a day or two in the hope of hearing from you, but have been disappointed. One or two of the chaps that wrote at the same time received letters. With Xmas getting so near, I often wonder how you are getting on with preparations, and how JE will enjoy his second Xmas. My thoughts have gone back

to 1938/9 and the wonderful parties that we gave. I have made a cake and a pudding and shall make the most of our limited resources.

In the last 10 days I have taken 5 examinations in Industrial Administration and have 5 more to go (3 hours each).

I wonder what the other officers are doing. I gather that they are now scattered to the 4 winds.

Be cheerful and God bless you.
Edward. X.

Whilst I had been busy taking course examinations, sitting in the camp library, others had been thinking towards the future after the war was over. One fantastic idea – I wish that I could say it was originally mine, but it wasn't, though I very soon made it my business to become involved in the shaping of what it was to become – was the creation of a club to aid underprivileged youngsters, that could be set up with funds generated by ourselves after things got going again post war. There were sure to be thousands of young people who would, for whatever reason, want or need a steer towards a brighter future. Perhaps their parents had died, or they had been evacuated to the countryside, or otherwise displaced or orphaned.

A meeting was called, and it was held up in the vast attic room of one of the blocks. There was a great hole in the roof, courtesy of that American raid, and it was freezing cold. And so, after one or two false starts, the idea of a Boys' Club began to be kicked about. The idea was put forward to everyone present and, after a timely intervention, I think by a paratrooper who came from the East End originally, it received enthusiastic support from everyone. It was eventually decided to call it after the town most local to the camp – Brunswick – and it was initially going to be sited in the East End of London. The Brunswick Boys' Club had a good ring to it. We all put the word about, and just about everyone gave a pledge of money, written on any scrap of paper that was available, to be redeemed with the same sum by way of personal cheque when they got back home. Upwards of £12,000 was pledged, an enormous sum for that time.

The astonishing thing was that every single one of those pledges, given under the most difficult of personal circumstances so far from home, was honoured after the war had ended, and was later matched by the government of the day.

To drum up some extra funds, some bright spark suggested that there could be a huge raffle with prizes donated by our camp colleagues. Some of those 'prizes' were extremely outlandish. Aside from the almost obligatory weekend for two at the Savoy, a brace of theatre tickets, and a year's subscription to *Punch* magazine, my offer (thinking back to my almost idyllic time at OCTU on the Isle of Man) was a couple of boxes of Manx kippers. I forget who won those kippers now, but I regularly had the odd box sent over to my home after the war, and thoroughly enjoyed them. Absolutely the best that you could ever want for.

When the war was over, we boxed up all of those 6,000 books from the camp library and got them shipped back to form a nucleus of reading material for the fledgling Brunswick Boys' Club.

News from home or the battlefield was something of a drug to all of us. We got most of our news about the progress of the war from the wall board. The Germans in charge of us had no problem in us receiving and distributing fresh news as it became available, whether from new intakes of prisoners or from the wireless. And so we got it typed it up – a typewriter had been allowed, although heaven only knows where it came from – and then it was pinned up for all to see. With new prisoners arriving almost weekly, there was a regular influx of fresh news, particularly as to where the Allied forward Units were by then.

POW Camp

Although that typewriter had been allowed to us, strangely, when we asked for some sort of Gestetner type of duplicator, it was immediately denied.

I had been waiting all of that time to have news of what happened to 7 RN and all my comrades after the day of my capture. With the arrival of another particular intake of officers – none of whom were from 7 RN – I learned a bit more. It seemed that on the 9th August, my battalion was relieved from the hell of that bridgehead at Grimbosq by the 7th Royal Welch Fusiliers from 53 Div. Our Brigade then withdrew back behind the line for a three-day complete reorganisation.

21st December 1944. (To my parents)
Dear Pop & All,
Needless to say my thoughts are very much with you at this time. I hope that our next Xmas will be a 1939 effort and that we will all be together again.
Love to all and best wishes for the New Year.
Eddie.

Only one letter did in fact reach me, perfectly timed for just before Christmas, and that was from a tenant of one of Elizabeth's mother's properties in Ripley, just around the corner from The Woodlands, in the main square of the town. May Capon wrote that she had seen JE and that *'he was getting to be a young nibs'* and that *'when visiting, he had taken a liking to a feather duster which he would not let go and carried it home aloft like a banner.'* She also mentioned that *'he is a darling boy and I must say a very determined young gentleman just like his Dad.'* That letter just made my day.

I attended a church service, held on the parade ground, on Christmas Day, and later on we had a slap up meal. There was pea soup, followed by fried meat roll with fried bread, and then some cheese followed by trifle. I even got a cup of coffee afterwards. I think that it was Canadian. In the evening we had German stew (more turnips!) with Christmas pudding and more of that Canadian coffee. I felt quite bloated.

> 27th December 1944.
> Darling,
>   Christmas has passed, and my thoughts have been constantly with you. I took my 6th exam paper on Saturday and the 7th on Boxing Day, in the coldest room I have ever written in. Only 3 more papers then I shall relax a little. On Christmas Eve I went to a church service, very pleasant, and in the afternoon I strolled across the camp to a carol service. As I walked, I thought about our walks across the fields to Blackfordby with (my dog) Smith and realised how much I failed to realise the wonderful conditions in which we lived. I had a really good day, but my stomach has contracted in no small degree. I made a tour around the people I know. The older inhabitants were extraordinarily generous with their gifts of cigarettes and under the circumstances we had a very good time. I daily expect to hear from you and for the time, not too distant, when we shall be together.
>   Edward. x.

At the Christmas Eve church service, we gave our best and lustiest to *Jerusalem*, much to the consternation and puzzlement of our captors, who I didn't think twigged quite what it was about. But it summed up our own feelings perfectly. Like many others around me, I howled all the way through it, as it had long been a favourite.

It was a huge anti-climax as soon as the New Year set in. For how much longer would we be there? When would it get a bit warmer? When would the Red Cross bring us some food, because those German ration packs were getting smaller and smaller. There was only so much that you could do to disguise a turnip, and by then they constituted the main element of nearly every meal. The only good news was that we were told that a truckload of Red Cross parcels had arrived at the station, but we had all heard that rumour before. If they were to appear, though, in the usual quantities, we should be OK until February.

Dear God, but it had been cold that winter. I had never known cold like it. It was not helped by the lack of fat that all of our bodies now carried and we were frozen right through to the marrow. We did not have a healthy diet at all, and our daily calorie intake was dangerously low by then, only alleviated when any Red Cross parcels were delivered, and they were becoming extremely spasmodic. As a result of the privations, it was not unusual for most chaps to have lost 3 or 4 stone by then. The theatre had packed up. Nobody had sufficient strength or incentive to keep themselves going in this sort of weather, let alone do things for general entertainment. Things seemed to be getting critical.

To cheer myself up and spread a bit of positive news to cheer others, I decided to announce that I had written off to order a new car for myself, much to the amazement of all my new camp friends. I reckoned that I would be needing one anyway when I got back to work in England, and it seemed a good way to demonstrate not just my patriotism but my confidence in the recovery of British industry once the war was over.

I reckoned, though, that it would be a good six months after the war ended before any company would be in a position to effect delivery, so my order went to Mr Henry Ford, who, since the outbreak of war in 1939, had turned his factory at Dagenham over to the manufacture of military vehicles. I had penned the appropriate letter and sent it off, enclosed with one to Elizabeth, asking her to stick a stamp on the envelope and post it.

20th January 1945.
Darling,
Again I have waited for a letter from you but have reluctantly decided that I shall not receive one before the war ends. I finished my exam in rather uncomfortable weather but did on the whole rather well on 9 papers but not at all sure about the others. I am now relaxing, but finding my

days very full, helping to run the next Industrial Administration Course, planning a new type of house to compete with the prefabricated ones, the odd game of bridge and poker and the camp entertainments. We had an American film about a week ago. Life is a little better nowadays with the better news and the fact that for the last 3 days I have had 3 blankets over me. The tobacco ration is rather chronic however.

How are you all keeping? I gather that the weather has been as bad with you as with us. However, it cannot be long now, I feel.

All my love.

Edward. x.

The thing that really got me down throughout my stay at Oflag 79 was the lack of incoming letters for me. I had not had one at all since that one in December. I had to assume that Elizabeth was writing to me, yet each week when I heard the shout *'Mail up!'* I toddled along to see if there was anything for me, but there never was. I did not understand what had gone wrong. Maybe it was down to the rapidly disintegrating German postal system, because although others were receiving mail, it was only a few others. The only glimmer of hope was that we could not be that far now from the end of the war. All my old bets, made when I was so full of so much enthusiasm and certainty, had never come off, so I was forbearing to join in the latest stakes to name the big day. I had had my fingers burnt too often for that. How idiotic I must have been to bet that the war would have been over in three weeks, when it still had two years to run – and it was not yet over even now.

The guards were letting more Red Cross parcels through now. I assumed that the Red Cross were not sending extra parcels, so it must have meant that the guards were not stealing so many. Some of the Germans were becoming really quite friendly, perhaps thinking of which side their bread was going to be buttered quite soon. I supposed that they were more privy to the state of play than we were, and it probably well behoved them to keep on the right side of us 3,000 chaps,

POW Camp

just in case. Mind you, they still manned the machine gun towers around the perimeter and I was sure that if anyone was so foolish as to make a dash for it at this late stage, they would still shoot to kill.

Spring was finally in the air, and the bone-chilling cold of winter in northern Germany was receding behind us at last. We had been told that the last winter had been one of the coldest on record. I could quite believe it. There was no heat yet in the sun when it shone, but at least there was now no more frost on the ground when I poked my head against the window pane first thing in the morning. The few fir trees around the old parade ground had lost their covering of snow which made their boughs bend low, and there were now flashes of green shoots here and there amidst the hues of brown.

Please, O Lord, could it be long now before all this was over?

We had a very formal German Roll Call on the 25th February. We were all pulled out of our blocks, muffled up with anything that we could find, and stood in lines three deep. The SBO had had to make a formal report to the German Commandant that a British officer had escaped. At that time, I had no idea how, and I was not sure why. It was news to me. Perhaps he had gone stir crazy – we all got like that from time to time – but it seemed hardly worthwhile now for him to make the effort and risk his life. It would hardly have affected the war effort, but I supposed that he was out to make a point. As a result we were stood to on that parade ground from ten in the morning to three forty-five in the afternoon. And so the latest performance of the symphony concert that I was due to attend had to be cancelled. Dashed inconvenient, what!

I don't know whether it was as a result of that officer escaping, or purely co-incidental, but we were all handed leaflets the following week, published by the German authorities, informing us that we would be shot if we tried to escape. The notice seemed to imply that the British, particularly, were the ringleaders and trying to wage some new type of guerrilla warfare, and it ended with the underlined sentences at the bottom of their screed stating hilariously:

To All Prisoners Of War!!
Escaping From Prison Camps Has Ceased To Be A Sport!!

They had no sense of humour, those Germans. But had we not known that all along?

We were by then right down to basic German rations only. Red Cross parcels had dried up completely by February. I suspected that they simply could not get them through, such was the mayhem out there between both sides. The Germans had admitted to us in one of their more candid moments that their railway system was now almost *'kaput'*. People in the camp were continuing to lose even more weight as a result of food deprivation. It was so difficult to keep going and remain positive. At least it wasn't raining, though.

But, a month or so later, on the 22nd March, much to everyone's amazement, there was indeed a delivery of Red Cross parcels. Last week there had been a telegram from the Red Cross in Geneva to the camp authorities, stating that another load of parcels was on the way, coming by truck instead of on the railway. The notice mentioned 4,000 parcels. We all wondered if it was a fake put out by the Goons to try to keep us calm. But no, it was true, and there they were. My first meal from my parcel was meat and vegetable stew. It was simply marvellous. Words failed me.

Two days later, we heard from an official German communique broadcast throughout the camp that the Allies were only about 60 miles away from us.

'Surely it CAN'T be long now?' was the question on everyone's lips.

26

White Cliffs

On the 10th April, we could all hear heavy gunfire in the distance, and the following morning there was a lot of air activity, little of it German. A number of the German garrison rather briskly took their leave of us and went off down the road towards Brunswick. We did not see them again.

13th April 1945. (Friday)
Darling,
    At last I can write to you, no longer c/o 'The Hun'.
    I was cooking some prunes at 0925 hrs. yesterday morning when I heard a terrific cheering and was told that the Americans were at the gate. I continued to cook my breakfast, nevertheless I felt very thankful. Although we have been expecting the event for some little time I was very pleased that the release had come bloodlessly.
    I have received quite a number of letters in the last few days but none later than December so I will not trouble to reply to any of your queries as I feel that your wish will be gratified (sic) in the course of the next 10 days. Needless to say, our food situation has greatly improved.
    Should this reach you within a few days, I hope you will be able to have the car in order and licensed and a stock of Guinness and oysters.
    All my love, Sweetheart.
    Edward. x.

PRUNES FOR BREAKFAST

But, oh, the anti-climax of it all! After so many months of hope and despair, on the 12th April, the Americans, their shoulder badge flashes denoting the US 9th Army, had drawn up to the main gate in a couple of jeeps. Behind them came the distant clanking noise of armour, the rattle of metal tracks on the approach road. A noise that was instantly recognisable and which we all remembered so well. The jeeps moved forwards and the gates were opened by those left of our guards. Hundreds ran to cheer the Yanks, but most of us did little else but breathe a sigh of relief. This had not been one of those infernal concentration camps of which we had heard so many wild but unsubstantiated rumours. This had just been a huge camp where mostly officers could be contained and be kept away from playing any future part in the war. I reckoned that our captors there knew all along that the final result was going to be in our favour, and so they treated us fairly decently, in as far as they were allowed by their masters. Red Cross parcels may have found their way to the guards and their families from time to time, but that would be ever the way of things, in war as elsewhere. In the end, the gates just creaked open and the guards stood to one side, their guns lowered, and that was it. Those in the machine gun towers came down to ground level, leaving their armoury up aloft. Then, as though symbolically, the camp commandant lined up his men, marched to the front of them, and saluted the senior American officer before handing over his pistol and stepping to one side. I had a feeling deep down that the Germans were as glad to see the end of the whole thing as we were. There was no bloodshed on either side, which was something that had been bothering me. I had seen enough blood shed to last several lifetimes. I needed to see no more.

We held a Thanksgiving Service on the central parade ground at 1600, attended by everyone in the camp, and some of the Americans who had liberated us. Later on, with itchy feet, I strolled out of the open main camp gate for the first time. It felt so strange to walk through those gates. I still remember, all these years afterwards, the prickly feeling that I got at the back of neck, as I crossed the line from the camp and stepped just one pace into freedom.

Much later that evening, with the fresh supply of food that the Americans had brought to us, we ate like kings! I always thought it so strange that the Americans, wherever they were sent, were accompanied by enormous mountains of food and other supplies. There were never shortages for those Yanks.

And so we went to sleep that night in the same old beds, in the same old huts, but that time, symbolically, with the doors left wide open. No lights, no shouts, just silence. A time of wonder, and precious thoughts of our loved ones, soon now to be reunited.

Next day, it did not take any of us very long to pack up our meagre belongings, in the hope of going home. But it was to be days yet before transport would arrive to take us away. There were, after all, over 3,000 of us to repatriate, and the war was not over yet.

It seemed amazing, quite uncomfortable, to be able to wander out through the main gates with nobody on duty in the watchtower to prevent us from doing so with a bullet in the back. After a day or so of waiting around, and with no more information filtering through to us, a group of us from my block went out into the nearby countryside to do a bit of foraging, and we had the opportunity to look around more extensively. It seemed so unnatural to be walking about, free and unguarded, over ground that we had only be able to stare at through the barbed wire of our camp. Later on in the day, I wandered over to the nearby aerodrome and there saw Bernard Stanhope who had taken his sketch pad with him, and was quietly making some drawings. I stood behind him for a few minutes, looking over his shoulder at the rather attractive sketches of the airfield and hangars. He made bold strokes that quickly produced an identifiable subject matter, and made it all look so easy.

PRUNES FOR BREAKFAST

Back in the camp the following morning, I bumped into an English officer, parked in a wheelchair at the doorway to an adjacent barrack block. He had been told that he was being repatriated by courtesy of the Americans directly to a hospital back in England. He, lucky chap (if you could call him lucky with a leg missing), was going straight away. I reckoned that I would not be the only person who pressed a quick note into his kitbag with the request that he post it when he got back to England. I was fortunate that he did so, and therefore that my family had news of me rather sooner than I had thought would be possible. I never even knew his name, but I should take the opportunity to thank him now for that kindness, once again.

> *16th April 1945.*
> *Darling,*
> *Letters and messages must be rolling in to you, and I expect you also heard the wireless news on Saturday evening. I am very fit, appetite almost back to normal and looking forward every minute to being with you. Almost the end of the long straight.*
> *All my love.*
> *Edward. x.*
> *P.S. Being posted in England by kindness of one of the hospital cases coming home today.*

It was not until the 15th that we got a movement order, and we all went over to the aerodrome and waited and waited, staring up in to the sky, waiting for those planes to come for us. Then the order was cancelled, and so we rather dejectedly traipsed back to the camp. We had seen and heard just one lone Dakota buzzing overhead, before it finally came in to land at the airfield. Was it the herald of a fleet of them? By the time that night was over, could there be dozens of planes on the airfield? I celebrated the possibility by having two American supplied boiled eggs for my dinner.

White Cliffs

But they did come at first light. Next morning, when our movement order was reinstated, the first 200 men marched proudly from the camp to the airfield and flew off home, their destination Newbury. Uplifting all of us was clearly going to take some time. I received my own movement order for the next day. It was cancelled. Then again for the next day. That was cancelled too. Eventually, my name was called, and it was my turn to go. And so it was that, at last, I was able to take my leave for ever from Oflag 79, my home from home for some eight long, hungry months, and officially the largest prisoner of war camp for officers in Germany.

We travelled again across the breadth of Germany, thankfully overhead this time, and in a little better comfort than when we had first arrived. From my perch in the Dakota, I was able to look down to see what remained of a completely shattered country, pock marked everywhere by the devastation of war. There was, it seemed, a sea of khaki at nearly every town or junction. Entire towns passed by my aeroplane window, and lay in total ruin below me, some with hardly an untouched building left standing. I mourned the loss of lives on both sides, but, at that moment, it was enough to know that we were going in the right direction, homeward bound at last.

We landed in Brussels that same evening, the 23rd April at 1645. After the traditional de-lousing (what a regular occurrence that had become) and hot – yes, HOT – showers, we were given some new kit and some money, all of which we had to sign for. Afterwards, we were led away and dined on steak and chips in an officers' Mess. I assumed that the steak was courtesy of the Yanks, who appeared to have everything.

There was a scare next day and my flight was cancelled.

The newspapers back in England had really been on the ball. I learned then that an entry had appeared on the 14th April that Oflag

PRUNES FOR BREAKFAST

79 had been liberated by the Americans. It must have been wonderful news for those 3,000 families to have been able to read that morning.

Bulletin No. 12
From the BBC Home Service at 2100 hours today 14.4.45

'FIVE MILES FROM BRUNSWICK ALLIED TROOPS HAVE OVER RUN OFLAG 79. THIS CAMP CONTAINS NEARLY 3,000 BRITISH OFFICERS AND 400 OTHER RANKS. NO NAMES ARE AVAILABLE YET, BUT DETAILS WILL BE SENT AS SOON AS POSSIBLE TO NEXT OF KIN. THE NUMBER OF THE CAMP WAS OFLAG 79.'

I hoped that my parents and Elizabeth saw that piece of news straight away. As for me, when I had reached Brussels on the 23rd April, I was able, at long last, to make a successful telephone call to Elizabeth. It had to be brief, and I seem to remember that we both put down our respective receivers in tears. I felt so bad about it that I rang her again later in the evening, when I had managed to reposition myself in an endless queue.

After a day of more administrative delay, or lack of transport, I knew not what, the 25th April saw my flight airborne at last, clawing its way up through the leaden clouds hanging thickly above Brussels, and very soon I was able to peer down at the English Channel, thinking of the last time that I had crossed it, in such very different circumstances about ten months earlier. With a great lump in my throat, I had to blink away the tears as we crossed over those white cliffs near to Dover, that bastion of all that remained English in my mind. Those cliffs represented to me the impossibility of our land ever again being taken by any aggressor. Adolf had not managed it, and I was sure that nobody else could, either.

White Cliffs

Our flight touched down at Dunsfold fighter aerodrome on the Surrey and Sussex county border, to be greeted by a magnificent reception hosted by the RAF and the local Red Cross. Oh, and yet another de-lousing.

Bone-tired as I had stepped down from the plane on to the Dunsfold runway, as I waited impatiently in the long line for that inevitable de-lousing, my thoughts strayed to Elizabeth and home. Afterwards, we were treated to a splendid meal, though there was far too much on offer for my smaller stomach, and then we were handed free travel warrants and I opted for the first available train heading north. Finally, after those long years away in the Army, I was on the home run to Derby railway station. There, I stepped down on to the platform and was greeted by my wife, my father, and my young son John Edward, the latter probably with no idea of what the big fuss was all about. I was driven from Derby to Burton, and, as we climbed the long hill out of town, I glanced sideways at the swinging sign of the Waterloo Inn, that which I had last seen so long ago and under such different circumstances. I closed my eyes in relief, savouring the homecoming to come.

For me, it was all over at last.

I learned that my good friend Norman Tarry had survived, and was appointed onwards to HQ 8 Infantry Brigade. He went on to have a distinguished military career right up to the very end, when the complete capitulation of Germany was declared. A jammy beggar, always managing to get billeted into some chateau or other, as always!

26th April 1945.
Letter from Capt. N T Tarry, HQ 8 British Infantry Brigade BLA.
My dear Elizabeth,
　　How are you?
　　I hope keeping fit in view of the fact that Eddie will soon be home with you. Do let me know when he does return. I often wonder

PRUNES FOR BREAKFAST

if he has been liberated yet. By heaven, it will be a great day when we did it, we should get awfully tight.

I do hope that your son and heir is still thriving. Eddie will see a great change in him.

Margy has had a card from Eddie asking for news of me and also some more of the old 7th. She replied to him but I doubt if he will ever receive it or the couple that I have written to him either.

The weather is perfect and it does make things that much better for us.

I must close, Elizabeth, just going forward again.

Do keep cheerful.

Yours ever.

Norman.

Norman had written to Elizabeth at Christmas time, not only sending a card, but advising that he was still with HQ 8 British Infantry Brigade BLA, by then over the border and well into Germany, but, as ever, still going forward, as he put it, though it was by then all so very close to the end. It would be a while yet, though, before he made it safely back home and saw my son, his godson, again.

I learned that many of those left standing in 7 RN had become scattered during the intense fighting as it raged back and forth, and that those few left alive were then assimilated into 177 Brigade. Thus, our dear 59 Division, which had trained so hard for four long years, and had come to Normandy as part of a reserve Division, then fought so valiantly in their short campaign, was effectively no more. We could, however, proudly hold on to our title of the only Duplicate Division to have seen active service in Normandy, but it made me very sad for a number of days afterwards.

After it was all over and I had time to draw breath, I found that Elizabeth had kept all of the letters that I sent to her from the POW camp. They arrived, I learned, at very irregular intervals, sometimes out of order. I put that down to the inevitable irregularity of the

German postal service, which must by then have been in complete disarray.

And her letters, or rather the lack of them received by me during my early months at Oflag 79? Elizabeth had written regularly to me ever since she received my note from Chalons all those months ago. We both decided that it was due to the vagaries of the German postal delivery system, and neither of us were really all that surprised that it was, by then, in the process of complete collapse, just like the rest of Germany. Nor, I supposed, did it really matter any more. I was back home with my wife, my son, and my family, and that was enough for me.

I did indeed eventually get my new car, a Ford Prefect in black, together with a small congratulatory certificate. Two years later, I exchanged it for one of their new V8 Pilots.

And so my story draws to a close. When it was all over, what was there left to make of it all? It had been a long five years, and my country had suffered enormously in order to right a very great wrong, and to ensure that we remained free from the yoke of oppression. As in the last one, the Great War, millions had died in that period, the greatest of all struggles. What the world would look like nowadays, should Germany have prevailed, I could not bear to even begin to consider. It was enough for me to say that I gave my best to the great effort made by all of my comrades, and that it was then the time to put everything behind me in the hope that I could once again take up the reins of my family life, as I had so often dreamed before I ate my final meal in that camp – my prunes for breakfast.

Epilogue

Instead of the more usual type of 'what happened afterwards' epilogue, I have decided that I can do no better than to quote verbatim the entry that my father made in his beautiful leatherette bound Armed Services NT Bible, which he presented to me as a small child after he returned from the war.

I still have that Bible, and the words that he wrote still move me every time that I read them. I take it out each year on my christening day, 29th May, and, sentimentally clutching my antique silver christening spoon emblazoned with the enamelled leaping fishes of Brighton, read through it once more. More than seventy years on, his words still have the power to move me.

Those hand written words go as follows:

To my dear John,

This was my first birthday present to you, given to you when you were too young to realise that your Country and Empire was fighting the greatest fight in its history. It will win, but before it has won, thousands of its greatest sons will have died for it. The war will be over when you read this, but I hope that you will grow to be as proud of your great Country and Empire as those that have gone before.

For the rest, I hope that you will always play the game, hitting hard, and when you lose, losing well, remembering always that it is the game that counts, not the result.

I hope you will always shoot straight, and learn to recognise nature, the birds, flowers and trees.

Epilogue

Remember to always treat women with respect and courtesy, and animals with kindness.

I would commend to you the Ten Commandments and, in this book, Corinthians 1, Chapter 13.

Your affectionate Father.

6 April 44.

In his own way, though I never really appreciated it, he must have been quite a special person.

Itinerary After Landing at JUNO Beach

From my research, and from the contents of my father's letters, I believe that the following places are shown in the correct order after he landed in France. Should there be errors, then they are mine alone.

Graye sur Mer – Landing Area
Banville
Esquay-sur-Seulles – Bn. Concentration Area after disembarking
Colombey sur Thaon – Bn. Forward Assembly Area
Le Manoir/Anguerny – Bn. HQ. with troops under canvas locally
Cambes – Bn. Starting Point
La Bijude
Epron
Auberge
Couvre-Chef – To regroup
Ryes – Bn. reserve Rest Area
Grainville sur Odon
Loucelles – Concentration Area
Brettvillette
Fontenay le Pesnel
Tessel – Rest Area
Bordel
Rauray – Bn. Rest Area, then Concentration Area
Villers-Bocage – Follow-up by 7 RN
Ferme de Guiberon
Ouffieres

Itinerary After Landing at JUNO Beach

Goupillieres

Grimbosq – Captured in an orchard close by

Versailles

Paris

Chalons-sur-Marne – Now known as Chalons-en-Champagne

Oflag X11B – Hadamar, NW of Frankfurt am Main, near to the town of Limburg

Oflag 79 – Waggum, north of Brunswick at the edge of the Brunswick/Wolfsburg Aerodrome as was, northern Germany. The camp was the ex-depot of a German parachute regiment, next to the Hermann Goering aircraft engine factory.

Glossary

88
Heavy German anti-tank gun of 88 mm. Capable also of being used against aircraft, it had an elevation ranging from -3 degrees to +85 degrees.

AMGOT
Allied Military Government for Occupied Territories.

APO
Army Post Office locator system for individual Units.

Bailey
A type of portable bridge, with steel and timber systems, capable of supporting the weight of a tank. Available with floating pontoons for extra length.

BLA
British Liberation Army. The new designation for Allied Forces post BWEF.

Bren
Light machine gun. Bipod mounted or hand held.

BWEF
British Western Expeditionary Force. Designation of Allied Forces after D-Day.

Glossary

Churchill
Iconic British infantry support tank, weighing in at 38 tons with 75 mm gun and 2 machine guns, turret mounted.

CO
Commanding Officer

Crocodile
Modified Churchill tank converted into a flame thrower, using specially thickened petroleum. See also "Funny."

Funny
Modified British tank, e.g. with a flail system installed forward of the front end in order to activate enemy mines. Sometimes fitted instead with a frontal bulldozer blade. See also "Crocodile".

Half Tracks
Armoured vehicle with wheels at the front and tracks at the rear. Used for better grip than just 4 wheels.

H-Hour.
The designated time for an attack, landing or other military operation to commence.

LST
Landing Ship, Tanks. Packed with tanks, heavy machinery, other vehicles and troops.

LCT
Landing Craft, Troops. Could be piggy-backed on a larger LST.

Moaning Minnie
British name for German multiple field rocket mortar, so called

because of its shrieking noise when fired. The German name was *"Nebelwerfer"*, or smoke mortar.

OCTU
Officer Cadet Training Unit (in this case the 166th on the Isle of Man).

OO
Orderly Officer

OP
Observation Post

Panther
Medium German tank, half the cost of a Tiger, built using conscript labour, but with only a 75 mm gun.

Panzer
German fast mechanised armoured Units – usually but not exclusively referring to tanks.

Pay Parade
Weekly arrangement where each serviceman was paid in cash via a sealed envelope.

Reveille
British waking up signal.

RN
The Royal Norfolk Regiment (e.g. 7 RN)

RTR
The Royal Tank Regiment (e.g. 9 RTR)

Glossary

Tiger 1
Heavily armoured German tank, outgunning Allied tanks with an adapted 88 mm gun.

Tracer
Bullets containing a small pyrotechnic charge which, when ignited on firing, show both trajectory and destination.

Acknowledgements

There are a number of people whom I would like to thank for their tireless efforts in supporting me through to the production of my final manuscript and beyond. When I first put finger to keyboard for my first book – a completely different genre – I really did not realise that I knew nothing, absolutely nothing, about the writing and construction of a book. I was about to enter a different world. With this second book, I am still feeling like a novice.

Firstly and most importantly, I must thank my wife, Sally, who has read each draft, made suggestions and generally supported me through the process, mostly without complaint! Whilst I have enjoyed the writing process, it must have been a trial for her.

My editor, Jennifer Barclay, has improved and honed my writing and presentation, let alone my punctuation. Her skills have proved yet again to have been much to my benefit. As with my previous book, I could not have done all this without her. How very lucky I am to have met her.

I read a number of books and spoke to a lot of people whilst doing my research for this book, far too many to mention, though I am indebted to them all. However, I should like to draw attention to the following:

Freeland, Lt. Col. J. H. *A History of the 7th Battalion, The Royal Norfolk Regiment, July 1940 to August 1944* (With thanks to Christine Searancke)

Knight, Peter *The 59th Division – Its War Story* (Original Edition)

Morss, Robert *59th (Staffordshire) Division in WW2*. Robert Morss

Acknowledgements

got me started on this historical venture of discovery. He was the first to point the way forward to me.

Reynolds, Major General M. *Steel Inferno. 1 SS Panzer Corps in Normandy*

My thanks also go to John Harding, my talented brother-in-law, who has so ably interpreted my wishes for the front cover of this book as well as producing a masterpiece on the front of the previous one. You can see his other work at www.johnharding.net and he welcomes commissions!

And lastly, I must thank Sheila Collis, Editor of *Island Connections*, for her continued support and encouragement, and for helping me to promote this book throughout the Canary Islands.

Thank you, one and all.

Thank You!

Thank you for reading this book. I hope that you have enjoyed the story of my father's wartime exploits. There was perhaps nothing earth-shattering about it, but maybe that is actually the importance of it, as I see it – an ordinary man being asked to do more than is ordinary, and doing it with relish and mostly with good cheer, for five long years.

    Writers need reviews; it is their oxygen. If you have enjoyed this book and if you have the time and inclination, please let me know what you thought. Even better, if you are able to write a short review – however brief – that would be wonderful. If you were then able to post it on to Amazon or your favourite book site, that would be even better. By doing that, you not only help out authors, but you help new readers to find us as well, which ultimately benefits everybody. Thanks in advance!

    If you have enjoyed this book, may I suggest that you try my first book – *Dog Days In The Fortunate Islands* – which tells the story of my retirement, with my wife and my dog, to begin a new and surprisingly exciting life in the Canary Islands. Told with humour and pathos, it is a light hearted journey that I hope will enthral and amuse you in equal parts.

Please do contact me for my latest news through my website:
www.johnsearancke.com